REPRESENTATION AND URBAN COMMUNITY

REPRESENTATION AND URBAN COMMUNITY

Andrew D. Glassberg

To my parents

First published 1981 by
THE MACMILLAN PRESS LTD
London and Basingstoke
Companies and representatives
throughout the world

ISBN 0 333 28878 5

Photoset in Great Britain by
ROWLAND PHOTOTYPESETTING LTD
Bury St Edmunds, Suffolk
Printed in Hong Kong

Contents

List of Tables

Acknowledgements

This study relies heavily on interview data with members of three London Borough Councils—Bromley, Islington, and Tower Hamlets councils. Their willingness to participate in this effort, and give freely of their time and hospitality, is what made this study possible. Their assistance was fundamental. In addition, I must make special mention of the leaders of the three Borough councils I have studied in this research. They also gave freely of their time, and provided me with access to their colleagues.

In addition to the elected members, officials of the three boroughs provided many helpful insights. I should make special mention of the library staffs of the Bromley Borough Library, the Islington Borough Library, the Tower Hamlets Borough Library, and the Greater London Council libraries at County Hall.

This study is a revised version of a Ph.D. dissertation in political science prepared for Yale University. My advisers at Yale, Professors Stanley Greenberg, David Mayhew, and Douglas Yates, provided encouragement to initiate, continue, and now to complete this work. My debt to them is considerable. My colleagues in the political science departments at Lehman College, City University of New York and at the University of Missouri—St Louis have provided continuing intellectual and emotional support for this work. They too receive my gratitude.

Friends and colleagues in London, from academia and local government, provided me with insights into the workings of London politics and society without which this study would be far poorer.

But despite the range of assistance I have had in completing this work, I remain responsible for all interpretations (and errors of interpretation) that are presented here.

Introduction

This is a study of urban politics and urban politicians at the "neighbourhood" level. It is set in three London Boroughs, and is based on interviews with actors in these three boroughs' local political systems, and examination of published material about the three boroughs' current political life and political history.

My interest in examining the functioning of units of government such as these grew out of policy arguments in the United States, debating the utility of "neighbourhood governments" in large metropolitan centres.

One of the fundamental problems in examining neighbourhood government in the US is its experimental quality. Because of this, all organizations which can be studied are primarily concerned, almost by definition, with institutional survival. Any assessment of the long-term impact of this governmental form, therefore, needs to look at political environments where the form has become a regularized feature of the political landscape. London provides an opportunity for such an examination, which American cities do not.[1]

In concluding his study of "neighborhood democracy in the United States", Douglas Yates suggests that one of the effects of the experiments he examines is "that it increases pluralism in urban democracy. In promoting 'local solutions' to neighborhood problems, decentralization permits the articulation of more diverse preferences and interests and thus enhances local self-determination."[2] This study is an effort to examine this type of proposition in an explicitly non-experimental setting. London provides a locale where this is possible. I shall return at the conclusion to a discussion of what the evidence from London can

tell us about neighbourhood urban structures, which are often
suggested for the US as well.

Although, as I shall be indicating in this study, local government in London, and throughout England, has gone through
many waves of "reform" and reorganization, one constant
feature of the political structure has been the existence of forms
of government below what Americans would usually think of as
the "citywide" level. Since 1963, these units in London have
been called London Boroughs, and the reorganization of London
became something of a model for later reorganizations of local
government in the rest of England as well. Although it is obvious
that these waves of reform indicate no unanimous consensus on
the appropriate forms of sub-metropolitan government, the
crucial aspect of the English experience, for the purposes of this
study, is that the existence of some such forms has come to be a
"given" of the political system.

The choice of three London boroughs, rather than including
any units from elsewhere in the country, was dictated by the
then imminent reorganization of functions and boundaries of
local authorities in the rest of the country. London reorganization was adopted in 1963 and implemented in 1965. The more
recent reorganization elsewhere in England follows the London
model in many ways. Discussions with political scientists and
political activists in London indicated that certain London
boroughs were developing reputations as "untraditional"
English local authorities, and were emphasizing much more
localist themes in their election campaigns and council activities.
These untraditional governing styles were reported to be concentrated in certain boroughs dominated by the Labour Party,
but where there had been a change in political leadership within
the Labour Party ranks.[3]

For purposes of this research, therefore, it was decided to
examine the potentially contrasting representational styles in
three types of London boroughs: a "traditional", "cloth-cap"
working-class, Labour dominated borough; a "traditional",
affluent, suburban, home-owning, Conservative borough; and
an "untraditional", "community-action-oriented" borough of
the type described above.

Although no systematic comparison of governing styles of all
of the London boroughs exists, several boroughs have been
studied intensively,[4] and there are also a number of studies

comparing a limited number of boroughs.[5] In addition, comprehensive published material is available on the political and demographic make-up of the boroughs.[6]

Using published sources, and consultation with English academic experts, boroughs were identified which fit the three categories listed above. A tentative list of Tower Hamlets, as an example of a traditional Labour borough, Bromley, as an example of a traditional Conservative borough, and Islington, as an example of a "community-action-oriented" borough, was made up.[7] Conversations with Labour and Conservative Party activists in London, and with present and former local government officers confirmed the "typicality" of these choices. Preliminary interviews with political leaders in each of the three boroughs, and examination of council records, confirmed reported variations in borough political styles. These preliminary interviews were conducted in January 1974, while the bulk of the interview data reported on in this research was gathered in tape-recorded interviews conducted during the summer of 1974. Analyses of local government records were conducted at these same times, and a follow-up examination of more recent material was conducted from the summers of 1976–9.

I The Problem of Community Representation

This study examines representation and community. It will investigate how local-level elected representatives vary in their personal theories on these two dimensions, and what impact these variations have on their day-to-day functioning. I shall also be examining the impact of these variations on the styles and policies of the councils on which these representatives serve. I shall argue that problems of representation are significantly different at the local level from those that arise in national politics, and even from those that arise in intermediate-level political structures, such as states in federal systems.

In examining these questions, I shall suggest that any analysis of varying representational modes, and of whole-council styles and policies, needs to take into account not only the individual perspectives of the council's rank-and-file members, but also the specific attitudes of the council's leadership, and the local political and economic context of the unit of government in which these participants act. Accordingly, I shall be devoting special attention to the views of council leaders, and shall be examining in some detail "contextual" variations and similarities among the London boroughs studied in this research.

I wish to suggest that any understanding of variations in whole-council styles and policies must take into account three elements: the variations in backgrounds and political styles of rank-and-file councillors; attitudes of council leaders; and the historical backgrounds and current "facts of life" of the units themselves.

It is also important to point out at the outset that the "dependent variables" in this study—whole-council styles and council policy decisions, are really two distinct items. It is quite possible, for example, that variations in the "independent variables" of borough background, leadership characteristics, and rank-and-file councillor attitudes may affect one without necessarily having the same impact on the other.

But before turning to the details of these questions, it will be necessary to clarify certain theoretical problems in the study of representation. As I indicated above, the problems posed by this concept are not necessarily the same in local political systems as they are in systems of broader scope.

A   A THEORETICAL PROBLEM—THE DISTINCTIVENESS OF COMMUNITY REPRESENTATION

Although one obvious difference between local and national representatives lies in the presence or absence of a superior political authority with powers to control the action of subordinate bodies, I wish to argue that the crucial distinction for the purpose of understanding variations in perspectives on representation is the possibility of a homogeneous population within a local government area, and the impossibility of similar homogeneity at the national level. I will focus particularly on the relevance of class homogeneity or heterogeneity in making this argument.

It is, of course, true that a national representative may represent a homogeneous constituency, but what I am arguing is that only in local politics can a representative serve in an environment where not only his own constituency is homogeneous, but the entire local authority area is composed overwhelmingly of people in similar class positions. Although I will be making this argument with specific reference to class in the English case, a similar point might be made about ethnicity, at least in the American situation.

As a result of this possibility, I will be suggesting that it becomes necessary for participants in local politics to develop at least implicit theories of community, as well as theories of representation. (In discussing community, it is useful to separate out the concept as an overarching social phenomenon —as in the gemeinschaft-gesellschaft distinction, for example—

from its use in everyday language as a term for an area of local distinctiveness. It is this second usage that I will be examining.)

I am suggesting that this particular sense of community, i.e., an area of local distinctiveness, poses special problems for representatives in local government that do not necessarily arise in national politics. At the national level a "class-conscious" representative, for example, will usually perceive a similarity, if not identity, of interest between the needs of his constituency and the needs of the class that populates his constituency. A representative from a working-class district, for example, can simultaneously attempt to advance the interests of the working-class and of his constituency on many policy questions.

This is not to say that conflicts of interest do not sometimes arise, only that there are many policies on which the cue "advance the interests of the working class" is sufficient guidance for choosing a position, without the necessity of deciding whether one wants to take a "national" or a "parochial" perspective. (As was pointed out earlier, a similar position might be possible in some societies with regard to ethnicity or other overarching social divisions of the population.)

In local politics, on the other hand, a representative with an ideological perspective identical to that described above will be faced with many more situations in which the cue "advance the interests of the working class" is insufficient advice for position-taking. The entire area served by a local government authority may be class-homogeneous. The representative from a working-class ward in a local government in which virtually all wards are working class needs an additional perspective to help him decide on policy priorities. (All-middle-class areas would, of course, pose a similar problem.) I will suggest that the representative's notion of community, explicit or implicit, provides this cue.

It might be useful at this point to show two possible, but conflicting, ways of resolving this problem. A local representative in the position described above might, for example, adopt the view that the relevant "community" he ought to concern himself with was the local government area as a whole. "Advance the interests of the working class" might mean all the working class, and if the local government area was all-working-class, then such a representative might feel that any distinctive advocacy of the interests of his own ward would be inappropriate. Indeed, he might feel that because of the class-homogeneity of the entire area, his ward had no distinctive interests of its own. Such an individual might be called in some sense "cosmopolitan" in his outlook, except that the boundaries of his cosmopolis would be limited to his local government area.

The concept being discussed here is, of course, not limited by formal political boundaries. The attitude would extend to the sociological boundaries of the working-class area. But in activating this attitude in real politics, the local government area can serve as a surrogate for the sociological community, if there is some rough equivalence between them. Such a rough equivalence might be found in a small town, for example, where a single dominant economic activity produces a community largely homogeneous in its population.

But large metropolitan centres are necessarily diverse, both in economic and class-composition terms. Within large cities, however, sub-areas are frequently homogeneous in their population composition. In a political system which provides some form of "neighbourhood government", therefore, it is possible to locate units whos population is class-homogeneous.

I am suggesting that the English system provides this in jurisdictions like its London boroughs and is, therefore, a particularly advantageous locale for investigating the question of how representatives deal with the problems described above.

As I indicated in the introduction to this study, the possibility of organizing units of this kind has been discussed for large American cities, and the decentralization/neighbourhood government effort has produced some arenas for studying how local political activists see their representational activities, and for investigating the linkage between their personal theories of representation and their views of community.[1] But because American experiments in decentralization have been tenuous and controversial, they do not provide the best setting for examining what "normal politics" is like at the community level. And it is "normal politics" in relatively small, homogeneous, units, which provides the best setting for examining representatives' behaviour. Homogeneity is the key, and larger, city-wide governments, would not provide a setting in which to examine its effects upon representation. England provides a setting where the equivalents of "neighbourhood government" are a stable and on-going part of the political environment, and where styles of representation at the community level can be

studied without the confounding factors of newness and uncertainty that characterize comparable American institutions.

In addition to the resolution discussed above, in which a
councillor would define "community" as extending to the
sociological boundaries of his area, a local government representative, faced with the same set of circumstances, might develop
what I will call an "ideology of localism". In this form, a
councillor, without necessarily changing his views on national
politics, can nevertheless press the particularist interests of his
own ward, even when that ward is not class-distinctive within
the local government area. I will argue that this form of
resolution is the product of a representative's assigning para-
mount importance to a particular conception of "community" in
his understanding of the political process.

In the first of these two examples, the representative's concept
of class and community combine; the "community" extends
throughout the span of territory populated by those of similar
class composition. In the second example, the representative's
notion of community is independent of his notion of class, and is
based not on the sociological composition of the population, but
on a geographic one; the "community" is made up of those who
live in a compact area, for which the ward is the political
expression.

The distinctiveness of the problem of representation at the
community level is also striking when one examines some of the
major theoretical formulations about representation, and con-
siders their relevance for local politics. At least since Burke, both
political practitioners and political observers have been troubled
by questions about the proper role of elected representatives in
governing systems. In what has become the standard empirical
study, Wahlke and his colleagues identified three styles of
representation: the delegate, the trustee, and the hybrid politico.[2]
Although they were writing specifically about American state
legislatures, their formulation has been applied to national and
sub-national legislatures alike.[3]

But in a less often cited distinction, Wahlke *et al.* distinguished
between representational roles—the delegate–trustee–politico
typology—and areal roles—the territorial scope which members
of the legislatures they studied saw themselves as representing.[4]
This second cleavage, which, I will argue, can be thought of as a
holistic–particularistic distinction (and which Wahlke *et al.*

divide into a district-oriented, state-oriented, and district and state-oriented typology),[5] takes on fundamentally different forms at the local level than it does when national political systems are under examination.

At the national level, a holistic focus of representation necessarily implies a view of society in which differing class and sectional elements can (or ought to) work together harmoniously. At the local level, such an implication is not necessarily present. As I argued above, this disjunction between national and local arenas will be particularly striking in those communities which, though internally homogeneous, are distinctive in national terms.

Thus, a representative who might seem at the extremes of particularism in national politics might appear holistic in his orientation towards local politics, with precisely the same value system in each case. Local-level particularism, on the other hand (what I identified earlier as an "ideology of localism"), seems to occur when a representative of a small and homogeneous area such as a ward sees his function as "defending the turf", a view which I will show has been growing in parts of the British political system. This ideology of localism can be quite independent of a representative's views on national politics, and this study will report on examples of local defence in parts of both the left and the right of British local politics.

But despite the resurgence of localist orientations, the most characteristic areal orientation, in both national and local politics in England, has been decidedly holistic in character, and political figures have overwhelmingly identified with a trustee orientation towards politics.

Both formal and informal forces in British political life have been supportive of a trustee orientation. Hanna Pitkin, in describing Burke's view, writes: "if superior wisdom and ability reside in the representative, then he must not subordinate them to the opinions of his ignorant, inferior constituents."[6] A. H. Birch has argued that the delegate model was never as popular in Britain as in the United States in part because of the formal arrangements of power. Sovereignty, he points out, continues to rest theoretically in Parliament, not in the people.[7] Under such a constitutional arrangement, the trustee is the more appropriate legislative role. In addition to this formal characteristic, greater national homogeneity has been presented as an explanation for the dislike many English politicians are said to feel for too vigorous a promotion of localist interests.[8] (Although, as I argued earlier, few would suggest that Britain is class-homogeneous as a nation.)

Finally, the strength of the party system is often presented as accounting for the lack of attention to constituency interest that the delegate orientation is sometimes seen to require. (Studies of electoral behaviour in England invariably show almost no impact of promotional work for the constituency on electoral outcomes.)[9] The assumptions and practices of British national government have permeated the local political process as well, although, as I shall be suggesting below, the structural characteristics of English local government are at some variance from those which operate at the national level.

Although Edmund Burke's view of the proper functioning of representative government has dominated British political rhetoric, British political practice has been more varied historically. Samuel Huntington has identified an earlier strain in British politics, which he regards as Tudor in origin, which emphasized the particularist representation of constituency interests as being of greater importance than the representation of a holistic conception of the public good presented by Burke.[10] Huntington's analysis, which is limited to national-level politics, indicates that this "Tudor" style disappeared in Britan, but has remained alive in the United States.

But despite the adoption of *attitudes* towards local government which seem congruent with national political trends, English local government has retained certain key structural features which Huntington argues were characteristic of the earlier "Tudor" forms at the national level, but which no longer exist at that level. Huntington argues, for example, that the idea that MPs should live in their constituencies, and the use of multi-member constituencies, were important structural backdrops to Tudor particularism.[11] English local government has retained both: the multi-member ward is the almost universal pattern for local authorities, and there is a formal requirement that local authority members live or work within the authority's boundaries, and often an informal requirement that they have some sort of direct connection with the specific ward they represent as well.

In addition, some of the structural characteristics often said to reinforce a holistically inclined "responsible party system" in

British national government are absent in local politics. The notion of a responsible party system presupposes not only cohesive parties but competitive parties.[12] Although the twentieth-century development of English local government has been characterized by a continuing extension of partisan politics into sub-national politics, there are obviously many places (if not most) where one-party control can be taken for granted.

Even where local party competition is vigorous, the party discipline imposed by the formal requirements for the maintenance of continual party majorities in the House of Commons are absent in local government. English local authorities, unlike Parliament, are elected to fixed terms of office, and are not even theoretically subject to removal by "votes of no confidence" precipitating new elections. This is not to say that the idea of responsible, cohesive parties is not practised in English local politics, only that certain of the forms which reinforce this pattern at the national level do not operate sub-nationally.

Thus, the maintenance of what have come to be traditional "post-Tudor" holistic patterns at the local level rests more on the maintenance of supportive attitudes than on the reinforcing effect of formal structures. We might expect, therefore, that challenges to these patterns would have greater possibilities of success in this arena, where constraints to such a challenge are fewer.

This weakness of formal structural constraints on particularism in local politics may be viewed as akin to the notion of "slack resources" developed in the study of American urban politics. (Robert Dahl presents the idea of slack as a concept not limited to the United States. He writes that: "the existence of a great deal of political slack seems to be a characteristic of pluralistic systems and the liberal societies in which these systems operate.")[13]

Those who might wish to challenge traditional holistic patterns have at their disposal at the local level (but not at the national), surviving institutional forms of the type which are congenial to particularistic local politics. But the existence of these slack "structural resources" is, of course, no guarantee that they will be put to use by anyone. But what has been seen in this section is that there are both distinctive problems of representation in urban politics, and institutional forms in English local government which permit the expression of new resolutions of these problems, when and if there are political actors who wish to attempt them.

B COUNCIL STYLES AND COUNCIL POLICIES— THE "DEPENDENT VARIABLES"

As I indicated at the outset, a major aim of this research is the identification of linkages between attributes of individual actors in local political systems and whole-system characteristics. This element of analysis is often overlooked. Wahlke *et al.*, for example, despite detailed attention to the roles played by individual legislators, never amalgamate their findings to say very much about the impact of their legislators' behaviour and attitudes on the overall functioning of the California, New Jersey, Ohio, and Tennessee legislatures. Barber briefly argues that "lawmakers" improve the effectiveness of the Connecticut legislature,[14] but, of course, he does not deal with whole legislatures comparatively and, as I have argued, the problem is a distinctive one at the local level.

At another pole of the literature, most work on policy outputs engages in aggregate data anlysis of whole-system performance and rarely comments on the characteristics of the individual decision-makers who function within the systems under study. In this tradition, measures of partisan competitiveness, available resources, and social needs are used to statistically explain variation in policy output. But neither Dye, in describing variation among American states,[15] for example, or Boaden, in describing outputs of English county boroughs,[16] in another report, tell us anything about the characteristics or attitudes of American state legislators or English county councillors.

In this study, I will be integrating these two traditions. While an examination of only three units makes the sorts of statistical analyses of Dye and Boaden inappropriate here, I will nevertheless be asserting that variations in styles and policies of the councils studied are explicable, and that the attitudes and actions of individual council members are one element in accounting for these variations. (As an aside, it is worth mentioning that analysis of English local government is affected by an intriguing semantic confusion over the meaning of the term "council". While in the United States this would refer only to the legislative body, in England it often means not only the legislative arm of local government, but the entire local government entity, including the bureaucracy. Thus, when someone says, "The Council is doing so-and-so" it is unclear whether the speaker means merely the local legislature, or the bureaucracy, or both. I will use the term council to refer only to the legislative arm, using the term borough for the local government entity as a whole.)

When I speak of "council styles", I have in mind whole-system attributes, the way the council as an entity presents itself to and is perceived by the borough it serves. I will particularly focus on the openness or closedness of council procedures, and the degree to which public participation in council decision-making is sought or discouraged. With regard to "council policies", I will be concentrating my attention on one specific arena of council policy-making, that of local economic development. The details of inter-borough variation in these two areas will be reported on in Chapter 5 of this study.

As I indicated earlier, I shall be suggesting that variation can be understood as being tied to variation in the three categories of "independent" variables examined in this research: borough characteristics, attitudes of council leaders, and attitudes of rank-and-file borough councillors. But I will also be suggesting that there are some common patterns of evolution among the boroughs studied, and that national political and economic tendencies operating in England serve to shape the direction in which council styles and policies both evolve.

C BOROUGH BACKGROUND, LEADERSHIP PREFERENCES, RANK-AND-FILE COUNCILLOR ATTITUDES—THE "INDEPENDENT" VARIABLES

I indicated at the very outset of this study that I would be reporting on local-level representatives, and the impact of their backgrounds and attitudes on the styles and policies of the local governments on which they serve. And the characteristics of rank-and-file councillors will form one element of the explanatory package I will be presenting. But in addition to the attributes of these rank-and-filers, I am suggesting that two other distinct elements have independent explanatory power.

The first of these, to be reported in Chapter 2, is what I have referred to as "borough background". I will be focusing particularly on the physical characteristics of the boroughs studied and their population configurations. These two elements, I will suggest, form constraints within which borough political leaders must operate, but they also provide clues to a set of distinctive local experiences and memories which help to shape the attitudes of the borough's decision-makers. For each of the boroughs, I will be further suggesting that changes taking place in their physical make-up, population composition and economic bases are producing changes in the local agenda of issues, and in the political resources which local leaders can bring to bear on their problems.

Although the boroughs chosen for this study were selected for their distinctiveness, they showed certain common patterns of economic evolution. But these commonalities in economic evolution have had distinctive effects in the three boroughs. What I will be suggesting in Chapter 2, therefore, is that both historical distinctiveness among the boroughs, and differential responses to current changes, make an understanding of the specifics of borough context crucial to any understanding of either individual councillor activity, or of whole-council styles and policies.

Council *leadership* preferences are a second distinct arena requiring research, separate from, but obviously related to, both borough characteristics and rank-and-file councillor views. Although council leaders are chosen by the majority-party councillors on the borough council (and are thus roughly akin to the Prime Minister in national-level English politics), I will be arguing that changes in leadership patterns in the three boroughs over time, about which I will be reporting in Chapter 3, can best be seen in the context of the economic and political evolution of the boroughs themselves. Thus, although leaders are formally responsible to the rank-and-file which chooses them, I will be presenting them as substantial independent actors. What I will be arguing, however, is that despite their independence from the rank-and-file they lead, their own styles and policy preferences can be understood as substantially dependent on the patterns of borough evolution, about which I will have reported in Chapter 2. In the concept of leadership I will be using, the attitudes and actions of the leaders I am examining will be seen as growing out of the particularities of the boroughs they lead, and the changes within those boroughs over time.

Because of the ties I will be asserting between borough characteristics and leadership patterns, I shall be presenting my analyses of these leadership patterns prior to my discussion of the attitudes and actions of rank-and-file council members. I will be particularly interested in two dimensions of council leadership: the attitude of council leaders towards political party, on the one hand, and voluntary organizations, on the other. I shall show more explicitly in subsequent chapters that I see politicians' responses to these two alternate stimuli as useful indicators of their general understanding of local political processes.

Although I will be beginning my analyses with discussions of borough characteristics and leadership attitudes, this is not to suggest that I regard the attitudes and characteristics of rank-and-file councillors as irrelevant. Rather, as I have suggested above, I will be presenting these attitudes as a third element which helps to explain variation in whole-council styles and policies. I have identified some councillors as adhering to a new political position which I have described as an "ideology of localism". In Chapter 4 of this study I will be presenting a fuller description of this, and other councillor-types uncovered in the course of this research. I shall be suggesting that two dimensions of councillor attitude are the most useful ones in developing an efficient councillor-classification scheme. These dimensions are "scope of ambition", the extent to which a particular councillor has aspirations for political involvement at political levels beyond the borough, and "scope of representation", the extent to which a councillor sees his prime representative focus as his borough as a whole, or his individual ward. Adherents to an "ideology of localism" are distinctive, I will argue, in simultaneously having a "broad" scope of ambition, intending to seek political opportunities beyond the borough, and yet holding a "narrow" scope of representation, seeing their ward as having distinctive interests which it is their proper function to articulate while they continue to serve in borough-level politics. Such councillors combine an interest in broader, usually national, political affairs, with a belief that the most local of interests require distinctive representation.

In addition to presenting a classificatory schema, I will also be suggesting that the different councillor-types vary systematically in their own attention to political party and to voluntary organizations: the same dimensions by which council leaders have been characterized. In addition, I will be arguing that the different councillor-types vary in the modes of recruitment which first brought them to council service.

What I shall be presenting throughout Chapters 2, 3 and 4, therefore, will be descriptions of the three elements of borough background, leadership preferences, and rank-and-file councillor attitudes which, I suggest, are the most useful dimensions for understanding variation in whole-council styles and policies.

D   EVALUATION

Throughout this research I will be reporting on patterns of political variation. These variations will be found among council leaders and rank-and-file councillors, and in the styles and policies of the councils as whole systems. Although I will be indicating patterns of constraint within which councillors and councils must function, I will nevertheless be suggesting that there is a range of alternative modes of behaviour open to the participants in these systems. Given such a finding, it will become appropriate to discuss the standards by which these alternative modes can be evaluated. As long as councils and councillors are at least partially free actors, any study such as this must consider the advantages and disadvantages of the styles those who have this freedom choose to adopt. Any such evaluation, of course, is dependent on the values which the observer brings to the process.

An effort such as this does not lack for benchmarks. Hanna Pitkin has suggested that there is an inherent paradox in the concept of representation, that the reason the "mandate–independence" controversy has never been "solved" is that we expect representatives to try to play both roles at times. But, she recognizes, the history of this controversy has been one of continual assertion of one or the other of these two positions as if it had dominant claims to political legitimacy.[17] As I will be indicating in Chapter 4, London borough councillor responses to questions about this tended to be ritualistic, with several

specific citations to Edmund Burke (and one to the Wahlke–
Eulau study!) made by councillors. Because of these ritualistic
assertions of the "trustee" orientation among the councillors
interviewed, I do not find this a useful evaluative distinction.

Instead, I will be using the criteria for representation in local
government set out by a variety of government commissions in
England charged with responsibility for recommending reforms
in the local government structure. Although, as I have indicated
earlier, the basic concept of borough government is a "given" in
the English political structure, this in no way indicates any
necessary satisfaction with the functioning of these institutions.

One sign of dissatisfaction with local government in England
can be found in the profusion of government commissions which
have been regularly proposing reorganization of local government structures for the past 20 years. Indeed, one formal
governmental commission in Britain itself suggested the need for
changes in the orientation of local councillors in England in the
direction of a more particularist representation of their wards.
In its report on *People and Planning*, the UK Committee on Public
Participation in Planning described the forces that lead councillors away from this focus:

> It would be easy to underestimate the pressures on the local
> authority member which pull him away from his constituency.
> He is elected to represent a comparatively small number of
> people, but as soon as he becomes a member of the council he
> has to think in terms of the council and its activities as a whole
> as well as being the representative of those who have elected
> him. If he becomes a member of a committee he may have to
> devote a great deal of time to that. If he becomes chairman of
> a committee, he has administrative functions as well. All these
> pressures tend to make him a part of a central administration
> and less able to devote time to the smaller area which he
> represents.[18]

This committee, appointed in 1968 to "consider . . . the best
methods . . . of securing the participation of the public at the
formative stage of development plans for their area,"[19] was
preceded by three other major commissions, the reports of which
have led to comprehensive reorganization of English local

government, first in London, and now in the rest of England as well.[20]

Each of these commissions began with an explicit assumption of disfunction in English local government, and of the need for substantial change in its structure. The introduction to the report of the Royal Commission on Local Government in England is typical in stating that:

> Local government areas do not fit the pattern of life and work in modern England. The gap will widen as social, economic and technological changes quicken.[21]

and that:

> the purpose of local government is to provide a democratic means both of focussing national attention on local problems affecting the safety, health and well-being of the people and of discharging, in relation to these things, all the responsibilities of government which can be discharged at a level below that of the national government. . . . We do not think that this purpose is being fully realised today.[22]

But despite recommending substantial changes in local government boundaries, and some reorganization of functions between two levels of local government, the reorganization of English local government has not produced any fundamental alterations of the structures for electing councillors. Throughout England, councils remain overwhelmingly partisan, and councillors at the lower tier of local government structures continue to be elected from small, multi-member districts with formal requirements for residence or business within the council's jurisdiction, and informal requirements of varying strength for ties to the particular ward the councillor represents. The utility of these commission reports for the purposes of this study, therefore, lies in their varying conceptions of what constitutes desirable councillor characteristics and behaviour. In Chapter 6 of this study I shall be using these alternative conceptions as benchmarks for evaluating the variations among councils and councillors I will have reported on.

As I indicated above, there have been three major local government reorganization commissions. The first of these, the

Royal Commission on Local Government in Greater London, was charged with responsibility for drawing up a new structure of local government for the London area in 1960. This commission (often referred to as the Herbert Commission after its chairman) placed particular emphasis on the need for attracting the "right kind of councillor"[23] to participate in local government. While to some degree the Herbert Commission saw this as a national problem (and argued that there had been a general decline in the quality of local government councillors because of an erosion of authority to the national government),[24] it also argued that the problem was more serious in London. People moving to London "with a distinguished record in local government elsewhere", the Commission found, were "advised not to waste time with local government, but to find something more useful, suited to their abilities and experience".[25]

The problem, from the perspective of the Herbert Commission, therefore, was not only to define the characteristics of the "good" councillor, but also to worry about how such people could be recruited into local government. The Commission was quite explicit about this:

> The control of the expert by the amateur representing his fellow citizen is the key to the whole of our system of government. . . . It is therefore important that one should find the right sort of councillor, and a . . . criterion of size, scope and area [of local councils] must be 'What best to attract good councillors.'[26]

The Herbert Commission developed a series of criteria for defining "good councillors" as well. Particularly relevant to this study are its arguments that the "good councillor must know his people, those who have elected him, their needs, desires and fears. He must also remember that he represents not only those of his constituents who have voted for him but also those who have voted against him."[27] Although this is not an explicitly delegate-model of representation, neither does it suggest a completely "trustee" view either. But in some ways more intriguing was the Commission's view that the "good councillor must learn to keep away from interference in the administrative execution of policy."[28] And "must, in the circumstance of today when politics almost universally pervade local government, act as an intelligent link between his party and the council, interpreting the one to the other."[29]

In outlining its views on how a councillor "may well be of use in individual cases"[30] the Commission indicated that "he may be useful in interpreting to his constituents the policy of the authority and the actions of its officers."[31] And "he can be useful as a liaison between his authority and voluntary associations in avoiding overlaps or in bridging gaps."[32]

What we see here is a view of appropriate councillor activity which largely consists of the councillor in the role of spokesman *to* his constituency, rather than vice versa. Even with regard to his political party, the "good councillor" is equally obligated to interpret council policy *to* the party as he is to explain party policy to the council. While the Commission recognizes some role for voluntary organizations, these are presented as service organizations, rather than as pressure groups which might themselves seek to influence council policy.

After arguing that it was unlikely that "any form of local government" would attract a large number of councillors who would perform these duties "to perfection",[33] the Herbert Commission reported that "a sufficient supply of councillors of ability" required a "certain minimum size and scope of authority", which is "wide enough to require (and indeed stimulate) their qualities and . . . satisfy their ambitions".[34]

Thus, the clear thrust of the Herbert Commission's views was that councillors needed a structure with enough power to induce "better" people to participate. Rather than emphasizing a representation of local interests, the key problem was competence.

The Herbert Commission's authority was limited to recommending structural changes in London local government. In following years, two national government commissions were appointed with responsibilities for recommending reorganization of local government in the rest of England. As with the Herbert Commission's report, public attention at the time was largely directed towards questions such as boundary redrawing, size of local government units, impact on political party control, and on division of powers between two tiers of new metropolitan-area governments. But, as I shall indicate below, these two commissions, the Committee on the Management of Local Government (usually referred to as the Maud Committee), and the Royal Commission on Local Government in England (usually referred to as the Redcliffe-Maud Commission, with the same chairman as the Maud Committee, now ennobled), did present some very different theoretical assumptions about the proper representational role of local government councillors.

The Maud Committee, in summarizing its conclusions about local government councillors, wrote that:

> the direct responsibility of local government for services designed to meet the needs of many sections of the population can only be effectively discharged if the people with first-hand knowledge of all sections of the community are represented on councils.[35]

This view of the desirability of at least some rough match between the socio-economic composition of the population and the membership of local councils is explicitly contrasted by the authors of the Maud Report with their own theories of proper representation in national legislative bodies:

> It might be objected that our ideas of government in Britain do not require that representatives should be identified directly with particular groups. They speak and act as individuals rather than delegates. The discussion of representation, however, generally concerns Parliament. The functions of Parliament and local authorities are very different. Local government by definition requires a closer connection between local representatives and the management of the services of a relatively small area; it is concerned only with local issues and not with such wide issues of state as defence or foreign affairs. The activities of local councils . . . [are increasingly] concerned with improving the quality of living conditions and ameliorating the personal difficulties of individuals in their areas. . . . These special features of local government, in contrast to central government, require personal experience of all the varied circumstances and opinions of the local electorate which are unlikely to be available if small sections of the population play a disproportionate role in local government.[36]

Thus, the Maud Report not only argues for the distinctiveness of the problem of representation in local government; it also stands in contrast to the emphases of its predecessor in London, the Herbert Commission.

Although the Maud Report elsewhere rejects the notion of explicitly investigating the "calibre" of councillors,[37] it is obvious that its members proceeded on the expectation that a council which was socially representative of the community it served would, on balance, produce "better" policies than one that was less representative.

The Maud Committee focused on the need for representative councils, in a socio-economic sense. The Redcliffe-Maud Commission, which followed it, placed more emphasis on representation, in the sense of articulating community feelings: "The most important function—and the only duty—of a local council should be to make known the views of the local community on any matter affecting it."[38]

Furthermore, the councillor was to be an appeals agent to whom the constituent could turn when dissatisfied with public services:

> A proper relationship between members and their constituents is a pivotal point in English local government; the former, by finding out at first hand their constituents' wants, learn how the services are working and how they can be improved; the latter have in the member an immediate point of reference if they do not get satisfaction from officers [council employees] . . . [The councillor] must be readily accessible as well as sympathetic.[39]

Thus, although both the Maud Committee and the Redcliffe-Maud Commission emphasized the councillor's representational role, they opted for somewhat different definitions of representativeness. The Maud Committee focused on the need for socio-economically representative councillors, while the Redcliffe-Maud Commission placed more emphasis on accurate articulation of the views of local constituents.

It is, of course, a question for empirical examination as to whether these two propositions—that local governments ought to be socio-economically representative; and that they ought to facilitate direct personal ties between councillors and those they represent so that views are accurately articulated—are congruent or not. I will be suggesting throughout this study that this relationship is a problematic one; that is, having a councillor socio-economically representative of his ward does not necessarily facilitate all types of councillor–constituent contact.

The members of both the Maud and Redcliffe-Maud Commissions saw a tension between councillors who were able to reflect community views and those who might be most effective at directing the technical work of the council. While they resolve this dilemma by arguing for a division of labour among councillors, with some performing one set of tasks, while other councillors emphasize the other,[40] I will also be suggesting later in this study that some councillors, particularly the "ideology of localism" councillors, claim the ability to do both tasks effectively.

But despite some differences in emphases between the Maud and Redcliffe-Maud Commission reports, the two together stand in striking contrast to the earlier Herbert Commission in the nature of their concerns about representation. Where the Herbert Commission placed its emphases on articulation of council views to party and public, the Maud and Redcliffe-Maud Commission emphasized the articulation of public concerns to the council.

In Chapter 6 of this study I will be assessing the extent to which the councils and councillors studied meet these varying criteria of "good" councillors. But the theoretical problems raised here are not limited to local government in England. Questions regarding proper definitions of representativeness, for example, have been strongly raised in American politics as well. Debates preceding and during the 1972 Democratic Presidential Nominating Convention particularly focused on these problems, and I will return to them in Chapter 6, the concluding chapter of this study.

I indicated in the Introduction that an interest in problems of American neighbourhood government originally stimulated this study. I will also be returning to this comparative concern in Chapter 6, with an examination of the now rather extensive literature on American–British comparative urban politics in light of the findings of this particular study. Problems of representation and of community are not limited to England,

and I will be arguing that the "solutions" found by political practitioners in London have relevance to the American experience as well.

2 The Three Boroughs

Although their present configurations date back only to 1963, London boroughs, in common with most units of government in Britain, have a strong sense of history about them. (The ceremonial mace is paraded into the council chamber at the beginning of meetings; the mayor is accorded ritualistic deference; and borough documents are marked with the borough seal, an emblem which tries to trace the origins of these late-twentieth-century entities as far back in time as possible.) This sense of history is not limited to formal trappings, but pervades the attitudes of the participants as well. It is important to note that the importance of recalled past history does not have any necessary ideological valence to it. Although we sometimes think that a sense of the importance of the past is a typically conservative attitude, it was the Labour councillors of Tower Hamlets who most strongly evinced this sense among the three boroughs studied here.

Social science usually strives for generalizability. This chapter, on the other hand, will emphasize the particular. It is an examination of the elements of distinctiveness (as well as possible similarities) among the three London Boroughs studied. This "borough-distinctiveness" will be presented as one of the important formative elements of councillor attitudes and actions, both in shaping the types of problems that councillors need to deal with, and in providing a history of local experience from which they can draw cues on how to do so. As I suggested above, tradition seems to play an important part in borough political life (even if it needs to be a created tradition) and it therefore becomes a useful exercise to examine distinctive details of local

life in any study attempting to understand local political processes.

This chapter is divided into two broad sections: the physical
characteristics of the boroughs studied, and the populations that
live within them. Although there is an obvious interaction
between these two elements, I will be arguing that they are
independently important in understanding the nature of the
boroughs, and in some sense act separately in setting the agenda
of issues the boroughs must confront.

The three boroughs studied here were originally chosen for
their reputations for diversity. This chapter will describe that
diversity, and argue that the boroughs' past patterns of distinctiveness act as constraints on patterns of politics in the
present. But this emphasis on diversity ought not obscure the
fact that the boroughs are, in the final analysis, operating within
the same national and regional political systems, and are located
in the same metropolitan area. As I will be suggesting in
subsequent chapters, there are patterns of common economic
influence which impinge on all three boroughs. Each of the
boroughs is becoming more integrated into regional and
national economic life. Borough "autarky" is declining.

What the patterns of traditional distinctiveness reported on in
this chapter do, however, is to make likely that the boroughs'
response to current economic stimuli will vary. The history of
the boroughs remains alive in the minds of its decision-makers,
and the boroughs' current physical and demographic make-up is
a consequence of this past history (see maps in Appendix 2).
Thus, although in later chapters I will be describing some
common forces acting upon the boroughs in the current period,
their traditions of past distinctiveness described in this chapter
are important elements in structuring their varied response in
the present.

A   THE APPEARANCE OF THE BOROUGHS

When researchers for the Greater London Council computed
composite indices of borough socio-economic characteristics in
1971, Bromley had the highest score and Tower Hamlets the
lowest in all of Greater London.[1] Islington was the third lowest
of the 32 London Boroughs. These statistical findings fit well

with some popular senses of affluence and poverty in the London region, but not with all. Tower Hamlets, comprising much of the East End of London, forms the area which conjures up images for many other Englishmen of Dickensian slums and social misery. Bromley, on the other hand, while mainly composed of neat and obviously well-off suburbs, would not usually be thought of as the height of English affluence. Indeed, the section of Bromley which would have the most well-known "sociological" image would be Orpington, a largely commuter village which, in the 1960s, became a metaphor, in the concept of "Orpington man", for a new classless Englishman, living a suburban life which increasingly separated him from the political cleavages represented by the Labour and Conservative Parties. And if one popular image was sought of what "Islington" meant, it would probably be "gentrification", that process by which young professionals move into working-class areas close to the central city, renovate old town houses, and make the area "trendy".

But popular images are not perfectly reflective of the reality of each of the three boroughs. Islington, despite a reputation as an arena for gentrification, remains a basically working-class borough with (as of 1970 statistics) the second lowest percentage of good housing of any of the London Boroughs.[2] And the vice-chairman of the Islington Council Social Services Committee recently reported that Islington still had 1700 housing units without indoor plumbing.[3]

By now, most of the historic East End slum districts of Tower Hamlets have been completely levelled, first by the Second World War Blitz, and later by actions of the local government. In place of traditional working-class row houses, Tower Hamlets is now typified by high-rise housing projects, occasionally punctuated by shopping streets and remaining pockets of old housing.

With regard to Bromley, while the notion of "Orpington man" may conjure up, at least for Englishmen, a coherent picture of homogeneous modern suburbia, the reality of the borough is far more variegated.

Perhaps most sharply of the three boroughs studied, Bromley is not a single entity, but a collection of diverse communities, which happen to be surrounded by a common political boundary. The current London Borough of Bromley is an amalgamation of five different pre-reorganization local authorities. Only one other London borough was formed from so many different constituent parts.

On the far western edge of the borough, in what had been the independent Urban District of Penge prior to the 1963 formation of Greater London, is an area which is physically and socio-logically working-class Inner London.[4] At the new borough's outer reaches to the south-east, in Darwin Ward, is territory that is still so rural that its councillor described agricultural labourers who vote for him because, as he (jokingly) recounts, they think his family was "meant to rule".

This distinctiveness within Bromley is reinforced by the physical distances which separate parts of the borough. It is geographically the largest in London,[5] patterns of transportation and communication lead to little natural contact between many of its sections, and no single weekly newspaper circulates throughout all of the borough's sections. One indicator of the geographic spread of the borough, and its diversity, can be found in the fact that despite the political consolidation of 1963, neither postal nor telephone patterns have yet made this switch. Mail to most of the borough is still addressed in pre-consolidation manner, as if sections of the borough were still independent boroughs in the County of Kent, and much of the eastern part of the new borough is not within the Greater London telephone dialling code area.

Although Inner London boroughs are far more compact, sharp distinctions in appearance and orientation separate parts of Islington as well. In the southern Barnsbury and Canonbury areas, gentrification has been underway for a long time, over 20 years by one estimate,[6] and sections look affluent indeed. The official guide of the borough describes "elegant Georgian houses taking a new and welcome lease on life",[7] and one can find many streets of completely redeveloped houses, with manicured lawns and freshly painted doors which have become standard symbols of the gentrification process. Even where these sections exist, however, the majority of the population in the wards concerned is still working class, now largely housed in the council house estates in the neighbourhood.[8] But a walk down the side streets of Barnsbury and Canonbury would convince most passing observers that they were in a neighbourhood of general afflu-ence.

Varying explanations have been advanced to account for the development of gentrification in Islington. The "intrinsic beauty of the Georgian houses, which exist in the low-income areas of Inner London"[9] has been cited by academic observers and implied in the official guide quotation reproduced above. Government renovation grants for such houses have reinforced the tendency to rehabilitate this type of housing.[10] Other observers have concentrated their attention on "planning blight", in which long-delayed plans for low-income housing or commercial redevelopment produce an uncertainty in the local property market which proves attractive to speculators, who buy properties piecemeal, rehabilitate them, and then sell them to middle-class owner-occupiers.[11] Once renovation of this type begins, of course, the prospects for large-scale "slum clearance" projects in the area drop sharply.

Such redevelopment could not take place without a ready market for the redeveloped housing, and such a market clearly does exist. The proximity of Islington to the London financial centre is often commented on by local political leaders as a reason why Islington has become attractive to middle- and upper-class residents, and office construction in central London meant that there were more such people looking for housing. In addition, construction restrictions on suburban housing, particularly the London Green Belt, have been regarded as an additional explanation for the development of gentrification in Inner London, since Green Belt restrictions make the expansion of the suburban housing stock more difficult.[12]

No one would be likely to get an impression that gentrification had taken place in most of North Islington. This is an area of largely old and unredeveloped housing, with a sprinkling of council house estates of both pre-war and modern vintage. In the older row housing, particularly, are the worst housing problems and the severest social problems in the borough. One observer characterized North Islington as a "non-community", with a population heavily made up of short-term residents living in extremely crowded conditions, and with many houses still lacking indoor plumbing.[13] The physical problems of the area are exacerbated by a shortage of open space rare for London, at least a shortage of open space of the usable park and playground type.[14] Many sections of the north of the borough do have another type of open space, however, where slum clearance projects have levelled old housing but where no new housing has yet been erected to take its place.

If Bromley is a borough of numerous distinct communities, and northern and southern parts of Islington are also quite distinctive in their appearance, then Tower Hamlets would, at first appearance at least, have the most homogeneous "look" of the three boroughs studied. In one sense this is peculiar since, as I shall argue in later chapters, residents and political leaders in Tower Hamlets have a very definite sense of "place". But this sense is, for the most part, a memory of the past, since redevelopment has eliminated the sharpest physical distinctions between sections of the borough. (There is still an unredeveloped pocket at the western edge of the borough, in Spitalfields Ward.) Within Tower Hamlets the most significant distinctions would be between different types of council house estates. In a borough now typified by high-rise council houses, the low-rise developments remain the most highly sought-after, in the reporting of local political leaders.

Several commentators have described the process of complete redevelopment and new council-house building as the working-class equivalent of the middle-class suburban move to a single-family, owner-occupied dwelling. Willmott and Young, in their comparisons of working-class life in Inner London and in suburbia, argued in 1960 that "Bethnal Green [one of the components of what is now Tower Hamlets] is changing fast . . . and may be growing more like the suburb every day."[15] Rex and Moore, in their 1967 study of race relations in Birmingham, describe this type of development as a consequence of working-class political power, used to create environments for the established working class (i.e., not the new immigrants) which can be their own version of suburbia. Thus, in their description, "we get a new public suburbia parallelling the private suburbia."[16]

This social consequence of council housing may help to explain why the issue is still central to the Labour Party today. A 1975 study by the national Labour Party showed that 63 per cent of the Labour groups in British local governments regarded building more housing as their top priority.[17] What varies among local Labour parties in Britain is what type of council housing they emphasize.

This variation is found between the boroughs studied, and also within them over time. In broad categories, councils may choose to emphasize high-rise council house estates, low-rise (and less dense) estates, or the rehabilitation and municipalization of existing private rented housing. And in addition to these physical options, local councils have had considerable discretion regarding who they would admit to their council housing. Rex and Moore, in studying Birmingham, describe how that city for many years eliminated new immigrants from consideration for council housing by adopting a "housing points scheme" which required at least five years' residence in Birmingham in order to be eligible.[18] Although national policy requires that priority in rehousing be given to "homeless families", councils can make choices in this area as well. Rex and Moore argue that Birmingham often rehoused such families in hostels rather than in regular council housing as a "deterrent".[19]

But other councils may have different emphases. Islington, in particular, now gives top priority for new council housing to homeless families, thereby causing considerable political controversy in the borough. As I will be suggesting in later chapters, each of the boroughs studied has undergone a process of socioeconomic transformation, and these transformations have had important policy consequences. In the area of housing policy, these have led to changes in Islington from an emphasis on area clearance and construction of new council estates to an emphasis on rehabilitation of existing properties.

This shift in emphasis has been accompanied by a change to an admissions policy which leads to more council housing for people who are not long-time residents of Islington. This category includes both migrants from the rest of Britain and also a considerable population of "New Commonwealth" immigrants who have settled in North Islington.[20] These two shifts in policy, of type of construction emphasized and of admissions criteria, have followed a change in the political composition of the Islington Labour Party and a subsequent change in the membership of the Islington Borough Council. These political changes will be described in later chapters, but it may be useful to note at this point that it is only in recent years that Islington has "agreed to rehouse furnished tenants from clearance area",[21] the type of tenants most likely to be newly arrived immigrants, and the Islington Council has publicly shifted its emphasis to rehabilitation and municipalization.[22] In addition to publicly owned rehabilitation, the Islington Council is now also encouraging the development of tenant-run cooperatives, with rehabilitation funded by the Council.[23]

In Tower Hamlets, on the other hand, the major shift has not been from new construction to rehabilitation, but rather there has been a shift of emphasis of the type of new construction engaged in, from high-rise to low-rise new construction. For housing controlled by the *borough*, Tower Hamlets has not been as receptive to new arrivals as Islington, and the area of largest concentration of newly arrived immigrants, the Spitalfields Ward, has both the highest percentage of housing units without "full amenities", and is also at the low end of the scale in percentage of the world's population living in council housing.[24]

It is important to emphasize this distinction between that portion of the public housing stock controlled by the borough and that under the jurisdiction of the metropolitan-area government, the Greater London Council. The London Government Act of 1963, which established the present structure, divided responsibility for public housing between the boroughs and the area-wide GLC. It envisioned, however, a gradual shift in control of most of the existing housing stock to borough control.

Boroughs have reacted differently to the opportunity to take over GLC housing estates. Islington, for example, has been far more interested in moving in this direction than Tower Hamlets. (Although at one point the London Labour Party urged the London boroughs not to accept the transfer of GLC estates from the ten Conservative-controlled Greater London Council,[25] Tower Hamlets was one of the few boroughs to steadily resist such transfers.[26])

The reasons for this variation in attitude seem to lie in the two councils' differing policies on who they wish to admit to the housing they control. Existing GLC projects, when transferred to borough control, come, of course, with their already existing group of tenants. GLC housing policies give priority to people displaced by GLC construction projects anywhere in the London area. As a result, these projects are rarely populated by "old-timers" from the boroughs where the projects are located.

Since Islington does not give "old-timers" that much priority for its own projects, there is not that much difference in the types of families housed in GLC or borough housing estates. Given this, Islington has little reason not to absorb GLC estates into borough control. Indeed, many members of the Islington

Council actively seek to gain control of GLC estates, since they believe that Islington does a better job of providing social services than does the GLC.

In Tower Hamlets, on the other hand, the admissions policies of the borough council produce considerable disparities in the types of people found in borough and GLC estates. Under such circumstances, the incentives for the Tower Hamlets borough council to take over GLC estates is much less, since it will require the borough to manage housing containing tenants which many in Tower Hamlets do not regard as "real" East Enders.

This variation in council policies is rarely ascribed directly to the difference in admissions procedures. Members of the Tower Hamlets Council, for example, are far more likely to talk about the adverse financial consequences for the borough which might accompany the absorption of GLC esates than they are to discuss who lives in those estates. As a practical matter, the consequences of these policy variations for the "look" of the areas involved are largely, but not entirely symbolic. Although the outside observer would not be able to immediately identify an estate as GLC- or borough-controlled, GLC estates tend to be larger, denser, and have more visible signs of vandalism than most borough estates. The relative appeal of borough estates in Tower Hamlets is enhanced by the borough's policy of providing greater subsidies per housing unit than does the Greater London Council. As a result, rents in borough estates tend to be somewhat cheaper than those in GLC properties.

Within a borough, therefore, a "prestige order" gets set up among varying types of estates. Although direct evidence is hard to come by, it is frequently asserted by observers of British politics that boroughs can, if they wish, structure the admissions policies for borough-controlled estates so that "problem families" get concentrated on certain estates, leaving the remainder of the borough's own estates free of such groups. No such "segregation" is possible within the GLC estates, since space on GLC estates is available as a first priority to individuals displaced by GLC construction. This produces mixed populations drawn from throughout the London area.

An outside observer can tell, therefore, from the general appearance of an estate in Tower Hamlets, generally what category a particular project falls into, and these distinctions are, of course, well-known to local residents. In addition to the social distinctions among borough-run estates, the distinction between GLC and borough estates is clearly indicated by signs and building markings which show which authority is in charge of a particular estate. In Islington, however, this distinction would be somewhat harder to make, since that borough has been considerably more active in taking over former GLC estates, and they would now be marked as Islington Council estates.

I mentioned earlier the argument made by Rex and Moore that working-class groups with political power used council housing as a way to create the working-class equivalent of middle-class suburbia, and that this process has adverse impact on the newly arrived immigrants, who are channelled into what Rex and Moore refer to as the unredeveloped "lodging-house areas".[27]

The variations discovered in this research between Islington and Tower Hamlets both support and refine this conception. In Islington, the northern part of the borough clearly seems to fit this pattern, although the new political leadership of the borough seems unhappy about it and asserts its interest in changing the pattern. In Tower Hamlets, on the other hand, although a small unredeveloped area can be found at the western edge of the borough which fits the pattern described above, the extent of redevelopment in most of the borough makes such a pattern unavailable. Instead, a distinction grows up between differing types of council housing: one portion which is borough-controlled, and largely houses "natives" of the area, and the other, run by the Greater London Council, largely populated by "outsiders".[28]

Although there is no way to know for certain how these differing patterns originally developed, it seems plausible to suggest that a pattern of partial redevelopment, such as observed in Islington, was less possible for Tower Hamlets because of the extent of Second World War destruction. Thus differentiation within public housing serves the "function" of making at least a rudimentary distinction between the local working class and new arrivals, which is elsewhere served by the distinction between council house and "lodging-house-area" neighbourhoods.[29]

Although the variations in appearance of neighbourhood within the two Labour-controlled Inner London boroughs studied are relatively subtle in nature, and the forces which

produce this variation are not always publicly acknowledged, no
such subtlety is needed to discover the variation between these
two boroughs together on the one hand, and the suburban
Borough of Bromley on the other. Bromley, as I indicated above,
is a very varied borough which for most purposes is not a
collective community at all. But despite the variation within
Bromley, its domination by suburban owner-occupiers is clear
both from housing data[30] and from direct observation.

With the exception of the Penge section at the far western end
of the borough, the bulk of Bromley is characterized by quiet
tree-shaded streets of single-family homes. Two sections of GLC
housing estates, built as "overspill projects" shortly before and
shortly after the Second World War, when Bromley was not yet
a part of the London area politically, are quite isolated from the
more traditional suburban neighbourhoods around them, and
have little impact on the owner-occupied neighbourhoods.
Although some analysts of these "overspill" estates in Britain
have argued that class antagonisms can be strong at physical
boundaries between working-class and middle-class communities,[31] specific studies of the Bromley estates have argued that
the relationship between the estates and the surrounding
neighbourhoods is one of "latent hostility", coolness rather than
active conflict, and that usually "reserve and indifference
prevail".[32] This particular study suggested that if the surrounding area is very affluent, which is the case in Bromley, the
council estates (which are low-rise, with broad expanses of lawn,
and neatly kept up) pose "no threat to the suburban ethos",[33]
and that, in any event, the "physical and social barriers that seal
them off from their surroundings are unmistakable".[34]

As a result, it is really unnecessary for the Bromley Council,
as a political body, to have much of any policy about these
already existing estates, and the legal powers of the borough to
resist additional GLC estates have sufficed to prevent more
being built, at least up to now. (If the GLC wishes to build a
new estate, the borough has the right to veto the project, subject
to override by the national government.[35]) The possibility that
the national government might indeed take such action is a
source of some nervousness for Bromley officials, but it has not
yet been much used, and has certainly not resulted in any
massive expansion of GLC public housing in the borough. The
borough itself builds small amounts of borough-run council

housing for local residents, but to the degree that borough-controlled council housing is an issue within Bromley, debate largely revolves around the question of whether the borough should begin to sell off parts of its existing council housing stock to current tenants, or whether such dwellings should be retained under Borough ownership.[36]

In Bromley, therefore, resistance to additional public housing is something of a political given, and controversy about land use and the physical appearance of the borough revolve around different questions. Here questions about patterns of private housing development predominate. These involve issues both of development on vacant land and redevelopment of some existing sections of large old houses into low-rise, owner-occupied apartment development. Much of Bromley's remaining large tracts of vacant lands lie within the London Green Belt area, on which intense development has been forbidden by national policy. Although maintenance of Green Belt policy is not without its critics, some arguing that keeping the Green Belt as it is reinforces London housing problems by making land scarce,[37] almost all Bromley political figures cite Green Belt restrictions as sufficient reason for opposing further development of large-scale private housing within the Green Belt area.

The Green Belt covers much of the southern portion of the borough, the section furthest from central London. Adjoining neighbourhoods tend to be quite affluent. At the north-western edge of the borough, however, especially in Copers Cope Ward, the usual pattern of political resistance to increased development is somewhat different. Copers Cope is an area of very large old houses, still primarily owner-occupied, with extensive re-development into the low-rise private apartment construction mentioned above now taking place. This private development, although the subject of considerable objection from neighbourhood political figures, does not rouse the type of opposition from the borough as a whole that publicly-financed council housing does. Indeed, some of the ward leaders seem to feel that the borough political leadership supports the redevelopment of the area.[38]

What we have here, then, is the distinction between opposition to "urbanization" per se, and urbanization which would change the class composition of the area. The latter is resolutely opposed by the borough political leadership, while the former is tolerated, if not tacitly encouraged, at least within limited geographical confines. The owner-occupied redevelopment of Copers Cope poses no party-political threat to the Borough Conservative Party, and it imposes neither immediate financial costs which would be incurred if the borough itself were to build council houses, nor the indirect future costs for social services which borough leaders fear would follow on from the erection of council housing by the Greater London Council.

I will be suggesting in later chapters that the patterns of political leadership in Bromley have undergone a change from one of a rather isolated defence of English rural and village traditions, to a suburban pattern of life more completely integrated into the London metropolitan area. The physical changes in Copers Cope Ward, therefore, indicate both cause and effect in this process. Economic changes and changes in family life styles among the affluent have reduced the demand among such people for the type of old housing available in Copers Cope. Owners of property and builders have incentives to redevelop this type of property to fulfil increasing middle-class demands for affordable private housing.

This demand is fuelled by the office development of central London and the strengthening, at least up to and during the time of this study, of London's position as a world financial centre. Such redevelopment might not be able to take place, however, without cooperation from the political leadership of the borough. Since the alternative to redevelopment of Copers Cope into middle-class apartment housing might ultimately be an evolution of the area into working- and lower-class housing (either by GLC redevelopment or, more likely, by the sub-dividing of large houses, as has happened elsewhere in London) the borough does not resist redevelopment in Copers Cope.

In other single-family home parts of the borough, however, where the style of the houses is not incompatible with modern middle- and upper-class living, the borough strenuously resists apartment development, even for new middle-class residents. Borough politicians argue strongly against GLC proposals to increase permissible densities, for example.[39]

The population changes that come with development encourage a political climate within the borough which supports further economic development, and which looks on a policy which completely opposes any physical change as inappropriate for a political unit which does not want to become a backwater. This change in political attitude is clearly reflected in the physical plans for the commercial area in Bromley town centre. The borough is engaged in a large-scale library and theatre project, and has proposed new traffic patterns to encourage easier access to town centre shopping and office complexes despite considerable local area opposition within the Conservative Party. As the opposition Labour Party commented, the patterns of commercial usage on Bromley High Street are gradually shifting from "greengrocers to offices and banks".[40]

This pattern of promotion of commercial development by the Bromley borough political leadership often arouses local opposition. As mentioned above, the "Bromley North Traffic Scheme" is one such example of a project with internal Conservative Party opposition. In another case, this type of local opposition was successful in at least temporarily blocking the conversion of a local airport from one used exclusively for recreational flying to one designed for "executive jet aircraft".[41] And although the extension of the London motorway system through Bromley was ultimately decided on (and defeated) at higher political levels, within Bromley itself those Conservatives along its immediate route were more intensely opposed than the Borough itself, which seemed to adhere to the general Conservative Party policy in London of supporting additional motorway construction.[42]

B THE PEOPLE OF THE BOROUGHS

There is, of course, an obvious relationship between the physical development of an area and its socio-economic composition. As I suggested in the previous section, the development of gentrification in Islington, for example, was dependent not only on an available stock of housing with the potential for this type of redevelopment, but also on a population pool which sought this type of housing. On the other hand, the absence of a possible housing stock available for gentrification in Tower Hamlets has meant that that borough has retained its essentially homogeneous working-class character despite its physical proximity to the workplace of many middle-class (and upper-class) executives in the London financial district.

But, as I suggested in the previous section, the composition of the population of an area also has impact in determining just what its reaction to incoming groups will be. Thus, Tower Hamlets presents an intriguing mixed history of an apparent receptiveness to new arrivals but a defensive posture today.

Historical studies of the East End of London have shown a long history of non-English migration to the area. In a pattern suggestive of many older American cities, one specific study of Spitalfields in the western part of Tower Hamlets suggests that this part of the borough has seen three distinct waves of migration: extensive Irish arrivals in the nineteenth century,[43] followed by heavy Jewish immigration in the decades immediately preceding the First World War,[44] and a post-Second World War migration from the "New Commonwealth",[45] itself sub-divided into three waves of West African, West Indian, and Pakistani streams.[46]

Interestingly, local political leaders in Tower Hamlets trace migration considerably further back in time and, with some pride, describe the area's receptivity to Huguenot refugees from France after the revocation of the Edict of Nantes. But despite this historical memory, most of Tower Hamlets today still remains a self-contained community, at least in the sense that it is heavily populated by people born in the area. Willmott and Young, in their study of Bethnal Green shortly after the Second World War, described a pattern of traditional passage of jobs from father to son in the borough's dominant labour union, the Transport and General Workers Union,[47] and how working-class residents made informal arrangements with rent collectors to find housing for their married daughters nearby.[48] Although this matrilocal housing pattern did not work so well for council housing,[49] Bethnal Green, according to the 1951 census, still had the highest percentage of residents born within the borough in which they then lived of any area in London.[50]

These patterns of residence and job succession fit the pattern Goldthorpe *et al.*, in their study of the affluent working class, described as "proletarian traditionalism",[51] a pattern of life they describe as "solidaristic collectivism . . . a disposition towards collective forms of action based on consciousness of belonging to a working-class community".[52]

Although the Blitz and redevelopment have considerably reduced the total population of Tower Hamlets, and changing employment opportunities have reduced the job-related solidarity described above, the area is still characterized by resistance to in-migration, and it is a largely successful resistance. The gentrification pattern of Islington is impossible because of the absence of suitable housing, a circumstance which not only keeps people out, but which also prevents upwardly mobile East Enders from remaining in the area.[53] But Tower Hamlets is also resistant to proposals for new middle-class housing construction, and many local leaders fear the possible influx of non-working-class residents as land occupied by the now slightly used docks along the Thames is made available for redevelopment.

The official newspaper of the borough began one account of redevelopment plans by saying, "Docklands for the East Enders is Council policy"[54] with the implication that this was perhaps not the policy of the regional and national government, although it ought to be. The construction of a small number of new private homes in one stretch of Dockland led to considerable local protest, with one community association exemplifying much of the local reaction by condemning a plan which, they argued, would make the area "reserved for rich people".[55]

It may be that those who now reside in Tower Hamlets are made up of that fraction of the traditional population which has consciously decided to stay in the area. The pattern of "overspill estates" described earlier has meant that many East Enders had a choice, at least at one time, of whether to stay in the East End or move to a suburban council estate. Willmott and Young describe how those who made the suburban move did so because of their dislike for apartment living and "for the children".[56]

It is reasonable to assume, therefore, that for many of those who stayed, the traditional values of working-class solidarity in a homogeneous working-class community seemed more important. One aspect of traditional English working-class life, commented on by many English sociologists, is a tradition of "reserve", with the "respectable working class" being cautious about inviting strangers into their homes.[57] Although some of these analysts distinguish between in-home behaviour and life in the streets, it is nevertheless possible to suggest that this style of life leads naturally into a political pattern of attempting to preserve neighbourhood stability as well.

In view of this pattern of resistance in Tower Hamlets, one must ask why it has seemed less prominent, or at least less successful, in Islington. Although the physical differences in housing stock are obviously crucial, this distinction between the two working-class boroughs studied may also be found in the composition of the two areas' traditional working-class populations. The Tower Hamlets working-class was quite isolated, working close to home[58] and living a life of "proletarian solidarity". In Islington, on the other hand, jobs were never so concentrated, and most of its residents worked in service occupations and therefore interacted more frequently with middle-class populations.

The northern part of Islington particularly has been characterized as a "non-community" with severe social problems[59] and overcrowded working-class slums.[60] In addition to heavy New Commonwealth immigration, it also received a considerable amount of recent migration from elsewhere in the British Isles, including a continuing heavy stream from Ireland.[61] This distinguishes Islington from Tower Hamlets, where the Irish migration was largely nineteenth century.

But in addition to these patterns of external migration, it has also been suggested that some of the new arrivals in North Islington are working-class people pushed out of the southern parts of the borough by the spread of gentrification.[62] Why were such individuals so much more readily displaced than their compatriots in Tower Hamlets?

When Willmott and Young compared working-class life in all-working-class environments with that in mixed socio-economic circumstances, they found that those individuals who lived in homogeneous working-class surroundings were more likely to have "self-respect".[63] They ascribed this self-respect to the combination of a long-settled working-class community and to a local political system which is ideologically based on the importance of manual labour.[64] Both of these conditions were more weakly met in Islington than in Tower Hamlets. Islington not only had a more recent pattern of immigration than most of Tower Hamlets and a consequent smaller proportion of locally born residents,[65] but the service occupations which dominated working-class employment in Islington were not the sort which would be as conducive to the support of an ideology of the importance of labour as the manual jobs held by East Enders.[66]

It therefore makes sense to think that not only was Islington physically permeable by the middle class, because of its housing stock, but psychologically permeable as well, because of lesser working-class self-confidence. Willmott and Young further argue, as I have mentioned above, that working-class self-confidence is dependent on residency in a homogeneous working-class community. Once gentrification of Islington began, of course, its working-class residents no longer lived in such a community. If we accept Willmott and Young's arguments, then the process of middle-class entry, once begun, would become self-generating as the older working-class residents became less able and willing to resist.

(In very recent years, however, the occupational base of Tower Hamlets has itself undergone considerable change. As I will be discussing more fully in the next chapter, working-class residents of Tower Hamlets have increasingly been switching from their manual occupations to service jobs of the sort traditionally more prominent among the Islington working-class population. The social base which has sustained Tower Hamlets working-class defensiveness, therefore, may be in process of erosion.

I will be describing the adaptation of the Tower Hamlets leadership to these new circumstances in Chapter 3. Unlike Islington, however, there has as yet been little gentrification in Tower Hamlets. Indeed, it may be that the very success of the "self-confident" working class of Tower Hamlets in promoting the comprehensive redevelopment of the borough as a place for working-class residents has precluded the entry of any substantial number of gentrifiers, even if the social bases which promoted this self-confidence in the first place are now no longer so strongly present.)

In Islington, without such strong traditions, entry of gentrifiers has been easier. As I will be suggesting in later chapters, the entry of these new residents, while they still form only a relatively small fraction of the borough's total population, has had very significant consequences, both for the composition of the borough's pool of political activists, and for the borough council's policies as well.

But the entry of these new arrivals into effective participation in Islington politics has been dependent on their adherence to the Labour Party, which still gets the almost automatic vote of the borough's working-class majority. In class-dominated English politics, it is something of an anomaly to find a large group of middle-class Labour supporters. The explanation for this phenomenon lies in the fact that the new arrivals, although middle class, come from a very specific sub-section of the middle class. Those who moved in first have been characterized as "people for whom external effects of a low-prestige address are minimal, people who are not in business, but in teaching, architecture, or similar professions".[67] "They may even feel that they will gain status with their friends by living in such an area, so demonstrating their lack of snobbishness."[68]

Such individuals are frequently upwardly mobile (and many political leaders among them stress their working-class origins.) As has been found in more general analyses of English patterns of partisan identification, such individuals have no problem in retaining the Labour Party adherence of their youth and school days.[69] While most of these upwardly mobiles are from out of the borough, the existence of available housing for them in Islington means that upwardly mobile working class natives of Islington can remain there. (In Tower Hamlets, on the other hand, Willmott and Young observed that such individuals are almost required, by their change of social class, to move out of the borough.[70])

The middle-class gentrifiers of Islington are obviously very different sorts of people from the middle-class residents of suburban Bromley. Here the housing patterns are more likely to be detached or semi-detached single-family homes rather than the redeveloped row houses of southern Islington. And the middle-class residents of Bromley are much more likely to have business occupations than the independent professionals in Islington. They are also much more likely to be Conservative in their political allegiances.

As I suggested earlier, there are some pockets of working-class populations in Bromley, a phenomenon common to English suburbia where "overspill estates" are a frequent phenomenon and where there are no middle-class boroughs without significant working-class populations.[71] But the dominant population groups in Bromley are middle class and home-owning, factors which, according to many English voting studies, independently reinforce Conservative Party support,[72] as well as raising rates of political participation.[73]

Organizational participation seems to be an important part of suburban life in Britain, as in the United States. Numerous general studies of English suburbia have emphasized the role of such organizations,[74] and specific studies of Bromley have confirmed this.[75] The Bromley borough council has been described as co-opting these organizations, and using them as vehicles for carrying out council policies.[76] This finding was confirmed in this research, both in interviews with local political leaders and in examination of council records.[77]

But despite the overall characteristics of suburban life and its relation to politics described above, variations within suburban Bromley can be found, both in type of resident and in responsiveness of the borough to local organizational pressure. The first section of this chapter described some of the differences among types of middle-class suburban housing found within Bromley, and these variations have political consequences. As I suggested earlier, the notion of "Orpington Man" was a common one in late 1950s and early 1960s British political commentary, and it suggests a classless suburbanite deserting both class-ridden major parties for the newly resurgent and class-ambiguous Liberal Party. One observer of this phenomenon in Orpington suggests that the success of Liberals in Orpington was primarily due, not to the absence of class feeling, but to conflict between two groups of middle-class populations within this fast-growing part of Bromley, "the established vs. the newcomer".[78]

In a more general context, attempts have been made to categorize the types of populations found in English commuter villages. One group of newcomers in such a categorization may fit the pattern for the rapidly growing parts of Bromley, the "reluctant commuter", a middle-class urban worker with some limited capital, ineligible for council housing but unable to afford middle-class housing in the centre city.[79] The expansion of single-family-home areas where such people can reside is limited by the Green Belt which, as I suggested earlier, limits "suburban sprawl" at the outer reaches of the borough. But it also provides a population base for middle-class redevelopment closer in, in areas such as Copers Cope.

Other suburban sections of Bromley, often of upper-middle and upper-class character, were built up earlier and have not had the same developmental or political patterns. Here one finds "the salariat", business and professional people with a "village in the mind", although it doesn't matter what specific village it is.[80] In such sections of the borough the Liberal revival was never particularly strong,[81] and any additional development continues to be successfully opposed by local residents, with the support of the borough council. As I will be suggesting in later chapters, politics within the Bromley Conservative Party can be seen in terms of the conflicts between these two differing types of suburban neighbourhoods and their differing populations, in a tension between additional London-oriented business and residential development on the one hand, and a desire to maintain the status-quo-oriented "village in the mind" on the other.

C   CONCLUSION

While to some degree the mix of population within the boroughs studied is a function of housing stock availability and a "logic of metropolitan growth" which pushes development outwards, the details of population composition are also affected by the policies of the borough governments themselves. Thus Tower Hamlets actively seeks to retain its working-class character by preventing the development of new private housing, while Bromley seeks to stay predominantly middle- and upper-class by preventing any significant increase in the amount of public housing.

But the policies of a local government such as a London borough are obviously subject to national constraints. Thus Tower Hamlets has been more successful than Bromley in maintaining its local "population policy" over time, since national governments in Britain have, for decades, encouraged the construction of public housing in the Outer London area, while no policy of active encouragement of private housing in working-class areas has been pursued. Similarly, national policy has been of considerable importance in structuring the population composition of the unredeveloped "lodging-house areas" in western Tower Hamlets and North Islington. Although both of these areas have significant concentrations of New Commonwealth immigrants, in no single ward have such immigrants become a majority of the ward population. Although there are a variety of reasons why this may be so, one significant factor in limiting the size of immigrant populations has been the enactment of immigration controls by the national government.

The population of Bromley is not homogeneously middle class in part because of national and regional overspill policies, but also because of the presence of a bit of Inner London within the borough's boundaries at its far western end in Penge. This old housing is now too large for single families and has long-since been converted to multi-occupation. Perhaps in order to prevent a recurrence of this pattern in another section of large houses which have not yet moved to this pattern of use, the borough government has at least tacitly supported the private middle-class redevelopment of Copers Cope. Within existing stable middle-class areas, however, the borough now resists additional development of housing, even when this involves no threat to the basic class composition of the area.

As these examples illustrate, it ought always be borne in mind that the population composition of these boroughs, or of any other specific local geographic sector, is not simply an "independent variable" affecting the politics and policies of the borough, but is also, at least in part, a product of the policies already adopted by the borough government, and by the national government as well. Both the existing physical characteristics of the boroughs, and their population compositions, have impact in setting the agenda of borough issues, and act as constraints on borough decision-making. In subsequent chapters I will be describing the political leaders who operate within these constraints, and the policies they advocate and adopt in responding to them.

3   Borough Leadership: Evolutions of Style

In Chapter 2 I emphasized the role of distinctive local histories in understanding the patterns of political development in each of the three boroughs studied in this research. In this chapter I shall be investigating the role of leadership within each of these borough's governing borough councils in structuring the ways in which the boroughs' governments operate.

I will be presenting "leadership" as an independent explanatory concept, separate from the role of both borough background factors and attitudes of rank-and-file borough councillors. But I will not be arguing that the council leaders about whom I will be reporting act as entirely free agents. Rather, I will be suggesting that patterns of leadership in the three boroughs have undergone evolutions in emphases, and that these evolutions can be tied to common forces of economic change operating throughout the Greater London area. I am not suggesting that economic forces are infallible predictors of political change, but rather that they are predispositional in character, producing environments more conducive to the development of some political patterns than of others.

Leadership theory has itself undergone evolution over time. In summarizing these trends, Ralph Stodgill, writing in the *Handbook of Leadership*, concludes that "theorists no longer explain leadership solely in terms of the individual or the group. Rather, it is believed that characteristics of the individual and demands of the situation interact in such a manner as to permit one, or perhaps a few persons to rise to leadership status."[1] I shall be working within this framework.

Although the boroughs chosen for detailed examination in

this study were not chosen for the characteristics of their council leaders, it nevertheless developed that each had undergone a process of change in leadership shortly before the initiation of this study. It was possible, therefore, to conduct interviews with past leaders as well as present ones, and to examine both official and unofficial accounts of leadership style under both "regimes" in each of the boroughs. I will be focusing in each instance on the leader of the council. The position of leader of the council is the one of real power in the English local government system. He is the leader of the majority party on the council and, although facing annual re-election, serves without time limit. In contrast, the ceremonial head of each borough, the mayor, is normally limited to a one-year term. The ceremonial distinction of being mayor is regarded as a reward for long service (usually although not exclusively in the majority party), and it is not unknown for a leader of a council to temporarily relinquish his leadership for a one-year honorific as mayor, and then to return to the position of real authority as leader of the council.

The position of the leader of the council has been strengthened by the adoption of structural changes by many local councils in England. Of particular importance is the adoption of a policy committee structure, analogous to the Cabinet in national politics. This committee brings together the heads of the various substantive council committees under the chairmanship of the leader of the council. (In earlier forms, each substantive committee acted more autonomously.) The adoption of policy committees was urged by the Maud Committee in 1967, and while not all English local governments have adopted it, all three boroughs studied in this research had such a committee. In their study of *English Local Government Reformed*, Lord Redcliffe-Maud and Bruce Wood characterize this evolution as one in which "more emphasis is placed on . . . leadership from the council's centre".[2] The leader of the council's power over his colleagues has been increased.

These changes will be examined in the context of one specific aspect of the leaders' behaviour: the organizations to which they feel they and their councils ought to be responsive. I will be suggesting that the two major alternative types of organization to which leaders might turn are their own political party organizations, or, alternatively, the at least nominally non-partisan voluntary organizations to be found in their boroughs.

I will be arguing that patterns of borough economic evolution have been conducive to changes in patterns of political leadership. One result of these changes has been a shift in the relative attention paid by council leaders to party organization and local voluntary organizations. Although I will be describing some similarities among the economic forces at work in the three boroughs, I will be showing that these common forces produce differential impact on the leadership styles in the three boroughs.

A   CHANGES IN THE BOROUGHS

In 1966, Ruth Butterworth, writing in the Australian journal *Politics*, characterized the political system of the old London metropolitan borough of Islington as an example of Labour "Single-Party Rule Politics" in which the council's mission was to "keep the rate low and their Labour majority constant".[3] In order to accomplish this, the local Labour Party "became exclusionary",[4] feared local activists[5] and had a council leadership made up exclusively of older members who had lived in the borough all their lives.[6]

Less than ten years later the new London Borough of Islington had a reputation (both externally and internally proclaimed) as one of the most radical in London, had a council leadership made up of middle-class professionals who were largely not native to the area, and had council policies which produced a seemingly endless stream of community meetings, and which proclaimed itself an "open council" (in implicit contrast with past practices). In a 1973 study which included the Borough of Islington in its sample, H. V. Savitch characterized the leader of the Islington Council as a "mediating leader", a member of the Labour left himself, but with several of the "old guard" continuing in strategic positions.[7] After the 1974 borough elections, many of the remaining "old guard" councillors were gone, and most of those who remained had lost their positions of influence.

Most interviewees in Islington attributed the rise of the left-wing of the Labour Party in the borough to a combination of two factors: the Conservative Party victory in the borough elections of 1968, after which some of the older Labour leaders retired; and their replacement, when Labour came back to power after the 1971 elections by professionals, new to Islington if not to the Labour Party, who moved into the borough as a part of the process of "gentrification", the renovation of neighbourhoods of older houses which had recently had dense working-class populations, and their replacement by new professional owner-occupiers. (The Conservative victory of 1968 is best understood in terms of the extremely low popularity of the national Labour government of the day. In 1971 the Conservatives lost every council seat in Islington, and this was repeated in 1974.)

But to describe the change in the Islington Council as automatically following from the entry of a numerically small group of middle-class professionals[8] would be too mechanistic an account. It would fail to take account of the need to explain why and how the new middle-class professional migrants into the borough saw local-level political activity as a useful expenditure of their time, and why they saw the local Labour Party as a congenial arena for this activity, once they had decided to undertake it. They might have limited their political activities to the sorts of national protests Parkin describes in his study of the Campaign for Nuclear Disarmament,[9] a movement in which many Islington activists took part.

The Islington example ought not be taken to suggest that change of leadership is dependent on political turnover or on demographic change. The second borough sampled, Tower Hamlets, chosen originally as an example of a "traditionally led" Labour borough, suggests the contrary. In 1974, the leader of the borough council since its inception in 1964, Alderman J. Orwell, was replaced by a 29-year-old councillor with only four years of council service, Councillor Paul Beasley. Unlike Islington, Tower Hamlets had never come under Conservative Party control (indeed the Conservatives had not elected a councillor since the London reorganization of 1963), nor had the borough seen an influx of new middle-classes as had Islington. Quite to the contrary, Tower Hamlets remains an almost entirely working-class community (professional and managerial workers made up only 5 per cent of the borough's 1971 population[10]), and all elements of the borough's political leadership seem committed to having it largely remain so. The overwhelming and continuous Labour control of the borough has meant that, unlike Islington, there has never been an occasion for the "forced" retirement of long-serving councillors, and many Tower Hamlets councillors serve for long periods indeed. (One interviewed councillor traced his own involvement in politics back to the General Strike of 1926 and his council membership to the 1930s.)

Leadership change in Tower Hamlets, therefore, took place within a continuing setting of working-class control of the Labour Party, and Labour Party control of the borough. In a certain sense, therefore, the leadership change within Tower Hamlets could be described as factional, in contrast to the socio-economically based shift in Labour politics in Islington. (Ruth Butterworth, in her aforementioned study of Islington politics, describes such a shift within that borough in the late 1940s, at a time when that borough was not experiencing the sorts of population changes that characterized it in the 1960s.[11]

. But to describe the Tower Hamlets leadership change as "merely" factional, reflecting neither policy changes nor new social trends in the borough, would be superficial. Although the potential policy consequences of the change in Tower Hamlets leadership are significant, I shall focus in this section on the social bases of the leadership change. Although the borough has remained virtually completely working class, the past decade has seen a significant change in the types of working-class occupations Tower Hamlets residents engage in. From a time when the borough's population was heavily concentrated in either local light industry or in docking, Tower Hamlets workers have been steadily shifting towards service occupations, and to jobs increasingly located out of the borough. Docking has been shifting eastward and down-river along the Thames and this has led to major changes in employment patterns. (Plans for utilizing the resulting disused Dockland form a major item for controversy within the borough.)

This shift in the occupational, if not the class base of borough life is reflected in the leadership change. From a union official in the Transport and General Workers Union, Alderman Orwell, to an employee of a large and well-known firm of solicitors in the City (London's financial district), Councillor Beasley, the leadership of the Tower Hamlets council has reflected the shifting occupational mix of its workforce. This change in occupational predominance, reflected in the borough's leadership change, has brought with it a change in the bases of borough political life, and policy needs.

In the last chapter I described the traditional forms of working-class life in Tower Hamlets. One of the characteristics of the more traditional worklife was an environment where workers in the borough's light industry or docks had little contact with middle-class Londoners. Working close to home, in small, self-contained communities of row houses, such workers' daily contact with other social classes was largely limited to a small number of workplace supervisors, individuals who left the borough when the workday was over.[12] (A number of Labour councillors interviewed rather contemptuously referred to their Conservative opponents in borough elections as being largely drawn from this group. "They don't even live in the borough" was a frequent characterization. English law permits candidates to stand in local elections who either live or work in the borough in which they are candidates. Since the 1940s, however, only local residents may vote.)

With the major exception of the boss on the job, therefore, traditional East Enders were largely on their own. Such a set of life experiences is easily conducive to the development of "them and us" view of the political and social world, with the "them" being an extremely limited number of upper-income individuals. In describing the political and social attitudes of traditional working-class settings in Britain, Goldthorpe argues that in older industrial areas "collective memory of 'the bad old days'" plays a considerable part in structuring attitudes and that "long-established working-class institutions [preserve] attitudes formed in the struggles of previous generations".[13]

For those in the growing service employment sector, the work experience is quite different. Far from the apparent self-sufficiency of traditional East End occupations, Tower Hamlets service workers usually travel out of the borough, and work in settings where much larger numbers of middle-class individuals are present. Particularly for those who work in the City, the security and stability of their jobs is bound up with the general economic success of complex financial institutions. "Working-class solidarity", therefore, loses the natural reinforcements of the earlier period.

In addition to changes in occupation, Tower Hamlets residential patterns have also been undergoing considerable change.

The process of massive residential redevelopment has meant that tightly-knit row-house neighbourhoods are now largely gone, and with them the occupational homogeneity that characterized such areas. While class composition remains homogeneous, the occupations of the residents of any given section have become much more heterogeneous. From a situation in which particular neighbourhoods could be clearly identified as being populated by dockers, or brewery workers, etc., most housing estates have workers with a great diversity of different jobs.

This shift in housing patterns has had great consequence for the local Labour Party. While its basic hegemony is not threatened, its older style of organization has been. As long as any given ward was populated predominantly by working-class people from the same industry (and often the same employer), there could be a virtual identity between local trade-union organization and local Labour Party organization. Indeed, in the "classical" pattern, particular unions were thought to have particular wards as their own "turf". In such a situation, the local union organization was the breeding ground and recruitment arena for many local councillors. Once the union had made its determination, the councillor could be pro-forma selected by the Labour Party.

With the growing diversity of occupations in any particular ward, the claim of any specific union to a particular seat is obviously muted. Indeed, individual councillors interviewed in this study reported that seats which had traditionally been the preserve of particular unions were now less identifiably so, and councillors had been selected from the wards in question who were not members of the "traditional" unions of the ward.

While this has not yet led to much in the way of informal "primary" contests in Tower Hamlets, it does suggest that the selection of councillor candidates is becoming much less automatic. For the borough leadership, this change means that rather than presiding over a collection of semi-autonomous unions fiefdoms, a more bargaining style of leadership is required.

In addition, the decline of "automatic" candidate selection processes implies a growing importance for position-taking by potential councillor candidates, and this suggests a growing preference for a borough leadership more overtly active itself in position-taking. Since local ward candidates can no longer rely simply on union endorsement for obtaining and continuing their councillor positions, it can be helpful to them to have a council leadership which more articulately provides them with issue positions to take back to their own wards.

In quite different ways, therefore, both the "traditional" Labour Party leadership of Tower Hamlets, and the "innovative" Labour Party leadership of Islington, have moved in the direction of party modernization, with a more articulate and accessible leadership. As the interview material to be described below will show, the new leaders of both Tower Hamlets and Islington seem concerned with presenting a public and external image of competence. The need to do so, I am suggesting, is an indicator of the decline of a style of leadership which rested so solidly on a homogeneous local base that it had little need for external approval.

The types of leadership shift described above are not limited to the Labour Party. While I argued above that an overtly "innovative" Conservative borough leadership was a cell without any obvious London cases, changes in Conservative leadership style can be found in London borough politics as well. As with Tower Hamlets, the "traditional" Conservative borough studied, the Borough of Bromley, has remained stable in its class and political composition for many decades. In the case of Bromley, this stability has been one of a heavily home-owning, suburban middle-class character.

One section of Bromley, the pre-London-consolidation Urban District Council of Orpington, was for many years a centre of Liberal Party activity and success for all of England. A Liberal victory in a mid-1950s Parliamentary by-election brought the term "Orpington man" into pop-sociological usage in England as a term for new, relatively classless and politically unattached voters among whom the Liberal Party was thought to be making steady inroads.[14] Although the Liberal Party's fortunes have risen and fallen over the intervening years, and although Orpington still remains an area in which the Liberals make a special effort to do well, by the 1974 borough council elections the Liberals had lost all seats on the Bromley Borough Council from the area, and the wife of the original Liberal Parliamentary victor was herself defeated in a Parliamentary race from the Orpington constituency in the autumn 1974 national elections.

But although the Liberal Party no longer does distinctively well in Orpington, or in the rest of Bromley for that matter (it now holds borough council seats from only one of the borough's 25 wards), some of the explanations which have been advanced to account for its temporary success in Orpington are of utility in understanding the evolution of Conservative Party leadership in Bromley borough as a whole.

Although contests over leadership of the Bromley Conservative Party were low-key and behind-the-scenes (as has typically been the case for the British Conservative Party as a whole) the tension between "the established and the newcomer", common to English suburban life,[15] is reflected within local Conservative Party organizations. Just as Liberals in Orpington were able to capitalize on rapid growth and appealed to suburban commuters, so the local Conservative Party, in its successful efforts to beat back the Liberal challenge to its middle-class base, has had to try to reconcile the needs of its traditional supporters among the long-term residents of Bromley's various villages, with the interests of its newer commuter arrivals.

One major symptom of this tension within an essentially class-homogeneous group has been conflict over the extent to which the aim of the borough government should be the preservation of things the way they are, and the extent to which it should promote additional middle-class development. This promotion might take the form of permitting the erection of "luxury" housing, increasing the extent of redevelopment of Bromley's town centre, and similar questions. While both groups would unite in opposition to additional low-income council housing, and view with alarm the potential for dictation from the regional government, the now-Labour-controlled Greater London Council, there is a clear difference in perspective.

Since support for development of this type is more in accord with the national stance of the Conservative Party, one aspect of leadership change in Bromley has been a shift away from a purely borough orientation. As the comparative attitudes of old and new leaders to be reported on below will show, there has been a shift away from a leader who saw his function as the defence of "village values" toward one with wider political interests and national political ambitions.[16]

Thus all three of the sampled boroughs underwent leadership

changes within their dominant political parties within the last several years, and although the specific bases of these changes differed from case to case, all could be described as having the effect of decreasing the particularism of local politics, and moving the political forms of each of the boroughs towards greater integration into a more uniform politics of London, and perhaps England as a whole.

To describe the changes in this way is not to suggest that attention to local issues was necessarily attenuated by the leadership changes described above. Indeed, in the case of Islington the change of leadership within the Labour Party has had a result of producing more emphasis on very local, ward-based problems by increasing attention to local voluntary organizations. Rather, the integration into the larger political world of London and of England has taken the form of a greater involvement of borough leadership in the political questions and styles of the outside world, rather than being rooted in an almost autarkical localism. I have suggested that these changes are rooted in the changing socio-economic patterns of the boroughs studied.

Islington changed from a borough with an overwhelmingly working-class population into one with a growing, articulate, and politically activist minority of middle-class professionals. The entry of these new residents into positions of political power was undoubtedly enhanced by the adherence of many of their number to the already majority Labour Party in the borough, even though the roots of their Labour affiliations may have been quite different from those of their working-class neighbours.

Tower Hamlets, although retaining its essentially working-class population composition, saw a profound shift in the types of occupations held by its residents, with a consequent under-mining of the linkages between ward of residence, place of employment, trade union organization, and local Labour Party, which had characterized traditional East End politics. New political forces developed which had to take account of a population increasingly employed in the service sector out of the borough, and of a partial political vacuum caused by the weakening of the traditional linkages described above.

Like Tower Hamlets, Bromley has also retained its basic class composition, although in Bromley's case its dominant population is middle class rather than working class. But with the

increasing development of suburban housing for London commuters and the spread of suburbanization to parts of the
borough which had not previously been a part of the London
commuting belt, the traditional village-based politics came to be
replaced by a more outgoing one, more likely to see patterns and
problems common to the entire suburban ring, and more
interested in emphasizing regional and national themes defending
middle-class interests. In the case of Bromley, this trend was
undoubtedly reinforced by its integration into Greater London
in the consolidation and reorganization of London area government in the early 1960s.

For each of the boroughs, the past decades have produced
changes in economic and population patterns which have
brought their populations into more systematic contact with
Greater London as a whole, and we ought not to be surprised to
see these changes reflected in the outlooks of those chosen for
positions of political leadership within them, even though these
changes are primarily found within the structure of a class-based
dominant party, rather than on competition between the parties.

B   CHANGES IN THE LEADERS

As mentioned at the outset, this research made the accidental
discovery of changes in leadership within each of the three
sampled boroughs. The most recent change occurred in Tower
Hamlets, where the leader of the Council since its formation
under the London Government Act of 1963, Alderman J.
Orwell, was replaced by a 29-year-old councillor, Councillor
Paul Beasley, who is now the youngest leader of the council in
any of the London boroughs. That this change was not the result
of Alderman Orwell's voluntary retirement or of a complete
change in attitude on the part of members of the Tower Hamlets
Council is indicated by Councillor Beasley's one-vote majority
over Alderman Orwell when the newly elected council first
convened in 1974. As mentioned earlier, Alderman Orwell is a
union official, with the Transport and General Workers Union,
while Councillor Beasley is an employee of a firm of City
solicitors.

In Islington, the break in leadership in the dominant Labour
Party occurred during the Conservative interregnum of 1968 to

1971. I have described above the reputation and attitudes of the pre-1968 Labour council in Islington, and although none of the formal leaders of the council from that period were available for interview, an individual widely identified as having been de facto leader remains active in borough politics and was available for interview, Councillor Bill Bayliss. Councillor Bayliss has served on the Islington Council and its predecessors since the early 1950s, and during the period up to 1968 he served as chairman of the Housing Committee and deputy leader. Councillor Bayliss is a teacher in Islington, and reports his parents and grandparents were working-class residents of Islington, living in the same ward as he now represents. His replacement, Councillor Gerry Southgate, is a management consultant, "only" a ten-year resident of the borough, and with prior political involvement in his previous residence, the Outer London Borough of Croydon.

In Bromley there has been continuous Conservative control since the formation of the borough in the London government reorganization. The leader (at the time of this study), Councillor E. D. Barkway, is an upwardly mobile individual. Of working-class background in Bromley (his father was a chauffeur), he is now joint managing partner of a merchant bank in the City. He has now served on the council for six years. In 1972, after only a relatively short period of council service, he replaced the then leader, Councillor H. W. Haden, a member of the council and its predecessors since 1960. Councillor Haden moved to Bromley in 1937 and manages a printing works.

In the preceding section I suggested that basic changes in each of the boroughs studied led to the choice of different types of leaders. This section will outline the particular ways in which the leaders studied differ in where they look for cues and/or support. The new leaders clearly differ in their basic style of leadership from those they replaced. The older leaders led less articulately. Perhaps feeling less need to justify themselves, their cue-giving to rank-and-file councillors could be simple, blunt, and sparing; the products of a belief on the part of both leaders and followers of a "natural" order of things in local politics.

The newer leaders, on the other hand, lacking the "natural" bases of support which their predecessors enjoyed "need" to be more articulate and more open in their leadership style. This is

necessary to justify the legitimacy of their positions in a
changing social environment. This distinction within local units
of a society bears resemblances to Durkheim's famous distinction between mechanical and organic solidarity for societies as a
whole. The first built on societies with few distinctions among
their members; the latter was found in societies characterized by
a division of labour. It is worth remembering that Durkheim
argued that societies based on mechanical solidarity required
"repressive" law for their government, while those based on
organic solidarity increasingly moved in the direction of "cooperative" relations.[17] While the analogy between specialized
sub-units of a single society, such as London borough councils,
and the entire societies Durkheim analysed ought not be pushed
too far, the distinction Durkheim drew between the repressive
and cooperative relations is suggestive for interpreting variations
in leadership patterns in London boroughs.

Attitude toward Party

One significant dimension on which the various leaders took
different views was on the role of political party as an element in
borough governance. Although English local government once
took place without much involvement of the national parties, the
history of partisan conflict in London local government is now of
long standing.[18] Nevertheless, leaders differ in the importance
which they ascribe to their political parties and the role they
view parties as properly taking. Perhaps the clearest example of
an older view was found in the position of Councillor Haden,
former leader of Bromley Council:

> When I first came on the council [in 1960] I knew men who
> were on the council who I regarded with great favour, who
> were men of stature and quality. And they were men, very
> often of independent politics. The idea in those days was to be
> independent, rather than to be affiliated with any party.[19]

In view of this favourable memory of non-partisan local politics,
it is perhaps unsurprising that even in the partisan atmosphere
of current borough politics, Cllr Haden does not see party
affiliation as a crucial distinction in evaluating councillors.

"Most members are pretty conscientious", he says, and disavows any distinction between the parties in making that assessment.

Not only is party not a particularly significant element in assessing individual competence, but it is less than completely determinative in that "it is possibly the state of the national parties", which is the most significant element in determining local election results. But he also insists that "there is a lot of personal following" for individual councillors. (It is important to note, in this connection, that it is the general view of both academic and mass media commentators on British politics that public opinion regarding the national parties is overwhelmingly the most significant element in affecting local election results.[20] They are widely treated as informal referenda on public attitudes towards the national government of the day.)

In view of such attitudes about the impact of party, it is consistent to find Cllr Haden thinking that "political parties have no power at all", and that "constituency associations [the basic units of the Conservative Party] can do nothing, it must be a council matter". But even within the council, the role of partisanship is somewhat muted for Cllr Haden. Councillors ought not take "individual questions affecting their wards" to the Conservative group of councillors "after all, councillors are expected to do their own work."

Contrast this picture of the role of parties with that of Cllr Haden's successor, Cllr E. D. Barkway. For him, party differences have considerably more impact. Labour councillors are explicitly evaluated in a much more negative way:

> The Labour group respond very, very much more to constituency pressure. For example, they are handed briefing notes from Transport House [Labour Party national headquarters]. In fact, at the group meetings, I believe they have a representative occasionally from Transport House.

These are bad things, in Cllr Barkway's view, and they are inherent in the Labour Party, he thinks, and not just a consequence of its minority position in Bromley.

But the greater prominence of party in Cllr Barkway's thinking is not limited to negative evaluations of Labour Party adherents and positive impressions of Conservatives. Within

Conservative ranks, he takes the party apparatus more seriously, even if he doesn't always favour its view. Unlike Cllr Haden, who thought that constituency associations had no power, Cllr Barkway thinks that the views of a constituency association "might carry weight to the extent that it would involve us in bringing the thing forward on our committee agenda".

This does not mean that the views of the party organizations necessarily carry the day:

> The Chislehurst Constituency Association (an area within Bromley) is very, very uptight about education. It happens to be their particular angle. And they come to us and nag away about one or two school problems in their area.

But:

> regardless of this political pressure there is an obligation on us to act in a responsible manner and I'm not going to throw away the council's money just to please the chairman of the constituency.

Thus the major distinction between Cllrs Haden and Barkway in their view of the position of political parties in borough life is not necessarily that one favours their role and the other opposes it; rather that a councillor who saw parties as essentially peripheral to the borough political process has been replaced by a councillor more likely to take them into account. In Cllr Barkway's view this would clearly extend to the nomination process. Despite a suburban Conservative tradition of redesignating sitting councillors who wished to continue to serve, Cllr Barkway recalls:

> A constituency party did see one ward and say that they needed a much stronger level of commitment from the man who's coming up for re-election than they'd had in the previous three years. And until they got that commitment they were very unhappy about the selection.

Furthermore:

> This is right and, in fact, I don't think we do enough of this.

Unlike Bromley, where Conservative council leaders could directly observe an opposition party on the council, the other two boroughs studied both had completely Labour council memberships at the time of this study. In both of these cases, therefore, a comparison of new and old leaders' attitudes toward the role of party is less easily made. Nevertheless, it is fair to say that the Labour Party, as an independent entity and not simply an appendage of class or union, plays a larger part in the thinking of the two new leaders than it did for the more traditional old leadership.

For Cllr Bayliss representing traditional Labour leadership in Islington, social class is a far more relevant political variable than political party affiliation. The crucial distinction, in Cllr Bayliss's formulation, was between working-class people and middle-class individuals "in commerce and trade" on the one hand, and "lower-middle-class professionals" on the other. Within the Labour Party, the conflict took place between the traditional working-class residents of the borough, and the newly arrived professionals. This conflict was mirrored in the Conservative Party, according to Cllr Bayliss: "There was a predominance of those in commerce and trade [in the Islington Conservative Party], but they also had a group who were Islington lower-middle-class professionals." The first group of Conservatives were similar to the Islington working class, while the professionals among the Conservatives had similar views to their opposite numbers in the Labour Party. With regard to professionals in the Labour Party, their allegiance to the party was quite suspect. According to Cllr Bayliss: "Before the war, these individuals would have been in the Communist Party, but the Communist Party doesn't have the fashionable cachet it once had."

The basis for division within the Labour Party was essentially class antagonism, and class envy. This was particularly true for Labour Party councillors in professional occupations. Cllr Bayliss argued that such individuals had seen a diminution of the difference between their own standard of living and that of the working class, and he felt they had a "dread of declining privileges". As a consequence, the middle-class professionals in the Labour Party deliberately advocated policies to aid the most disadvantaged residents of the borough, rather than the employed working class. Cllr Bayliss felt the middle-class Labour councillors adopted such policies in an attempt to maintain a distinction in the standard of living between themselves and the working class. (The Conservative middle-class "in commerce and trade", on the other hand, continued to enjoy personal possibilities for economic betterment that the professionals did not, and so they were not so subject to fear of working-class advancement.)

While the views of Alderman Orwell, the "traditional" leader in Tower Hamlets, had none of this upside-down view of class conflict, in his formulation the Labour Party was not an essentially independent entity either. Where Cllr Bayliss saw the party and conflicts within it as the appendage of class, Alderman Orwell viewed the Labour Party as an outgrowth of the trade unions. Of course, this view has much history behind it, and the Labour Party is, in many ways, a direct outgrowth of the British trade union movement.

For much of the twentieth-century history of the East End of London, the natural homogeneity and self-contained nature of communities made any distinction between union and party unimportant. This overlap was reinforced by the nominating procedures of the Labour Party in Tower Hamlets, which provided for independent nominations from unions affiliated to the party, and from ward organizations. (This procedure mirrors, at least in a formal way, the procedure by which Labour Party aspirants are placed on lists of potential Parliamentary nominees.) In order to receive the nomination, in Tower Hamlets one needed the support of both formal structures:

> nominations from the Trade Unions are complementary rather than in addition to (those from the wards) because if you can only get a nomination from the Trade Union from your own ward or from the ward [party organization] you wish to stand in, you've very little chance in the final selection.

One notices immediately, in looking at Alderman Orwell's view, that a concept such as "the trade union from your own ward" is a meaningful one to him. Of course, in Britain, as in the United States, trade unions are not organized simply by geographic area, but by occupation or employer. Only in an environment in which occupation and geography coincided could such a view take hold. And once a changing economic environment eroded the tight connection between workplace and residence, the political system based on it was itself in danger of erosion and replacement.

The new leaders of Islington and Tower Hamlets both differed from their predecessors in seeing the Labour Party as an independent concept, but their views of its functioning were far from identical. In Islington, the current leader, Cllr Southgate, presented a rich description of factional conflict within the Labour Party, but denied that this was the exclusively class-based conflict seen by Cllr Bayliss.

In Southgate's view, factions were fluid and changing, and grounded in many diverse factors. His catalogue of explanations included exclusionary practices of past Islington Labour Party organizations, age of councillors, experience on the council, and even ethnic group tensions. With such a multi-dimensional view of internal party strife, it was natural to interpret local politics as a changing mosaic of alliances, in which differing groups and individuals temporarily came together to form alliances, which almost as rapidly broke down.

Islington had three separate Labour Party organizations, one for each of the Parliamentary constituencies. The North Islington party was historically on bad terms with those from central and south. Even though the North Islington party was changing, as it ended its exclusionary practices and new members joined, there was still tension between the three parties, and between each of the parties and the council:

> We have very strong feedback from each of the constituency parties. They are constantly passing resolutions or giving us their views.

> So much of these resolutions deal with matters of detail. We [on the council] complain that those resolutions are not the resolutions we look for in stating a point of view on policy.

Factional competition was reflected in the nominating process as well:

> It's mainly done by the wards. . . . They would ask questions about what they know, the councillors' attendance record, for

example. There is a great deal of competition. It's not like th
Parliamentary selections, where you can have an adoptio
meeting and where the [party] members just readopt [th
incumbent].

Thus, the Islington Labour Parties were complex and con
flictual organizations, exerting independent pressure on th
council, and the role of unions in the nominating and influencin
procedure is not mentioned.

Although the new leader in Tower Hamlets, Cllr Beasley
differed from his predecessor, Alderman Orwell, in not presen
ing a picture of virtual identity between union and party, hi
views differ from those of Cllr Southgate in Islington as wel
Unlike Southgate, Cllr Beasley, though recognizing factions i
the Tower Hamlets Labour Party, assigns no particular di
ferences in point of view to them. Because all individua
involved were Labour "There is no political difference as such.
In Beasley's view, the idea that Tower Hamlets was an al
Labour council meant that "people are not under pressure [fror
competition] and therefore they'll tend to look at things overall'

In councils where political control was more divided, Beasle
thought "there are party political situations to be taken int
account".

But Tower Hamlets could avoid these. For Beasley, the notio
of "political differences" between adherents of the same part
seems unlikely. The fundamental cleavage was between Labou
and the Conservative Party. But Beasley did recognize distinc
tions among Labour councillors:

> I think the difference really was over how you adjust for th
> future. I think what people want is a little more open
> mindedness in many ways. I think if you've done a job for
> fair length of time, I think their ideas get a little stale. I thin
> the impression goes out that they're a stale council, not ver
> interesting, when a lot of what they've done is really ver
> good. I think in areas involving voluntary organization
> which have new ideas, I think people want to feel that we wi
> be a bit more receptive to them.

The difference between the factions of the Labour Party, fo
Beasley, were on matters such as differing openness to voluntar

organizations. But these differences, in Beasley's view, were primarily functions of age and length of incumbency, rather than being rooted in deep-seated ideological, class, or geographic bases. But Beasley did see differences within the party, in contrast to Orwell's more solidaristic interpretation. And it was appropriate that these differences get expressed. Thus it was important for Beasley that nominating procedures had been changed, so that wards would get a greater choice of individuals when designating councillor candidates: "In the past, control was in the hands of a very small group of people", Beasley reported disapprovingly. For Orwell, this would not have mattered.

I suggested at the outset that political leaders had alternate strategies open to them in mobilizing support for themselves and their policies. In a partisan political environment, the political party is a major and obvious vehicle for such an effort. In a strong-party system, such as Britain's, we would expect to see this vehicle extensively used. However, the existence of a party structure is no guarantee of its use, and the political leaders studied in this research, although operating within a single metropolitan area and under generally the same formal rules, vary considerably in their interpretation of the proper role of party, and in how they see parties operating to influence them and their councils.

In each of the three boroughs, the newer leaders saw party as a more independent and important force, operating to influence the politics and policies of their borough councils. In Bromley, a more partisan political style replaced a "village-oriented" outlook. In Islington and Tower Hamlets, partisanship, in the form of Labour Party dominance, had long since been taken for granted. But in Islington, a leader to.whom the fundamental cleavage was not party but social class was replaced by one where party, and party factionalism, had an independent life of its own. And in Tower Hamlets, a leader who saw party as an extension of union activity, was replaced by one who did not see this identity.

Stein Rokkan once suggested that as party systems develop in a country, they gradually extend downward, eventually permeating lower levels of the political system.[21] The research reported on here suggests an extension of that principle. Even within local political systems which have been formally partisan for a long time, continuing integrative economic forces serve to increase the salience of these partisan attachments for local political leaders.

Attitude toward Voluntary Organizations

Non-partisan voluntary organizations form a major obvious alternative set of institutions to political parties for political leaders seek to mobilize support and gain information. As with party, considerable variation was found in the role leaders ascribed to such organizations, and their feelings toward them.

The patterns of these variations, however, do not exactly match those reported above. Indeed, in some respects Cllr Beasley's views about party and its relationship to voluntary organizations resemble those of the man he replaced, Alderman Orwell, more than they do those of his fellow "new" Labour leader, Cllr Southgate. This similarity is reflected in their shared views of the Labour Party as a "party of integration".[22] For Alderman Orwell, this "integration" occurred naturally. Cllr Beasley, perceiving that the natural bases for integration had broken down, saw it as his job to restore cohesiveness by building links between voluntary organizations and the political party. This could best be done by getting Labour councillors themselves to become heavily involved in voluntary organizations:

> We're very fortunate in having councillors from the wards who know everybody. The way different organizations are set up, for example, tenants organizations, local festivals, law centres. As things evolve, the local councillor is generally involved in some way before the thing is set up.

Such a view, in which organizations, although good things, ought to and do exist under the aegis of Labour Party councillors, is a different perspective from that of Cllr Southgate, the new Islington leader, for whom the order of influencing is reversed. For Southgate, voluntary organizations come first, they then seek to influence the council, and finally, they seek to get their leaders selected as council candidates.

Cllr Beasley, as with Alderman Orwell before him, is some-what suspicious of organizations that are not Labour Party-linked. He described how some organizations were really fronts for the Communist Party. Some members of the Communist Party:

> tried to join little fringe groups, not in the name of their own party, but in the guise of a trades council, or a tenants' association, and then push their point of view that way. But the interesting thing is, a lot of people could see through that, and those organizations went sour.

Such a view is not entirely dissimilar from that of Alderman Orwell, who described organizations in Tower Hamlets in the following terms:

> We get pressure groups, yes, we get squatters' associations, tenants' associations, conservative organizations. We have all sorts of pressure groups to deal with and we've dealt with them as far as we possibly can. . . . I find this, that most of the pressure groups, the people who are doing the pressuring, are not from the area, they are mainly professionals from other areas who want to get in on the action.

The difference, of course, is that Cllr Beasley's distinction between those organizations with which he is willing to deal, and about which he feels positively, omits only the relatively small number of groups organized by Communists, while Alderman Orwell's interpretation would exclude most of the voluntary organizations in the borough.

If the distinction between the attitudes toward voluntary organizations of the two Tower Hamlets leaders is one of degree, the distinction between the old and new leadership in Islington is one of polar extremes. Both Cllr Bayliss and Cllr Southgate agreed that voluntary organizations were playing an increasingly important part in the political life of their borough, but they differed completely in their evaluation of this phenomenon.

Cllr Bayliss's views were, in some respects, an amalgamation of the positions of the two Tower Hamlets leaders. While some organizations, those formed by councillors, received positive

evaluations from him, most organizations were seen by him as
organized by professionals, and towards those he was very
hostile. Indeed, in his view, working-class residents of Islington
tended to dislike such organizations in general:

> The working-class people have always had a great suspicion
> of pressure groups. After all, any four people can get together
> and form an association and say, for example, we represent
> the people of Upper Street.

One of his major complaints about the new middle-class
councillors was that they were too responsive to such organizations:

> The professional middle-class types who came onto the
> council very recently themselves were originally all members
> of pressure groups: that's how they took over. And they were
> very susceptible to pressure. If any group, even if it consisted
> of five members, wrote to them complaining, wrote a very
> hard letter threatening to go to the press [the middle-class
> councillors], would fall over backwards to meet their demands.

But his major complaint remained that these organizations
formed vehicles for takeover of ward Labour Party organizations:

> You never know when the takeover is coming. A large number
> of these middle-class people sort of organized non-political
> groupings and then, using that as a sort of springboard, all
> join together, join various Labour Parties, and then took over.
> They would be consumers associations, so-called, resident
> associations, so-called, amenity groups, and so forth, and they
> just moved into the Labour Party and took over at the
> nomination time.

Although Cllr Southgate, the new Islington leader, shared
Cllr Bayliss's perception of the importance of such groups, his
evaluation was, unsurprisingly, completely different:

> There are far more community groups springing up now.
> They're very much a feature of the last ten years, and they
> generally say, "we want to do this", not "we want you to do"

but "we want to do this and we expect you to help us do it". And these are the sort of groups who increasingly come to councillors.

If one wanted to be responsive, speed was important:

> One of the things we have learned is that you must respond to these community groups in a short space of time. You cannot say to them we'll consider it in a year's time or the next budget. You've killed the group practically or you've forced them to go elsewhere or you've turned them into an anti-group. Focused their attitude into a row rather than to do something constructive.

And, in Southgate's view, Islington councillors were being increasingly responsive. In responding to a question on councillors' role orientation, he replied:

> That's the distinction Burke made, isn't it, about being a representative or not. I think it's kind of difficult to answer that because of the changing attitudes in developing the role of participation and consultation [of organized groups]. . . . What is actually happening is that we are, to a degree, becoming mere delegates, and responding to the community.

One notes that not only does the input from organizations change councillors' role perception, in Southgate's view, but that organized groups can legitimately stand for the views of the community. This, of course, is in direct conflict with the perceptions of the former leadership as expressed by Cllr Bayliss.

But Southgate shared the view that professionals played a large part in stimulating such organizations. He recounted how many of the newer councillors were first active in neighbourhood groups before coming to council membership, and he reported that in Islington "We have a lot of young people in middle-class occupations who are the children of working-class parents and who identify with left-wing attitudes and who are very involved in community work." So, it is really Southgate's evaluation which separates him out from the former leadership, and not really his perception of what was changing in Islington: "I think nowadays things are changing a great deal in that doors are very much more open now and so people have learned that they can come in and get things done which didn't happen so much in the past."

It is also important to note one important feature of the new Islington leadership's view which really separates it out from all of the other Labour leaders interviewed. This is Southgate's view of organized groups as being more comprehensive in their scope than the Labour Party; the very opposite of a party of integration. In describing how councillors kept informed on developments in their wards:

> Some of these groups, for instance, the Child Poverty Action Group and the Consumers Group, you'll find predominantly Labour Party there. You know, they're not front groups, they are predominantly Labour Party. But they have much wider —if they play that role I think they *have a much wider contact than just through the party*. (emphasis added)

And not only did groups have a wider range of contacts than the party itself, but rather than simply respond to existing groups, Southgate thought that the Council itself should stimulate the development of such organizations. He proudly reported that Islington:

> Certainly has been leading in genuinely trying to develop concentration on participation without just holding a public meeting and saying, there you are, take it or leave it. We are appointing officers to help people involve themselves in the hierarchy of the council, financing local groups, attendance of liaison officers, and all this sort of range of opportunities [for group participation].

Thus the new Islington leadership saw itself as going beyond simply reacting to groups which spontaneously arose, but actively sought to encourage more of them to develop. In contrast to the attitudes of both new and old leadership in Tower Hamlets, these groups were legitimated not by putting councillors on their boards, but by funding them with local government money and involving them "in the hierarchy of the council".[23]

We find, therefore, several distinct leadership attitudes towards voluntary organizations in the two Labour-controlled boroughs. In the "traditional" view of both Cllr Bayliss in Islington and Alderman Orwell in Tower Hamlets, such groups are tempting targets for professionals seeking to manipulate the working class. Although neither specifically used the term "outside agitator", they might well have. Cllr Beasley, the new Tower Hamlets leader, represents an intermediate point of view, in which the dangers feared by Bayliss and Orwell are not completely absent, but neither do they operate so strongly as to inhibit a positive working relation with local voluntary organizations. In common with Bayliss, Beasley seems happier when these groups include councillors as full participants, if not actual organizers. Cllr Southgate, the new Islington leader, represents the other extreme. Not only are groups strongly to be encouraged, but they are, in a sense, more "legitimate" than the Labour Party itself, because they cover a broader scope. Because of this ability of voluntary organizations to be more broadly representative, it becomes an appropriate function of local government not only to respond to them, but to stimulate and encourage their further development.

So far, this discussion of the role of voluntary organizations has omitted any mention of the third borough studied, the Conservative-controlled suburban borough of Bromley. In a sense, relationships between local government and voluntary organizations in suburbia are less problematic than those in central city areas. For one thing, the geographic arrangements of suburbia, with fairly clearly understood sub-communities, encourages the development of local residents' associations. The predominance of home-owning undoubtedly further encourages this. Thus, there seems to be something more natural and less controversial about such groups in suburban areas: they are a part of the landscape, and accepted as such by the borough council. In addition, one important divisive element in the Inner London boroughs studied, the question of whether outside professionals were dominating organizations ostensibly representing working-class interests, does not recur in suburbia. None of those interviewed questioned that associations of home-owning residents were organized by the inhabitants, and for the interests of the areas in which they were organized. Questions about their legitimacy were much less likely to arise.

All three of the boroughs studied have been in the process of shifting from more-autonomous to less-autonomous sectors of the London metropolitan region. I argued earlier that this shift was likely to have political consequences. In the case of the two Inner London boroughs, one indirect consequence of this change was a relatively greater role for voluntary organizations in the political life of the boroughs, as leadership in those boroughs changed in the direction of greater responsiveness to such organizations.

For suburban Bromley, however, the consequence of changes in demography and economics has had different consequences. Although a suburban area such as Bromley begins with voluntary organizations playing a larger role than they do in Inner London, and although that greater importance continues, there has been, in some respects, a *relative* lessening of influence as other factors, such as political party, come to play an increasingly important role. This shift is reflected in the differing views toward such organizations held by the old and new leaders of the Bromley Council, Cllrs Haden and Barkway respectively.

For Cllr Haden, voluntary organizations were clearly a good thing:

> Organizations are very useful. People like to live in a community and join things. People accept that nothing is perfect in this world, but they can do their bit to help. The residents associations, the village associations, they are most helpful. Critical, but helpful. They can alert us to problems, they are very interested in planning. I encourage this, I tell them, you tell me, I can't be around all the time.

Important organizations, therefore, were essentially "village" based, representing the interests of sub-sections of the borough:

> The Village Association (in my ward) is doing what it was set up to do. It acts as a kind of watchdog for the village.

Of course, the classic function of a watchdog is to keep out intruders, and this is a good metaphor for the function Cllr Haden assigns to them in Bromley borough life.

In consequence, it is hardly surprising to find that Cllr Haden, while leader of the council, encouraged councillors to become active in organizations of this type in their own wards, and to use them not only as forums for gathering information, but also as occasions to "help people in real need". Voluntary organizations, In Cllr Haden's view, not only served an information-gathering and political mobilizing function, but also, to some degree, served as alternative vehicles for providing local services, thereby reducing pressure on local government.

For the new leader, Cllr Barkway, the position of voluntary organizations, while still generally positive, had more shadings of doubt. For one thing, Cllr Barkway saw organizations primarily in terms of their political consequences, and the potential for their exercising a service function in lieu of council activity is absent from his presentation. In addition, they ran the risk of being too limited in their outlook:

> Are residents' associations useful? Oh, yes, I think so. I mean they do tend to take a rather narrow point of view. I think they do tend to get—to determine an attitude and then they will not vary it. . . . But on the whole one could say that all participation is good participation. I think we do encourage that.

So, although "all participation is good participation", local organizations often overlooked borough-wide priorities. In describing reaction to a proposal for a new pattern of one-way streets in Bromley town centre, Cllr Barkway commented:

> If I use the word extremist, you ought to see it in this context; that matters of extreme local interest suddenly are fanned up, for one purpose or another. It is amazing how something which really in itself is somewhat innocuous and affects only a very few people can suddenly become a borough-wide issue. The Bromley North Traffic Management Scheme, which probably affects two or three roads, and yet there's suddenly a vociferous outburst, where for years anyone living on that road has known that it was likely to occur.

In addition to the sudden appearance of a "vociferous outburst", possibly stimulated by the opposition party, voluntary organizations behaved differently, in Cllr Barkway's view, depending on the class and political composition of the neighbourhood involved:

> In the areas where you get a large element of owner-occupation, the white-collar areas . . . in those areas you do tend to get residents' associations of one kind and another.

> In the non-white collar areas there is a tendency to get spasmodic pressure activity.

This latter type was particularly likely to lead to the sort of "extremist" behaviour described above. Cllr Barkway's views of organizations, therefore, were not the same as Cllr Haden's rather undifferentiated approval. For Barkway, such organizations, although useful, had this utility contingent on not becoming "extremist". In addition, organizations might send large delegations to council meetings, or engage in organized letter-writing campaigns. This could lead a councillor to "play to the gallery, and he will say what is right to say because he knows he's pleasing the few people that have drawn his attention to the thing".

Unlike Cllr Haden, but reminiscent of some of the Inner London Labour leaders, Cllr Barkway expresses apprehension that organized groups may not always be representative of the communities they purport to represent. But his primary doubts remain political: the councillors from the working-class enclaves in the borough will be too parochial, the organizations from those areas will engage in spasmodic and potentially "extremist" activity, and even Conservative councillors will too often "play to the gallery" when spurred on by organized groups in their wards.

The evaluation of voluntary organizations by Council leaders, therefore, seems related to their prior attitude toward the role of political parties. In working-class Labour Inner London, voluntary organizations were seen by new leaders as important mobilization mechanisms, in some ways replacing Labour Party or local trade union branches in raising issues and in gathering support for council policies. In middle-class suburbia, on the other hand, the relative importance of such organizations (but not their absolute importance) was decreased with the growth in partisan structuring of suburban political life.

C SUMMARY

I indicated at the outset of this chapter that underlying economic and demographic changes created preconditions in which changes in leadership patterns became possible in each of the three London boroughs studied. Without suggesting a mechanistic relationship between such underlying factors and leadership styles, this research has uncovered patterns of difference in leadership attitudes which do "fit" with these underlying changes. Such a pattern suggests that "leadership" may not be as autonomous an explanatory concept as it is sometimes presented as being. Such a suggestion mirrors Vroom and Yetten's view that thinking of leadership simply as a personality variable overrates that dimension, and their experimental finding that considerably more explanatory power is attributable to "the situation" than to "individual leadership tendencies".[24] The growing economic integration of a major metropolitan centre like London, and the consequent decreases in neighbourhood autonomy, have consequences for the political system at the local level.[25] One aspect of these consequences can be observed in the attitudes of local political leaders, and in the comparison of their attitudes with those of the leadership they replaced.

In each of the boroughs, political party becomes a more important independent concept for leaders of the borough councils. In the two Labour-controlled, predominantly working-class boroughs of Islington and Tower Hamlets, voluntary organizations came to play an increasingly important role as working-class solidarity, "naturally" expressed through class feeling or through trade union organization, became less salient.

These Inner London boroughs present a paradox. The integrative trends which erode the traditional bases of working-class political organization give rise to the localist pressures of neighbourhood-based voluntary organizations. Middle-class professionals in Islington, for example, whose political involvement begins in national movements such as the Campaign for Nuclear Disarmament and Anti-Apartheid Movements, find themselves strongly pressing the interests of a particular street in a single London borough. What is happening in such a situation is the development of an "ideology of localism" among such participants. But this ideology is not strictly parochial, it could be expressed in any community. Indeed, an individual such as Cllr Southgate has been locally active in at least two different areas, and such a pattern was by no means unique among the middle-class professional Islington councillors. The role of local leadership in such a situation is to be responsive both to the specific local points being raised, but also to the regional and national trends which produced the climate in which such developments could take place.

In the suburban borough studied, on the other hand, voluntary organizations increasingly had to share attention with party organizations, as non-partisan "village" politics came to be replaced by more structured partisan conflict. Suburban defensiveness becomes more generalized and less village-particular, and more appropriately expressed in national party-political terms.

In each borough, as the "mechanical solidarity" of borough life decreased, a more outward-looking, regionally and nationally oriented leadership took power. These alterations in leadership patterns have consequences for the political style and policy preferences of the borough councils as a whole. But before examining whole-council style and policy, it will be necessary to consider the extent to which attitudes held by council leaders are congruent with those held by their rank-and-file colleagues.

In the next chapter I will be describing variations among rank-and-file councillors. It will be seen that the changes in leadership orientation are partially, but by no means completely, reflected in the attitudes of these councillors. Leadership attitudes and rank-and-file councillor views operate as distinct independent variables in shaping overall borough political life.

4 Rank-and-File Councillors: Patterns of Distinctiveness

In the previous chapters I have reported on certain commonalities among council leaders in the three boroughs under study. Although leadership patterns were historically distinctive in the three boroughs, and remained so, each borough was found to have a leadership which steadily moved borough politics into greater integration with Greater London as a whole. As the economy of the region became more integrated and local economic "autonomy" decreased, some elements of distinctive local political style at the borough level eroded as well.

In this chapter, however, the focus will be on patterns of distinctiveness among councillors.[1] Review of interview material from the London councillors sampled indicated that councillors could be divided into four basic types. Although there were obvious divisions between councillors who represented working-class wards and those who represented middle-class wards, and although these distinctions had a quite direct translation into Labour or Conservative Party affiliation, I shall argue that party alone is an insufficient explanation for variations found among the London councillors studied.

Indeed, cleavages within parties were in some respects sharper than those that divided the parties. Although councillors almost universally subscribed to certain basic tenets of their party's political positions, these did not indicate how they would carry on their function as local government councillors.

The most efficient classifications of the councillors, that is, those divisions which most accurately classified councillors into discrete representational types, were two variables which I shall call "scope of representation", and "scope of ambition".[2] The first of these two variables involves whether or not a councillor saw his primary function as representing the interests of his ward, or whether or not he thought that councillors ought to be responsive to the interests of the borough as a whole.

The second variable which I have identified as being of central importance in classifying borough councillors is "scope of ambition". In this classification, a councillor was classified as "broad" in scope if he indicated interest in political involvement beyond the borough level, and "narrow" if the extent of his political aspirations were fulfilled by borough politics.

As I shall suggest below, these two sets of classification variables bear some resemblance to both traditional delegate–trustee and cosmopolitan–local distinctions, but are certainly not identical to either.

Combining the two classification variables produces a four-fold schema shown below in Table 4.1:

TABLE 4.1 Borough councillor classification schema

		Scope of representation	
		Ward	*Borough*
Scope of ambition	Narrow	classic parochials	traditional rank-and-file
	Broad	"ideology of localism" councillors	traditional aspirants

In this classification, the crucial element of a "ward" scope of representation is the recognition of distinctive ward interests, and a perception of these interests as legitimate (and therefore appropriately acted upon by ward councillors). A "ward" scope does not preclude the recognition of borough-wide interests, but clearly does require the councillor to see the interests of the ward and the borough as not necessarily the same at all times. On the other hand, a councillor who was aware of the claim of distinctive ward interests, but who did not regard such claims as correct or legitimate, would not be regarded as having a "ward" scope for the purposes of this schema.

It should be recognized that the use of the political terms

"ward" and "borough" serve only as rough approximations for the geographical scope a councillor might see himself as representing. Thus a councillor might well see himself as representing a small number of wards, which he identified as forming a distinctive sub-community within the borough, and nevertheless be classified as having a "ward" scope. Similarly, a councillor might use the borough as a surrogate for some.larger area he wished to represent and still be classified as "borough" in scope. As an empirical matter, this latter alternative did not appear among the councillors studied in this research, although the former pattern was often observed.

Scope of ambition, the second classification element in this schema, was categorized as "narrow" or "broad". Councillors with a broad scope of ambition indicated a desire and/or intention to participate in socio-political activity beyond the borough level.[3] A councillor who expected to make a "career" of borough council service would not, therefore, be regarded as having a broad scope of ambition even if he hoped to rise to leadership positions within the borough council structure. But broad ambition, for the purposes of this study, is not being limited to the formal governmental structural hierarchy. While a councillor who hoped to be elected to Parliament would obviously be classified as broadly ambitious, so would a councillor who hoped to be widely influential through pressure-group activity at the national or regional level.

As I suggested above, this schema bares certain resemblances to cosmopolitan–local and delegate–trustee distinctions, but is not identical. Indeed, it suggests that at least in one sense, the classic categories of cosmopolitans and locals need not be mutually exclusive. Those councillors whom I have described as adhering to an "ideology of localism" have characteristics of both simultaneously. These councillors have developed a framework of ideas which suggests national consequences for ward activism, thus seeking "cosmopolitan" goals through local political activity. But because purely local concerns are not the extent of their political interests, these councillors are also more broadly ambitious politically.[4]

At the opposite corner of the table, "traditional rank-and-file" councillors also have elements of both cosmopolitan and local orientation. These councillors, who as I shall indicate below are almost entirely Labour Party adherents, have a wide scope of representation[5] but narrow ambition. Although they adhere to a nationally integrative working-class ideology, they are not personally involved (nor do they expect to be) beyond the local level.

The delegate–trustee distinction, while also clearly related to scope of representation, is not identical either. Indeed, in their original writing in *The Legislative System*, Wahlke *et al.* specifically distinguished between legislative roles and scope of representation.[6] While we might anticipate that councillors with a ward scope of representation would be more likely to regard themselves as delegates, they are not logically required to do so. A councillor, after all, might see his function as the articulation of quite local interests, and yet not believe that the resident electorate properly understood what those distinctive local interests were. Such a representative could, therefore, have a ward scope of representation and nevertheless maintain a trustee orientation.

Before investigating the behavioural and attitudinal consequences of the classification scheme, it is appropriate to examine whether these categories are simply party distinctions in another guise. As I suggested above, "traditional rank-and-file" councillors are almost exclusively members of the Labour Party. This is the only category in the typology, however, which is party-distinctive. The frequencies with which adherents of the parties can be found in each councillor-type category are given in Table 4.2.

TABLE 4.2   Councillor type by party

Classic parochials	*Traditional rank-and-file*
Labour— 10	Labour— 21
Conservative— 7	Conservative— 1
Ideology of localism councillors	*Traditional aspirants*
Labour— 6	Labour— 7
Conservative— 4	Conservative— 6
Liberal— 1	

Other distinctions, however, begin to suggest some of the explanatory elements of councillor type. An examination of councillor type by borough does show the beginnings of such a pattern, and is shown in Table 4.3. Since the three boroughs studied here were chosen for their politically distinctive styles, it ought not be surprising to find that distinctive councils have distinctive councillors as well. Of particular note is the concentration of Tower Hamlets councillors among the "traditional rank-and-file" type, and their complete absence from the "ideology of localism" category.

TABLE 4.3   Councillor type by borough

Classic parochials	*Traditional rank-and-file*
Bromley—8	Bromley—4
Islington—5	Islington—4
Tower Hamlets—4	Tower Hamlets—14
Ideology of localism councillors	*Traditional aspirants*
Bromley—5	Bromley—8
Islington—6	Islington—3
Tower Hamlets—0	Tower Hamlets—2

That this is not simply a consequence of the types of wards found in Tower Hamlets can be seen in Table 4.4. The table uses a classification scheme of ward types developed by the research arm of the government of the London Region, the Greater London Council Intelligence Unit. Wards were grouped into "Central London", "Inner London", and "suburban" categories on the basis of a factor analysis of census data.[7] It can be seen that although "Inner London" wards are heavily represented by traditional rank-and-file councillors, many such wards are represented by other councillor types.

TABLE 4.4   Councillor type by ward type

Classic parochials	*Traditional rank-and-file*
Inner London—9	Inner London—18
Suburban—8	Suburban—4
Ideology of localism councillors	*Traditional aspirants*
Inner London—6	Inner London—6
Suburban—5	Suburban—7

TABLE 4.5   Councillor type by councillor social class

Classic parochials	Traditional rank-and-file
Middle class—9	Middle class—4
Working class—8	Working class—18
Ideology of localism	
councillors	Traditional aspirants
Middle class—11	Middle class—8
Working class—0	Working class—5

The data used to generate the ward-type table are largely made up of social-class indicators. The data used are, of course, aggregate. It is possible to examine the impact of social class in another way, by observing the distribution of councillor types by the social class of the councillors themselves. This can be found in Table 4.5. For the purposes of this table, councillors were classified as "working class" or "middle class" on the basis of occupation. The classification scheme was based on the UK Census, which classifies occupations into socio-economic groups.[8] A sharp distinction can be observed between the class compositions of the upper-right-hand and lower-left-hand cells, indicating, in at least a preliminary way, the relationship of individual councillor class characteristics to councillor type. This can be seen in Table 4.4. I shall be suggesting that this relationship is not accidental, but is related both to mode of councillor recruitment, and to supportive structures available to councillors during their legislative careers.

Recent studies have indicated that a ward scope of representation is not the norm in recent British local government experience,[9] although it is reported to have characterized nineteenth-century local politics in England.[10] Because of this, I shall focus in detail on the two "untraditional" types of councillors who share this orientation, the councillors I have identified as "classic parochials", and those I am calling adherents of an "ideology of localism". (For convenience, I shall sometimes refer to this second category of councillors as "localists".) I will then more briefly note the characteristics of the two more traditional categories of councillors, the "traditional rank-and-file" and the "potential traditional leaders". Finally, this chapter will attempt to assess the significance for local government and politics of the entry of these new types of councillors.

A   THE CLASSIC PAROCHIAL

Scope of Representation

By definition, the classic parochial is ward-oriented and un-interested in political participation beyond the borough level. What the bare bones of definition fail to convey, however, is the extent to which a councillor's ward orientation is a matter of individual choice in the councillor's eyes, or whether it seems to him to be required by the political realities of his constituency. Consider, for example, the suburban Conservative councillors in Bromley, one of whom, in answer to a question on whether some councillors push too hard for their own wards, responded:

> I wouldn't say they push too hard. They push very hard. They are elected from a ward and they have to be parochial or else their ward [party] members will say . . . what the hell's going on on our doorstep.

Or another Conservative suburbanite who describes his ward as having:

> A narrow, insular view of itself.

And describes the local residents association as:

> one of the largest residents' associations in the country. As a result they have a fair amount of power on their own. . . . They're powerful enough to bypass me.

And as a result:

> The main job [of a councillor] . . . is trying to preserve [our ward] broadly in the conditions as you see it now. Seeing that such changes as do come are to the advantage of the residents.

The ward orientations of such councillors might be described as mandated, with the councillors having no alternative, at least in their perception, to concerning themselves with the special needs of the wards they represent.

Quite in contrast with this view is the view of an Inner London Labour councillor in Islington, whose ward-orientation is based on his opinion that:

> We've been left out of the way money's been spent in the borough. . . . But perhaps that isn't so much a matter of councillors from other areas pushing harder, but of not having sufficiently good councillors from this area.

For this councillor, ward orientation is a matter of personal belief in its appropriateness, rather than a requirement imposed upon him by the local electorate.

If the Bromley councillor quoted above expected trouble if he did not promote the interests of his ward, a Tower Hamlets councillor expected trouble if he did. One councillor who reports that he actively promotes the interests of his ward, because he felt his ward was deprived, reported that conflict:

> could come up over this community centre. Some wards have had this set up for them, and other wards say, we need this badly, particularly in [my ward], which is quite behind in this sort of thing.

But a councillor promoting his ward in this way could expect resistance. This same councillor reports that the likely outcome of raising ward-conflict issues such as the one above would be "clash with the [party] group" on the council. That such clashes ought not be taken lightly in Tower Hamlets is suggested by the report of another "parochial" Tower Hamlets councillor who suggests that when a councillor wants to advance the interests of his own ward: "if a member's got any sense, he will discuss things with the ward on either side of him and get their allegiance." But despite this rare report of neighbourhood coalition-building, this councillor still reports that: "when you push too hard, then you find the other people clam round you and squeeze you to push you under."[11] He also reports that he was twice expelled from the Labour group on the council for failing to follow party discipline.

Thus the parochial councillors in the three boroughs studied evince quite different patterns of stimulus in becoming parochial. Although the examples quoted above are not reflective of every single case, they nonetheless show a pattern: the suburban wards of Bromley are perceived by many of its councillors as requiring a ward orientation; the politics of Islington permits but certainly does not mandate such a pattern and the political environment of the Tower Hamlets council is sufficiently hostile to ward promotion so that those councillors who practise it anyway face risks and expect failure.

But it must be borne in mind that these images are the councillors' perception of reality, rather than a necessarily accurate picture of reality itself. As Table 4.2 indicated, no borough is unilaterally made up of councillors of either ward or borough scope of representation. But Tower Hamlets comes close to being universally borough-oriented, and the examples described above suggest a continuing hostile environment for those who take a different view.

Scope of Ambition

A ward scope of representation was, of course, only one element in the definition of the "classic parochial" councillor. The second defining element was a councillor's narrow scope of ambition. In a sense this is a natural combination (although as the typology suggests, it is not a necessary one). Most parochial councillors simply reported that representing their ward was the extent of their interest in politics, and many expected only temporary involvement even at this level. This combination of low ambition and intention to serve only a single term was particularly pronounced among working-class Labour councillors in this category. Conservative suburbanites in Bromley were more willing to stay on their borough council for longer periods, even though they had no intention of involving themselves in any other levels of political activity. This finding is unsurprising in view of the differential reception parochial councillors get in the Tower Hamlets and Bromley councils. (I have suggested elsewhere that the pattern of leadership in Bromley as a whole is changing, and that support for a ward-oriented councillor style is decreasing at the borough leadership level. But despite this change, the Bromley parochials come from a sufficiently secure ward base so that they can continue to practice this style without feeling that they must either change or leave.) Islington parochials occupy a middle ground. While they lack the supportive structures that encourage parochialism in Bromley, they are not subject to the hostility the style faces in Tower Hamlets.

As I will be showing in the next section, "parochials" often get recruited into their political activity by very specific grievances. Their ambition is to resolve the particular problems that originally led to their involvement. If such councillors aspired to political activity beyond the borough level, they would cease to be "parochial" (and examples of such attitude change will be shown later in this chapter). Whether the "parochial" style is sustainable over the long term even on the borough council level depends on the atmosphere of the particular council. As I have indicated above, the prevailing "ethos" of the boroughs studied differed in this regard, and a Bromley parochial would therefore have a greater political life expectancy than one in Tower Hamlets.

Recruitment

While narrow ambition and/or intention to serve for only a limited period of time are not uncharacteristic of British local politics, a ward scope of representation is. It thus becomes particularly important to inquire into the recruitment patterns which produce these apparently atypical councillors.

Inner London Labour parochials tended to begin their political involvement as an extension of other, non-political group activity. The most common example would be as participants in a local tenants' association with a set of grievances against the borough council. One Islington councillor reported problems in the rehabilitation of the block of flats in which he lived:

We started a tenants association here. We had councillors at our meetings and I could see I could do more being in the

Labour Party. Now I see I can get councillors to work for me.

In another Islington example of specific local grievances being translated into political action, a newly elected councillor reported:

> We formed the tenants' association because one of the children on the estate was killed and we wanted a piece of land for kids to play on. At the time there were elections, and two of the Labour councillors came to see us and said, certainly, they'd do everything to help us get the piece of land. We went and canvassed for them and got the highest-ever poll in this ward. Afterwards, the councillors came round and said, "Why don't you join the Labour Party?" I joined first, and then the one next door, and we gradually got the whole committee of the tenants' association. And we found that when it came to the council at town hall, the neighbourhood councillors voted against us, including the councillors from this ward. And we thought well, all right, if this is what it's like, we'll do it ourselves, and we went round the estate and got people to join. I felt people didn't know enough about the Labour Party, the councillors, what rights they had, and I thought the best way to teach them was to join the Labour Party.

And at the next election, the ward got new councillors.

Although the tenants' association was the most common form of organizational base for the working-class parochials, other specific local issues could also serve as stimuli to begin political activity. One Tower Hamlets councillor reported beginning significant political involvement as a result of a proposal to close the local hospital where the councillor was employed. This councillor's organizational efforts regarding the hospital brought her into contact with the borough government, to which appeals were made for assistance. It also led her to political activity within her ward, and a council nomination.

In one of the few specifically ethnic references encountered in this study, one Islington councillor reported beginning his involvement as a result of the nomination by the Labour Party of an Irish candidate for the local Parliamentary seat. A feeling that the Irish were under-represented politically led this previously apolitical man into the local Labour Party. His continuing activity within the party, which he saw as helping the now-elected MP, eventually led him to a borough council nomination in his own right.

As these examples illustrate, the recruitment of working-class parochials seems to depend on the existence of very specific and idiosyncratic local grievances. When such grievances concern council houses, local tenants' associations can either be formed or rejuvenated. Since the issues involved in such questions almost inevitably bring tenants into more direct contact with the borough government, it ought not be surprising that some of the activists in tenant organizations get politicized by the experience. But the existence of local circumstances that will set off such a pattern of involvement are sporadic and unpredictable.[12]

Conservative suburban parochials operate from a more stable organizational base. Residents' associations, made up of home-owners, are in regular contact with borough councils and are certainly ward-defensive in character. That some individuals will move from activism in such associations into the somewhat more partisan arena of borough-council activity is more predictable than the sporadic working-class patterns described above.

It ought to be borne in mind that the extension of full-scale partisanship to suburban politics is still a relatively recent phenomenon, and that some parochial suburban councillors see their council involvement as simply an extension of other forms of community voluntary-organization activity. Just as one does one's bit in local charitable organizations, etc., so one might become a ward councillor. One such councillor reported he was stimulated to political activity by being a leader in the local Boy Scout movement! Even though patterns of politics in Bromley are changing, in many Bromley wards the local Conservative Party is still an extension of these other forms of voluntary organizations, and so a parochial councillor coming out of such an environment can see ward-defensive politics as "natural". This is in sharp contrast to the conflictual origins of political activity for most Inner London parochials.

Attitudes toward Groups

In view of their modes of recruitment, it is hardly surprising to find parochial councillors largely supportive of the activity of

organized groups in their ward. But perhaps even more significant than their perception of groups as positive entities is
their perception of groups as powerful organizations. (As will be
seen in later sections of this paper, such an attitude is by no
means universal, especially in working-class Inner London.[13])

It was natural for groups to be in at least potential conflict
with the council, in the view of working-class parochials. That
was their function:

> The borough won't meet with just one person, but a body of
> 20 or 30, they'll meet representatives of it, and put their points
> of view both ways.

And groups had power, which meant that a skilful councillor
had to be wary:

> If anything comes up on the council which we feel doesn't go
> along with what the people [in the groups] think, then we
> oppose it. I won't say you can't have your own personal
> feelings on it, but we try to test the water, feel the temperature,
> and act accordingly. If it's a hot issue, they expect us to be in
> the forefront.

In Tower Hamlets, where the overall council reception to
articulation of ward interests was not especially positive, one
parochial "solved" the problem by producing a de facto merger
of partisan activity and pressure-group activity:

> Our ward [party] meetings begin as a political meeting, but
> as the evening progresses this becomes less so, and it ends as a
> tenants' association meeting.

This sense of the power of groups could also be found among
suburban Conservative parochials. After describing a rich
variety of groups within his ward, one councillor reported:

> They'll invite me to go to one of their meetings. . . . I go to
> their meetings and get involved. . . . There are a number of
> interesting questions and so . . . if anything crops up either
> they come to me, or I go to them and get the consensus
> opinion.

Suburban groups were sufficiently powerful so that councillors could not act unilaterally toward them. Consensus was needed.

As I indicated at the outset of this section, one suburban parochial described the access of groups in his ward as better than his own. The local residents' association was "powerful enough to bypass me". Another suburban parochial, although somewhat less pleased with the power groups held, reported that "they oppose everything they can". But even when he felt their arguments were without much merit, the groups nevertheless had power, in his eyes:

> We have all sorts of suggestions for parking meters. Now I was in favour of parking meters . . . because of the shortage of space. Well [a local merchants' association] opposed it. . . . We met with them and listened to their suggestions and they listened to our compromise. We did away with parking meters.

So even in those cases where the councillor was not himself supportive of ward group activity, groups could be influential. It will of course be clear that in the example above, the "compromise" adopted by the council was, in fact, the merchants' association position.

The essence of the parochial councillor's attitude toward ward groups, therefore, was a healthy respect for their power. Although parochial councillors occasionally were themselves unsupportive of organized groups in their ward, it is unsurprising to find that, for the most part, no such problems arose. One suburban Conservative parochial provided a summary of his attitudes toward ward organizations which can stand for the entire group of councillors: "Their views are . . . the views I have."

Attitude toward Party

Just as it was unsurprising to find that parochial councillors were generally sensitive to groups within their wards, it is also unsurprising to find that councillors of this type are not particularly partisan in their orientations. This is perhaps implicit in their combination of narrow scope and narrow ambition.

Indeed, to the extent that party does play a role in the thinking of such councillors, it is often in their making a distinction between the purely local party, and the larger organizations which involve themselves in national politics, an activity these councillors are not particularly interested in engaging in.

One parochial councillor exemplified this distinction by "always trying to divorce the local scene from the national. It [local politics] is all about amenities and drains and planning permissions, schooling, and housing."

A suburban parochial Conservative reported that despite extensive involvement in neighbourhood activities, involvement which led to his selection as ward councillor, he had "only fragmentary knowledge" of distinction between the parties as to how they operated in local government, and as far as national politics was concerned, "I enjoy watching but I don't see myself as involved."

Of course in a political system which operates with competitive and partisan elections, it is impossible for councillors to be entirely outside the party whose label they bear, but for some of the parochials the connection is tenuous indeed. At the extreme of non-involvement would be one Islington councillor who reported that "When we joined the Labour Party, we didn't know what a councillor was, we didn't know the difference between Tory and Labour. As far as we were concerned when we went to town hall, we dealt with officers." For this councillor, the crucial decision was the one to become actively involved and "fight the council". The decision to do so through the Labour Party seems almost an afterthought, based primarily on Labour predominance in the area.

Although no other councillor was this weakly connected to party, several other councillors indicated that party was not especially salient to them. One parochial reported a recent switch from Conservative to Labour Party support, while another, now a Labour councillor, indicated a growing dissatisfaction with Labour, and a desire to join some new "centre" political party. This same councillor also reported that in his view, one of the Conservative council members with whom he had served on committees was the most valuable member of the council.

In the perception of some parochials, this sort of inter-party "compliment" could be returned. One Tower Hamlets Labour councillor, after indicating that Communists made up the principal opposition in his area, nevertheless reported that "I have never been opposed. The Communist Party agent said to me, 'I know you've always done your job, we're not going to oppose you.'"

For some parochials, the principal perception of party was one of conflict between the local ward party organization on the one hand, and larger partisan units on the other:

> There is a definite gap between our [ward party] down here and the National Executive of the Labour Party. I've been to the Greater London Labour Conference, and . . . we feel that as you get up the tree [of the party hierarchy], they get more remote from the man in the street.

I already suggested that one councillor in Tower Hamlets "solved" his problem of how to legitimately raise tenants' association matters by a de facto merger of the tenants' group with the ward party organization. Similarly, for suburban parochials in Bromley, the local Conservative Party branch is like another neighbourhood organization. Just as one joins the residents' association, just as one is active in scouting, so one joins the local Conservative branch organization.

Thus, one suburban Conservative parochial reported:

> You start off getting involved in a committee, the sports committee [of the neighbourhood], you get yourself involved in church activities, you get yourself involved in the local chamber of commerce . . . and I had always been interested in the work of local government and somebody has to do it. . . . I'm interested in debating, I like to go along to lots of public functions. . . . I joined the Conservative Association by working on association committees.

For this councillor, the notion of party is not sharply distinguishable from any of the other neighbourhood organizations in which he was active. For other parochials, as the examples above show, the concept of party was even more weakly developed. But all parochials would probably subscribe to the sentiments of one of their number when he said: "A lot of people would say your first allegiance is to the political party that put you in, but I think your first allegiance is to the people who voted for me, my ward.''

What marks this as the distinctive parochial attitude is not the sentiment itself, but rather that it indicates just how the councillor conceptualizes party: a mechanism which other councillors think to be more important than he does.

B   IDEOLOGY OF LOCALISM COUNCILLORS

Scope of Representation

This category of councillors, made up of individuals with a ward scope of representation but nevertheless broadly ambitious, are a new phenomenon for British urban politics. As shown in Tables 4.2 and 4.4, none of these councillors come from working-class occupations, and none come from Tower Hamlets. Distribution of this group by party and borough is given in Table 4.5.

TABLE 4.6   Ideology of localism councillors by party and borough

Bromley, Conservative	4
Bromley, Labour	0
Bromley, Liberal	1
Islington, Labour	6
Tower Hamlets, Labour	0

It is important to mention at the outset a crucial distinction between the Labour councillors from Islington who fall into this category, and the Conservative councillors from Bromley. In many ways, the Islington councillors in this category set the tone of the Islington council. When councillors were asked whether their own council had any distinctive features, both members of this group, and other Islington councillors, recognized that there was something unusual about the current Islington council. Although the terms used to describe the phenomenon differed, there was general agreement that different sorts of people had been elected to the council, and that this produced a significant difference in what the council did. This group of councillors felt itself to be growing on the council, and to not only be in leadership positions, but to be consolidating its position.

The adherents of the "ideology of localism" among Bromley Conservatives, on the other hand, had all failed in their political ambitions, or been disappointed by the path taken by the Conservative Party. Rather than feeling in control, it was clear that their way of approaching local politics was in a minority in their own party and borough.

The single Liberal councillor in this category (and the single Liberal councillor in the sample as a whole) was an exception. He was quite comfortable with his party's position, and had been successful in national Liberal Party activities, but the party itelf remains small and no real factor in the government of any of the three boroughs studied. (The Liberals had once been powerful in the Orpington section of Bromley, but by the time of this study they had lost all elective office in the area.)[14]

By definition, "ideology of localism" councillors share their ward scope of representation with the parochials discussed in the previous section. But in contrast to the parochials, these "localist" councillors describe their ward-oriented activities in the context of a broader political focus. I mentioned at the outset of this chapter that for councillors of this type, activities within the ward were seen as having national consequences. This intellectual tie between the local and the national perhaps springs from the heavy involvement of this type of councillor in national pressure-group activities. Among the councillors in this category were a councillor who had been a national official of an anti-apartheid group, another from a committee concerned with national education, and a third who had run a branch of the Campaign for Nuclear Disarmament.

In view of this range of nationally oriented activities, it is perhaps surprising to find such individuals adhering to a ward scope of representation, indeed, to find such individuals active in local government at all. This apparent paradox can best be understood in the context of both broad social trends and the personal experiences of the councillors.

The broad social trends, in which committed activists, particularly those on the left politically, have turned their attention toward micro-level involvement, are well-known and certainly not limited to Britain.[15] But in addition, some parts of London, and parts of Islington in particular, have been undergoing "gentrification". This process of housing renovation and immigration of middle-class professionals has brought into Islington a group of new residents with a predisposition to activism.[16]

The borough, therefore, has a new pool of potential involvers from which to draw. As with the parochials, it is possible that some specific local situation will stimulate them to move from "potential" local activity into actual involvement, but once their involvement begins, their prior experiences lead them to have different perspectives than did the parochials described earlier.

One councillor, for example, sounds very much like the parochials when she described how she "campaigned against a council plan to shut down swimming baths to save money. I've got four children who used that bath very strenuously." But quite unlike the parochials, she had a broader context in which to place this experience: "I had worked as a social worker and felt that the old council operated a very restrictive policy. I worked with a unit that deals with the most underprivileged families . . . who need special discrimination to even bring them up to normal level." And she could compare services in Islington with those available elsewhere: "There was a sharp distinction between services available in Camden borough, where I also worked, and in Islington. I think the Islington councillors were too judgmental."

Another councillor who moved into a street in the midst of gentrification was "appalled by local conditions in the area when we moved into Islington". In addition, this councillor, with a history of political involvement while at university, "found the local Labour Party pretty boring initially".

We can see in both of these examples a combintion of personal stakes in changing the character of local representation and the broader context. For the first of these two councillors the personal stake was quite straightforward: a desire to keep open a swimming facility which her family regularly used. For the second, the personal stake may be somewhat more subtle but no less real. A political activist, accustomed to involvement and wishing to continue it, found the style of the Labour Party in her new neighbourhood to be "pretty boring". We ought not be surprised to have found her attempting to change it.

But in addition to these personal stakes, the broader context is also obvious: a desire to "do something" to aid individuals and families at the bottom of the economic order. Perhaps the essence of what I have called the "ideology of localism" is a belief that the best way to accomplish such an improvement is with more forceful articulation of very local matters.

It will be seen in the next section that those councillors I have identified as "traditional rank-and-file" argue strongly against a ward scope of representation on the grounds it would be unfair: some wards would benefit more than others. Parochials, we can see, would be unconcerned about such an outcome, indeed it is often the one they seek. But "localist" councillors resolve this problem quite differently. In their understanding, it is not just their own ward, but all wards, which should have more forceful spokesmen, and the council should provide settings in which this could happen. According to one localist councillor, the council itself should "hire rooms within the wards" where grievances could be expressed to councillors. Such a setting would increase the number of problems brought to councillors, a very good thing, from this point of view.

In some wards where "the community is very organized", "councillors have become very identified with the problems", and this is "rightly so". In other wards, "councillors have been remarkably quiet" and have not obtained the same benefits. As another localist councillor put it: "A ward member is doing his duty when he's taking up problems that are brought to him," but "some members go about it in a haphazard way." The remedy is to get a different type of councillor from these wards, according to the localists, rather than to reduce the extent of articulation of ward interests.

Scope of Ambition

So localist councillors differ from parochials in their motivations for practising a ward scope of representation, but both localists and parochials share the characteristic. Both types are ward-oriented. Where they differ, by definition, is in the range of their socio-political ambitions. (I have used the concept of socio-political ambition, since not all localists expected or intended to pursue conventional electoral political advancement. For example, I have classified as ambitious a councillor who was becoming active in efforts to improve national prison conditions, and another, who although not seeking national elective office, was eager to achieve position with the national Labour Party hierarchy.) The crucial aspect of "ambition" for the purposes of this study is as an indication that the councillor involved sees politics in a framework beyond the borough level.

As I also suggested earlier, political party affiliation made a great difference in the degree to which ambition was likely to be achieved. Of the four Conservative councillors classified as localist, three had sought Parliamentary designation but had been rejected, and one had temporarily resigned from the party in disgust over its procedures for selecting Parliamentary leaders. Indeed, one of the unsuccessful Parliamentary candidates, who had recently moved into Bromley after a history of council activity elsewhere, indicated how leadership aspirations and a ward scope of representation may be incompatible in the Conservative Party.

A member of the council leadership on his old council, but now a self-described "backbencher", he observed that:

> One of the reasons I am a backbencher is that because it's how I want it. I have thought in the past that if [you are] a responsible chairman . . . that once the committee has made a decision you've got to identify with that and stick with it and even uphold it. . . . Whereas as a backbench member it gives me much more wide-ranging powers of attack to support my constituents' point of view.

Thus we see how this particular councillor saw himself as having to choose between pursuit of his ambition and ward representation.

Labour "localists", on the other hand, were not faced with this dilemma. The Labour contingent included many councillors with aspirations to Parliament or the Greater London Council, and none described these ambitions as being in conflict with the articulation of ward interests. One Labour councillor, for example, saw no conflict between pushing in the borough council to get additional council-funded play groups in her ward and her, "coming to feel that national politics is where you are most effective".

Recruitment

Distinctively among the councillor categories, localists provided detailed accounts of self-generated involvement in council politics.[17] Particularly among Labour members in Islington, there were stories of the taking of control of ward meetings at which councillors would be nominated, to ensure that councillors they regarded as unsympathetic to ward interests would be replaced. Although most councillors in the other categories reported often ritualistic disclaimers of having sought council office, many of the localists willingly reported how they and colleagues organized to change the complexion of the council.

Indeed, several of the Labour localists reported difficulty in even joining local Labour Party organizations in Islington, despite the fact that they had been active in party affairs elsewhere before moving to Islington. One such councillor reported that she believed that one of the councillors she characterized as "old guard", who lived on the same street as she, had prevented her joining the party because so many pressure groups had been meeting at her home.

This councillor finally was admitted to the local Labour Party and reports that "I was very disillusioned with the sitting councillors. . . . We used to sit and listen to some of the old councillors' reminiscences about thirty years ago, meeting after meeting, hour after hour." After deciding to challenge the sitting councillors "The nomination was a bloody battle."

The procedures for candidate selection first require the adoption of a "short-list" from which the final candidates will be chosen by the ward party. Instead of waiting to contest the nomination at this final selection meeting "We decided to make up a ticket and to put up this ticket at the short-listing meeting rather than at the subsequent meeting, which was a tactic that, up to that time, had not been used. It took them completely by surprise."

As I suggested earlier, the localist councillors in Islington see themselves as on the ascendancy:

The same process [as the one described above] has already been gone through in central and south Islington, and now it's spread to the north.

The majority of the newer councillors are people who have worked within the community in one way or another. . . .

They have a good working knowledge of grass-roots problems in Islington.

And they now control the council.

In contrast with the conflict reported by localist Labour councillors in Islington, Conservative localists from Bromley report much more conventional patterns of recruitment. Several report a history of activity in local Conservative constituency associations, after which they were asked to stand for the council. So in contrast to the pattern in Islington, where the pre-existing leadership fought vigorously against the entry of councillors with localist orientations, the existing leadership of Bromley seemed quite willing to have such individuals on the council.

Perhaps the best explanation of this distinction lies in the fact that Conservative localists are quite conventional in their council activity. They look after the interests of their own wards, but there are many other councillors who do the same thing. They become unconventional only when they seek advancement to higher office while still adhering to their ward scope of representation. And, as I described above, when they seek to do so they are rejected. Their actual service on the borough council, however, is not unusual and poses no threat.

Labour localists, on the other hand, are quite distinctive. They are not only ambitious, but they act in unusual ways on the local borough council as well. While there undoubtedly have always been some parochials on the Islington council, they were far less challenging to the leadership than the new councillors, whom I have characterized as adhering to an ideology of localism. Unlike the parochials, the Islington localists not only want to represent their own wards actively, but they want to see other wards get the same type of representation. They thus pose a distinctive threat to pre-existing leadership, and it is not surprising to discover a pattern of resistance to their entry.

Attitudes toward Groups

Because it is the Labour localists who are so distinctive, the remainder of this section is basically a description of their activities. As I suggested earlier, it is in their attention to groups that localist councillors are especially distinctive. But their relationship to groups within their own wards is quite different from that reported on earlier for parochial councillors. Whereas parochial councillors often got their personal stimulation to begin political activity as a result of situations in groups to which they belonged, localists are much more likely to be promoters of group activity, rather than simply emerging from groups which already exist.

Even where a point of personal self-interest is a major part of the stimulus for political activity, localist councillors also stimulate the creation of additional groups. Thus the councillor described earlier, who began her direct political involvement as the result of a proposal to close the swimming facilities used by her children, also reports extensive involvement in setting up play groups in her ward prior to her council activity, and in stimulating new tenants' associations to form since her election.

The promotion of tenants' associations on council estates is an especially common form of group-promotion activity engaged in by localist councillors, most of whom are middle class and do not live in council housing themselves. Indeed, some opponents of these new middle-class councillors are especially critical of this activity, feeling that working-class councillors who lived on council housing estates themselves, would not need the "artificial" intermediary of politically active tenants' associations in order to know what was happening on the estates.

In response, localist councillors criticize their predecessors for failing to engage in this activity. One councillor described efforts to stimulate tenant activity in cooperation with a local community worker:

> I work very closely with a community worker in the area. . . .
> He'll get a case coming to him from somebody saying they're being winkled. . . . He'll do intensive visiting of all the tenants and try to encourage them to form a tenants' association toward protecting themselves. . . . And then when he's got it organized, he'll call me in and then they put demands on me.
> . . . I see him in opposition to me. I mean, I wouldn't be happy if he didn't keep on pushing me further and further.

And despite her own preference for this style, this councillor recognized that other councillors would disapprove:

Unfortunately, that tends to be your older councillor, who's been on the council longer. He tends to be your working-class councillor who would oppose this sort of participation with people. Really, I mean this is what it is. It's grass roots participation.

Thus the role of the localist councillor was not only to respond to groups, but to stimulate their formation as well.

In general, then, localist councillors were especially supportive of group activity, saw their function as stimulating groups, and took pride if they believed themselves to be successful. One localist councillor, reporting that an "umbrella organization" of several different tenants' groups had been formed, reported:

It's really an exciting development. . . . It's a grass roots tenants' campaign. [In most organizations] people go in and out, drift in and out, if they have a problem they go and have the problem solved and then they lose interest. Here there's a hard core of people who are consistently there.

This drive to both stimulate and regularize group participation is perhaps the most fundamental characteristic of localist councillors' attitudes towards groups in their wards.

Attitude toward Party

If localist councillors are supportive of group activity, especially that type of ongoing group activity they see as politically relevant, they are much more ambivalent about the role of party. Of course all of them have identified with party sufficiently to join and run for public office with a party label attached. I earlier described parochial councillors as not particularly attached to party, and sometimes as seeing a conflict between party and ward. For the localist councillors I am describing in this section of the paper, their attitude is quite different. Several were active in Labour Party affairs, one was chairman of the constituency party organization. But two elements characterized localist attitudes toward the party: one, that intra-party conflict was to be expected; and second that it was really the role of the council and councillors to deal with problems, not the party as an independent entity. (This latter point marks a particularly sharp distinction from the "traditional rank-and-file" councillors I shall be describing in the next section.)

As I described above, localist councillors provide detailed descriptions of intra-party conflict, often involving organized efforts to displace councillors. Conflict is described in ideological terms, "the left wing versus the right wing" of the Labour Party, and unlike the parochials who sharply divorced local politics from national, many localists were prepared to see a continuum of issues from the ward to the national level. Although some councillors were concerned that their entry displaced working-class councillors, they felt that the "reputation of the party" would be better served by councils which had activist policies, rather than by councils whose class composition closely mirrored the population. But the "reputation of the party" required the council to be the forum. The council should work directly with organized groups, not relying on the party structure to serve this function alone.

All of the above, of course, refers to the Labour councillors among the localists. I mentioned earlier that Conservative localists were not all that distinctive until they actually sought higher-level positions. But it is fair to say that both Labour and Conservative localists challenged party traditions in some sense.

The only exception to this pattern was the sole Liberal Party councillor who fell within this study's sample. This councillor happily reported that the Liberal Party as a national entity was opting for "community politics", where the national party would emphasize concrete local issues. In such an environment, the combination of ward scope and broad ambition seemed perfectly natural, and this councillor had been nominated for Parliament several times by the Liberals. Although his position as a localist probably caused him the least tension with his party of any of the councillors in this category, it still left him as a member of a numerically weak third party. At the time of this study the Liberals controlled only a single ward in the three boroughs studied.

Whatever the individual successes of practitioners of this style of politics, it had not yet reached the point at which it was a sufficiently compelling departure to lead to any wide-scale restructuring of inter-party competition. Thus it is understandable to find localist councillors concentrating their attention, as they do, largely on intra-party matters.

C THE TRADITIONAL RANK-AND-FILE

Scope of Representation

As Table 4.1 indicated, the traditional rank-and-file being discussed in this section are overwhelmingly members of the Labour Party. Indeed, it could be argued that "parochialism" is the traditional rank-and-file position for Conservatives, at least those in the suburban London borough of Bromley. It should also be recognized that at the time of this study councillors of this type were heavily concentrated in the borough of Tower Hamlets. This can be seen in Table 4.2. But while the evidence of this study cannot be definitive, there is ample reason to expect that this position, one of broad scope of representation but narrow ambition, also used to characterize rank-and-file councillors in Islington.[18]

I can identify four characteristics which lead this type of councillor toward believing that a broad scope is the appropriate scope of representation. First, and perhaps most important, is a notion which I will call "working-class solidarity", a belief that the needs of the working class are largely undifferentiated, and therefore ought to get an essentially undifferentiated response from the borough government. In practice this means, as one councillor put it, "equal shares all around".

A second characteristic attitude found among these councillors is a belief that individual councillors are not very powerful, that attempts to promote the specific interests of one's own ward will be largely unsuccessful. Councillors, in this understanding, will "check" each other, to prevent any individual councillor or group of councillors from gaining advantage for their own area. Councillors often pointed to the fact that any one ward has only a small proportion of the total council membership, therefore individual councillors or small groups "can't really affect policy". If they try, "other councillors will pull him up short", and, as a result, "pushing for the ward is soon stopped".

A third element of this structure of beliefs is a sense that council officers, the full-time non-political appointees who run local government services, really have the authority to decide, and that this is appropriate. Thus officers will prevent councillors from "getting too much" for their own wards. As one councillor put it, "We do it by priorities. Officers have the final say."

One final element of the traditional rank-and-file attitude is actually something of an exception to the idea that one cannot push local matters. This is the notion that it is all right to push local grievances, as long as they are directed against private interests and not public ones. One councillor described how a private redevelopment project was viewed with consternation by the residents of the ward he represented. But despite this "If the council was going to redevelop the area I would have been prepared to go to the [ward] people and try to persuade them [to accept it]. But since it was a private developer I was not prepared to do this."

Under such circumstances, resistance within the council to planning permission for the private developer was thought possible and appropriate. But, of course, under current circumstances most of the matters which are brought to councillors in heavily working-class areas are not of this type. Rather than reflecting grievances against private interests, they involve actions, or prospective actions, of the council itself. For the traditional rank-and-file, criticism of these must be kept within bounds. Too intense an articulation of ward complaints is wrong.

Scope of Ambition

The ambition of councillors in this category is, by definition, low. There are several reasons for this, but perhaps the most frequently cited are feelings of inadequacy for higher office. These are characteristically phrased in terms of lack of education. Most of these working-class councillors left school at the school-leaving age of their time, 14 or 15, and they feel conscious of gaps in their knowledge.

A second element is a recognition that advancement is difficult and that ambition is unseemly. "I don't like to make my opportunities", one councillor said. Another felt that advancement was difficult, but his explanation for why this is so is instructive: "The demand for safe seats in Parliament is high, now that MPs are well-paid."

A third element which might be regarded as reinforcing low ambition is that these councillors are tied to their borough council service, and like it that way. "I'd like to serve as long as possible" is a typical response. I mentioned at the outset of this paper that long-standing Tower Hamlets councillors have a strong sense of history about their local government services. One councillor in his seventies said:

> Apart from my immediate family, I'd say this was part of my life. . . . It's built up from the days when we used to go walking in these very old properties, putting in light and that sort of thing. And it's gotten to the stage now where I'd be lost without it.

And if one would be "lost without it", one does not voluntarily leave.

Recruitment

Almost universally, these councillors report entering politics through union activity. Several reported speaking up at union meetings and being sought out by union officials on the lookout for relatively articulate members. Several others were union organizers and, as their unions affiliated with the Labour Party, they were drawn first into local party activity and then on to the council. One councillor reported organizing the Beefeaters, the ceremonial guards at the Tower of London. Since the guards live in a geographically compact area (within the walls of the Tower!) their support enabled him to be elected from that ward to one of the predecessors of the Tower Hamlets council in 1928.

Two points ought to be made about these patterns of recruitment. One is the vital significance of trade union–party ties in drawing individuals such as these into elective office. It seems clear that most of them would never have thought of political involvement if there had not been this gradual path from union branch meeting, into local political party, and then on to the council.

Second is the fact that many of these councillors, who have served for very long periods, represent the first generation of union activists in their occupations. Although no other councillor had as colourful an organizing career as did the one who organized the Beefeaters, several councillors reported being the first union member at their job, and then organizing others. This pattern of entry can happen only once, and leaves a gap which other types of councillors come to fill.

Attitudes towards Groups

At the outset of this section I indicated the importance of working-class solidarity to these councillors. In this context, organized groups, other than union and party, can seem threatening, unnatural, and illegitimate. It is outsiders who raise issues: "extreme left groups [run by outsiders] get all the attention". It is the job of the councillors to resist this, to "keep the borough for people who live in it". Groups distort priorities: "They could make you forget you're there for everyone's benefit." And groups get responded to coldly and formalistically, unless they are well-known to councillors and under their direct observation, if not supervision. For other groups which raise issues "We advise writing to the Town Clerk."

Working-class people are seen by these councillors as apathetic about group organization, unless stirred up by outsiders: "Tenants' associations are largely social." "I know more than the residents." "Few people came to complain to me about [a rent increase]." A councillor is like a shop steward: "It's like in a factory. If you've got a militant shop steward who puts himself out well, he's a good boy; if you've got a lazy one people just sit and suffer." In any event: "Once you've given people a council house you've satisfied them."

As this composite of councillor comments indicates, groups are largely unnecessary from this perspective, and therefore largely irrelevant or illegitimate. (Trade unions are, of course, an exception to this characterization, for Labour Party traditionalists. As I have described in earlier chapters, the "traditional" links between union organizations and party tied the two closely together at the local level. As I will indicate in the next section, traditional councillors had strong positive feelings towards party, and unions get included in this feeling for most of them.)

Attitude toward Party

If traditional councillors were wary of most voluntary organizations, this wariness did not extend to their conception of the role of political party organization.

There are two basic reasons why this is so. One is that party is seen as an important arena for fairness, for democratic decision-making, an important value for these councillors. Councillor after councillor was at pains to point out that decisions within the party, whether at ward meetings or at party group meetings, or at any other level, were taken by majority vote. It seemed a point of pride that the party functioned this way.

A second function of the party, for these traditional rank-and-filers, is as a location for the demonstration of working-class self-respect. One councillor described his parents, who voted Conservative, as "trying to pretend they were not working class". By being affiliated with an overtly working-class organization, this councillor saw himself as counteracting that mistake.

It is in this context that many traditional rank-and-filers were disturbed by the entry of councillors such as the middle-class localists described in the previous section. "Professionals can't represent the working class", one councillor said, and the Labour Party was, and ought to remain, a working-class party in these councillors' view. Party was an opportunity for working-class pride and for demonstrations of self-sufficient effectiveness.

D TRADITIONAL ASPIRANTS

Scope of Representation

Every organization must have leaders, and they cannot come from nowhere. Although the localists described earlier may become significant Labour Party leaders in the future, the Labour Party has not been leaderless up to now. And within the Conservative Party, the advancement possibilities of localists does not seem especially bright.

The individuals in this final councillor classification—councillors who have a wide scope of representation and are ambitious for higher position—form the cadres from which party leaders have traditionally come.

Austin Ranney, in his study of patterns of Parliamentary recruitment, suggests that local government councillors form one major stream of recruitment of national Parliamentary candidates. This tendency was stronger within the Labour Party than among Conservatives, with 47 per cent of Labour Parliamentary candidates having such experience, compared with only 36 per cent of the Conservatives.[19]

Indeed, many of the councillors in this group have already moved beyond the "potential" category by running for higher office, either the Greater London Council or Parliament. Two councillors in this group concurrently serve on both their borough councils and the Greater London Council. (One other councillor, nominated for Parliament from what he regarded as a winnable seat, noted that it was legally permissible to remain on the borough council even if he was elected to Parliament, although he didn't really seem to expect to do so.)

As with the traditional rank-and-file councillors described in the last section, traditional aspirants also believed in a broad scope of representation. But distinguishing them from rank-and-filers, this view was often put in the context of efficiency. Thus one councillor indicated that ward concerns were "non-policy" matters and, as such, not worth attention beyond committee action. In the view of another, "policies need to be settled on a broad basis", while a third expressed the essence of this type of councillors' view when he indicated that "you're thinking nationally all the time." The basic concern here is not that one ward might take advantage of another, which was the prime worry of the traditional rank-and-filers, but rather that too much attention to local issues would deflect attention away from matters of greater substance.

In one introspective example, a councillor changed his view about the proper scope of representation while serving on the council. Asked if council members sometimes push too hard for their own ward, he responded:

> Yes, I've been guilty of that myself. As far as I was concerned, Dockland was Dockland wards' concern and nobody else's.

But obviously you can't do things that way, because it's involving the whole of the borough. Since I've been on the council I've seen further ahead, and I've had to change my opinion. We've got to use Dockland for the good of the whole borough, not just the local ward.

And later in the interview:

Once you get to higher levels like Parliament, you no longer have time to think about local things, about small things in London.

Here we have a councillor who, during his first term on a borough council, changed his orientation from a rather strict concern with the interests of his own ward, to a view where it was possible to imagine that you might "no longer have time to think about local things".

Scope of Ambition

As I indicated above, the councillors in this category were ambitious by definition, and many have already acted upon that ambition successfully. In contrast to the localists, whose ambitions were largely prospective, half of the potential leaders had already sought higher office, been nominated by their parties, and contested elections. Although several Labour councillors were concerned about the effect that Parliamentary service might have on their political views—"I'm concerned about mellowing in Parliament"; "There are few real Socialists in Parliament"—these concerns did not deter them from seeking political advancement. Indeed, the essence of the potential leaders' position was expressed by a Labour councillor who bluntly said: "I am ambitious. I am more interested in national politics."

Recruitment

The recruitment patterns of these councillors are not distinctive except in one important respect. That is the absence of working-

class councillors among the Labour members of this category,
except among the oldest councillors in the category. It has often
been noted by students of British politics that the class composition of the Parliamentary Labour Party has been slowly
changing. The findings of this study suggest that one reason for
this is that one traditional recruitment pool, of ambitious
working-class, local-party activists, may be drying up.

This is consistent with Austin Ranney's report that the reason
why more Labour than Conservative Party parliamentary candidates had local government experience lay in the frequency of
such experience among union-sponsored candidates. Sixty-four
per cent of all union-sponsored Parliamentary candidates had
such experience.[20] As Ranney argues:

> Having served on a local council probably helped applicants
> win places on the unions' parliamentary panels. It may also
> have seemed to some constituency Labour Parties an ad-
> ditional reason for adopting union nominees: for it was good
> evidence that they were more than union hacks put on
> Parliamentary panels because they were not good enough for
> high union office.[21]

Although Ranney does not elaborate on this point, it is obvious
that this pattern of advancement is dependent on the entry of
such figures into local politics in the first place. And, I am
suggesting, this initial aspect of working-class involvement is in
serious erosion.

Attitudes towards Groups

The "potential leaders" interviewed in this study were largely
sympathetic to the functioning of organized interest groups.
This might seem paradoxical in view of the strong objection
traditional rank-and-filers felt to such groups, an objection
based on the fear that interest groups were too parochial. For
potential leaders, this dilemma did not have to arise, since most
of them saw interest groups as also having broad scope. Since
the groups they perceived shared their own wider orientations,
they were not a negative force.

As one councillor put it: "Groups raise long-term questions.

They're entitled to." Or another councillor who clearly sub-scribed to a "group theory" of politics: "I believe in the voice of the people, but nobody really represents the people as such. What you really have are a number of interest groups which represent particular interests." Even councillors themselves were just another interest group, in his opinion.

Thus groups were largely legitimate for this category of councillors. But in addition, they aided efficiency. Interest groups accurately aggregated individual problems, and made them easier to deal with: "When people raise problems at the residents' association [as opposed to individually] it's likely to be genuine." Or another councillor, who indicated that she, and council officers, in her perception, "prefer to deal with groups rather than individuals".

Attitude toward Party

With regard to attitude toward party, it is reasonable to assume that the councillors in this category will be largely supportive of party structures, since they hope and expect to rise within them. Their view of party was, unsurprisingly, placed in a broad national context. Indeed, one aspirant was determined to show how work at the local level could be nationally important, and he proudly reported that his ward party organization had been responsible for starting a national movement to ban fireworks! Put simply, as one councillor did, potential leaders clearly believed that "you can't avoid the influence of national parties on local affairs", and they didn't want to do so.

E   CONCLUSION

It has been the purpose of this chapter to describe the types of councillors uncovered in this study, and particularly to point out the growth of two types of councillors with strong orientations toward a ward scope of representation. Although it is obvious that any individual councillor reaches his own set of orientations from a multiplicity of "causes", there are at least three elements which seem significant in influencing councillor type. These three are: councillor social class; type of ward represented; and atmosphere on the borough council.

With regard to social class, middle-class councillors have clear resource advantages in practising untraditional politics such as the "ideology of localism". They are better educated and more articulate. Their wide range of group affiliations gives them an arena for ambition outside traditional politics. The ambitious middle-class councillor can afford to take more "risks" in the traditional political arena since, if he is unsuccessful, there are always other options. An ambitious working-class councillor, on the other hand, has fewer alternatives and thus may perceive a need to act with more caution.

But ambition is possible for the traditional working class. The ties between union and party provide frameworks for political participation. (In addition, several councillors mentioned that having jobs in nationalized industries was helpful, since they were legally required to give time off for council purposes. In this respect, those in the working class had an advantage over some middle-class councillors, particularly small businessmen, who complained about the constant conflict between job and council activity.)

Atmosphere on the borough council was clearly important in either providing opportunities for the adoption of certain types of roles, or in inhibiting their development. Practitioners of the "ideology of localism" clearly have an easier time now on the Islington council than they would in Tower Hamlets.

The type of ward a councillor represents provides him with a structure of opportunities and constraints. New councillors in Islington saw opportunities for organizing in politically un-organized housing estates. Some Bromley councillors, on the other hand, felt constrained by the already existing effective organization of powerful residents' associations of home-owners in their wards.

But these elements are not fixed for all time. Ward charac-teristics, and even the social class of elected councillors, are subject to change as demography of wards and boroughs changes. And even atmosphere on the borough council is subject to change, as leadership patterns on the councils evolve to better "fit" changing demographic and economic realities of the boroughs.

But what of the consequences? What difference does it make what types of councillors serve on a borough council? I think it is necessary to differentiate between the impact on borough policies, and the impact on recruitment patterns for higher political levels. In working-class areas, the entry of localist councillors may produce council policies more responsive to the poorest residents of the area, but this entry of new types into council activity also dries up advancement for working-class aspirants as the union-to-council-to-higher-levels chain is broken.

In middle-class areas we observe a more stable pattern. Ward orientation is acceptable as long as it is not coupled with aspiration for higher levels. But when the council leadership needs to assert its authority over ward interests, the lack of ties to higher levels reduces the effectiveness of suburban ward-defenders.

The variations in attitude and action of the different types of councillors studied in this research do, therefore, have consequences. And those consequences affect not only the policies of the local authorities in which they serve, but the national political structure as well. In the next chapter I will be examining the consequences of these patterns for the styles and policies of the borough councils as a whole.

5 What the Councils Do: Styles and Policies

Most studies of legislators and legislative behaviour focus upon the styles and actions of individual participants in the process, and give relatively little attention to whole-system characteristics. In this chapter I wish to suggest that a pattern of linkages can be found between the characteristics of individual participants described in earlier chapters and the collective processes and policies of councils as a whole. In addition, I will argue that the characteristics of the units themselves, the demographic, economic and historic backgrounds of the three London boroughs studied in this analysis, operate to form a pattern of constraints and opportunities which shape the styles and possibilities for action of the borough governments.

I will be discussing council activities in two basic categories, the styles of procedure by which the councils conduct their affairs, and the policies adopted by the councils. In this first category, of procedural styles, I will be looking particularly at variations in the openness of council decision-making. I will be suggesting that variations in openness/closedness can be detected not only in such overt patterns as the council's propensity to take decision in public or in private, but also in the extent to which the formal rules and informal norms of the council encourage (or discourage) individual councillors from pursuing these questions outside council meetings. The critical variable in this regard will be whether access by the press to the council (and councillors) is encouraged or not.

The second basic category within which whole-council activities will be discussed is the variation in policies adopted by the three councils studied in this research. I will be focusing particularly on one area of policy, the attitude of the local authority toward its further development, and specifically its economic development. It is obvious that a sub-national government, such as a borough council, is not an entirely free actor in determining its development policies. As I suggested in Chapter 2, opportunities and constraints in this field are often a consequence of long-standing national policy decisions. (Indeed, it can be argued that in the case of Britain, recent decades have seen increasing supra-national constraints operating as well.) But having said this, the evidence gathered in this research suggests that London boroughs are not simply passive transmitters of national development policy. Although the general outlines of their growth and change are set by forces of greater scope, boroughs have clear options about whether they seek to promote or retard these forces.

A   COUNCIL STYLES

As I indicated above, the concept of "council styles", as used here, involves the ways in which the councils studied conduct their business, and the incentives provided by the council as an institution to its individual councillor members to adopt certain ways of conducting their own council work. These styles can be seen as forming a continuum from openness to closedness. At the "open" end of the spectrum, councils do their work and expose their conflicts in public and establish mechanisms to encourage the public articulation of differences as well as the formal expression of citizen inputs into council work. At the extreme of closedness, councils are secretive as institutions, and have formal and informal policies which encourage individual councillors to present themselves as united, and discourage too many public occasions on which the local citizenry might challenge this appearance.

As I suggested above, any aspect of sub-national government, especially in a formally unitary system such as Great Britain, is partially constrained by national decisions. The degree to which a local government can be either open or closed is no exception. Thus, for example, decisions of the national Parliament now require local governments to conduct their formal business, at both the whole-council and committee level, in public sessions. This obvious promotion of at least a degree of openness can be regarded as partially contradicted by the nature of the traditional English libel laws, which pose constraints on investigative journalism, and therefore on the coverage of all levels of government. (There is also a strong history of excluding journalistic coverage of local government.[1]) This pattern of exclusion, a combination of customary closedness of council meetings and reluctance of local newspapers to report much about council activities, has been noted by many observers of British local politics. Wallace Sayre reported finding little information about local government in London in the London press, on radio, or on television.[2] Edward Banfield reports a tradition of excluding the press from official local government bodies,[3] and Paul Peterson and Paul Kantor report that London borough weeklies have little influence on borough politics.[4] In the few cases where weeklies attempted to engage in more comprehensive reporting and attempted to influence events, they had little influence, according to Peterson and Kantor.[5] In his comparison of the functioning of local government in the United States and England, L. J. Sharpe indicates that the access of the American press to information, and its interest in reporting on local events, is an important reason why he characterizes American local government as, on the whole, more open than that in England.[6]

In a country with democratic, party-competitive institutions such as Great Britain, councils which contain representatives of more than one political party cannot possibly fall at the extremes of closedness, if only because the opposition party will not permit this, and the formal rules and informal norms require that the opposition be given opportunities to disagree publicly with council actions. But party competitive norms do not prescribe how one-party councils, such as those in Tower Hamlets and Islington, are to be administered, nor do they govern the modes of behaviour within majority (or minority) party groups on the councils with divided partisan membership. Thus, although neither the councils as collective entities, nor the political party groups within them are totally free actors, the external constraints on their openness, or lack thereof, in the conduct of council business, are open to significant variation from one jurisdiction to another. This variation can best be seen as a consequence of three basic factors: the characteristics of the boroughs—their demographic and economic bases, and their political history; the patterns of leadership which each council worked within; and the attitudes and backgrounds of rank-and-file members of the councils studied.

I have suggested in previous chapters that variation in participants' attitudes toward political parties and voluntary organizations formed two crucial dimensions which affected the ways in which council leaders and rank-and-file members saw their functions. I now wish to suggest that variations on these two dimensions also affect the ways in which participants can be located on the openness/closedness dimensions referred to above. Those participants with positive attitudes toward political party, that is, those councillors and leaders who see political party as the fundamental organizing force which structures their council activities, tend to fall, in the British context, at the "closed" end of the continuum.

The definition of "closedness" being used in this chapter does not in any way exclude vigorous competition between differing political parties for public support (and votes) during election campaigns. Rather, it refers to the ways in which councils conduct their business while in office, particularly the relationships within party groups on the council, and the ways in which councils interact with their citizen populations during their terms of office. Indeed, it is precisely because of the nature of inter-party competition, with its emphasis on appearing before the public (and the opposition parties, if any) with a united front, that an emphasis on the ties between party and local government produces tendencies toward closedness.

This emphasis on party can take several forms. Party can be seen as the organizing force which not only formally nominates council candidates, but also guides their actions once in office. In a somewhat differing but complementary conception, the job of participants in local government can be understood by its practitioners to require that they use their local government positions to enhance the standing of their party in its national partisan endeavours. But for both of these purposes, a united front of party members, "closed" ranks, is an appropriate stance.

The second major dimension on which I have previously characterized council participants is in their attitude toward voluntary organizations, "pressure groups" within their boroughs which seek to influence council policy, rather than having an ongoing stake in formal partisan support of one or another political party. (I have earlier suggested that it is necessary to differentiate between labour unions and other voluntary organizations in this regard, at least in the British case. The systematic ties between labour unions and the Labour Party means that for a great majority of British trade unions, they do indeed have an ongoing stake in formal partisan support of a particular political party. Thus, when I refer to relations with voluntary organizations, I am normally excluding labour unions, unless they are specifically mentioned.)

Since the essence of voluntary organizations' relations with borough councils is their demands on councils for resources and for policies they desire, it is natural to find that councillors who see themselves as spokesmen for such organizations will desire "open" council procedures in which voluntary organization demands can be heard. Because organizations other than labour unions lack formal ties to either the council as an official entity or to its political-party components, such organizations require a council setting in which the raising of issues from outside the council's formal structure is regarded as legitimate, and is encouraged. This is the very essence of council openness, and we can expect "localist" councillors in particular to argue for and support council procedures which would open access to ward-based voluntary organizations.

In previous chapters, both leaders and rank-and-file councillor samples were found to have varied in their attitudes towards these twin sources of political cue-giving, the political party and the voluntary organization. I would now argue that those who look primarily toward party will show tendencies toward "closedness" in the council styles they support and pursue, while those whose primary orientation is toward voluntary organizations will tend toward openness.

But in addition to this variety in party/voluntary organization orientation, I also suggested that councillors could usefully be classified on two other dimensions as well—the scope of their ambition and the scope of their representation. At this point I will focus on "scope of ambition", and argue that variations on this dimension produce variations in councillor attitudes towards the desired openness/closedness of council procedures. (I will later be suggesting that variation on the other councillor dimension discussed in the previous chapter, that of "scope of representation", is related to councillor attitudes towards economic development. That argument will be made in the next section of this chapter.)

"Ambitious" councillors are more likely than their less ambitious colleagues to desire open council procedures. There are two distinct councillor types that I have classified as "ambitious", the "localists", who rose out of neighbourhood pressure groups and developed what I characterized as an "ideology of localism" linking neighbourhood concerns with broader national politics, and councillors I characterized as "traditional aspirants", who entered their borough council through traditional paths of party and union, but whose personal political goals extended beyond the arena of borough politics. (It should be borne in mind that the definition of "ambition" used in classifying councillors centred on the individual councillor's desire to seek involvement in higher-level political bodies, and not simply to rise within his current borough political structure.)

It is this desire to seek higher political office that moves both "localists" and "traditional aspirants" to support more open council structures. In order to rise to higher levels, to be selected as a Parliamentary candidate, for example, recognition of one's abilities and attitudes becomes a fundamental need. An "open" council structure, permitting (and promoting) articulation of policy positions, is therefore a help to an "ambitious" councillor in making himself known.

I am arguing that the three strands of influence which affect council styles: borough backgrounds, leadership preferences, and rank-and-file councillor attitudes, provide varying pre-dispositional tendencies towards openness or closedness in council procedures. The historical/political backgrounds of all-working-class areas such as Tower Hamlets in the present (and Islington in the past but not in the present) lead to "needs" for working-class solidarity, a solidarity which translates itself into relatively closed council procedures. A borough like Islington today, however, with considerable variation in its socio-economic mix and a substantial influx of middle-class pro-fessionals, can be expected to be a borough of considerable inter-class controversy, with the now-dominant middle-class, professionals (in both the council itself and in the population base) supportive of more "open" council procedures. In Bromley, the historical traditions of "village" politics would lead us to expect a council "open" to certain types of inputs from established residents' associations.

These borough background factors, however, are mediated by national political norms. In several respects these norms are norms of closure. A generally uninquiring local press, and traditions of internal government secrecy, mean that public information levels regarding council activities are likely to be low. In addition, a disciplined party system is not likely to be very tolerant of openness which might expose intra-party factionalism and policy disputes. The impersonal background factors of borough backgrounds and national political norms, therefore, provide mixed clues as to whether individual borough councils are likely to be taking "open" or "closed" stances toward the boroughs they administer. It is precisely in an environment such as this, with mixed background factors, that the role of individual predispositions of council leaders and rank-and-filers become important in shaping political styles.

With regard to borough leaders, common trends of economic integration into Greater London have had diverent political consequences. In the case of Islington, leadership shifted to a councillor for whom voluntary organizations were perceived to be a more comprehensive organizing force in borough life than was political party. In the scheme presented above, we would anticipate that such a leader would want to move his council toward the "openness" end of the "openness/closedness" continuum. In Bromley, on the other hand, changes in council leadership led to an increase in emphasis on the role of party. We would anticipate that such a shift would bring with it a shift in the direction of closure in the Bromley council's ways of doing business. Tower Hamlets occupied an intermediate position. Although the new leadership continued to see political party as the prime organizing force of borough political life, the new leader was clearly more open towards participation by voluntary organizations (in addition to traditional union participation) than the old leader had been. We would expect, therefore, to find his preferred council styles falling somewhere between those of the Islington and Bromley leaders.

Rank-and-file councillor type also had impact on whole-council styles. "Localist" and "traditional aspirant" councillors had interests and attitudes consistent with support for "open" council styles, while "parochials" and "traditional rank-and file" councillors could be expected to be more tolerant of "closed" styles. Since the mix of councillor types varied from borough to borough, we would expect the net impact of rank-and-file councillor attitudes on overall borough council styles to vary in similar fashion.

The Impact of Borough Background on Council Styles

I have presented the three boroughs as having traditionally distinctive political styles. (But I also suggested that all three of the boroughs have been subject to common forces of recent economic change.) While it is reasonable to assume that the traditional styles are themselves the product of earlier economic and social forces, they also acquire a "life of their own", and can be expected to continue to have meaning for participants in local political processes long after the original forces which gave impetus to these traditions have disappeared.

Thus traditions of closedness in Tower Hamlets can be traced to traditions of working-class solidarity and the development of "them and us" understandings of the workings of British society. Such attitudes are tied to a sense of working-class self-sufficiency which the old economic base of Tower Hamlets encouraged and reinforced. Among the political expressions of this solidarity were the actions of predecessor councils to the current Tower Hamlets London borough council in collectively resisting external pressure. Thus, the imprisoning of the entire Poplar borough council in 1921 for its unwillingness to implement taxation demands of its hierarchical superior, the London County Council, formed a significant part of the learning, if not the memory, of many older members of the Tower Hamlets council of today.[7]

As I suggested in Chapter 2, Tower Hamlets councillors often exhibited a strong "sense of history" regarding their borough and its component neighbourhoods. The sociological literature cited there also suggests that relatively small neighbourhood units were of prime importance in structuring residents' sense of self-identity. These traditional attitudes among residents and councillors have received twin shocks in recent decades. Massive reconstruction and population (but not class) shifts have destroyed much of these physical and psychological communi-

ties. The London Government Act of 1963, which created the
present London borough structure, produced Tower Hamlets
from a combination of three old metropolitan boroughs: Poplar,
Stepney, and Bethnal Green, each of which had had its own long-
standing Labour Party and political establishment. Under such
circumstances, it was inevitable that the early years of the
amalgamation would be characterized by factions based on
these older geographical lines. As a result, those councillors in
Tower Hamlets who now appear to be the most traditional, were
really quite "modern" when they worked within the Tower
Hamlets council to end the geographical separatism that no
longer had any basis in class, party, or formal political
boundaries.

The task of the post-London Government Act politicians in
Tower Hamlets was to build "one borough". Closedness, the
development of at least the facade of unity, was useful for this
process. Thus, even the "modernizers" within the Tower
Hamlets structure were led by their sense of distinctive local
needs into styles of action which discouraged the open expression of factionalism (which they feared would re-open geographic divisions) and encouraged a rather closed presentation
of council solidarity to the outside world. As this example
demonstrates, it cannot be taken for granted that "change" and
"modernization" necessarily lead in the direction of political
openness. The need of the immediate post-reorganization Tower
Hamlets leadership was for unity, and a "closed" style was
useful in creating this unity, and consistent with the traditions of
the area.

But Tower Hamlets has begun to undergo certain changes in
its economic base and population composition. While these have
not affected its basic class composition, and still do not form a
part of the "sense of place" of older councillors, they are
relevant here, not because they eliminate the effects of tradition,
but because they set in motion political forces which are
supportive of certain changes in council style. This could clearly
be seen in the shifts of characteristic attitudes in the borough
council leadership.

For example, I pointed out earlier that a shift of economic
base from single-industry-dominant communities to communities of much more varied working-class occupations, meant that
the automatic tie between union branch and ward party was

being broken. As a result, position-taking could be expected to become a more necessary part of councillor activity, at least for some councillors, as councillors came to need their own bases of support more and more. Councillors who in the past could be placed on the council by their union now needed to make independent names for themselves. Such needs require opportunities for publicity, and an entirely closed council structure does not provide such opportunities.

What we might then expect to find in Tower Hamlets, therefore, is a tradition of closedness in council styles, but a tradition whose strength is in the process of being weakened. In Islington, by way of partial contrast, we would expect to find such traditions far more completely atrophied. Because of its history of mixed service occupations among working-class residents, a traditional occupational mix quite unlike that of Tower Hamlets, Islington has been much less resistant to the in-migration of new middle-class professionals.

The entry of new residents such as these could be expected to move the borough council toward more open styles in at least two different ways. For one thing, middle-class professional *residents* could be expected to be far more demanding consumers of information about the borough council than would be the case for the virtually all-working-class population of Tower Hamlets. Even if the new Islington residents made up only a relatively small fraction of the entire borough population, we would expect them to provide a "market" for increased information about their local government.

Second, middle-class professional *councillors* could be expected to be proponents of more open council styles. Unlike the trade-union base which characterized Tower Hamlets (and Islington) traditional Labour councillors, middle-class professionals on the Islington council came to their council activity from a local voluntary organization base. One of the prime activities of such organizations was criticism of council policies. We would expect the leaders of such organizations to continue to be articulate once elected to the council. Indeed, several of the traditionalists who remain on Islington council complained about the increased length of meetings which had developed in the years since substantial numbers of middle-class councillors joined Labour ranks on the council. Articulation of local interests, the stock-in-trade of the new Islington councillors, is incompatible with closed council styles. As such new councillors came to dominate the Islington council, we would expect to find that its styles had evolved far more thoroughly than Tower Hamlets in the direction of publicly visible procedures.

As both the Islington and Tower Hamlets examples above indicate, economic changes, population shifts, and changes in the political base of members of the borough councils led both boroughs to move their stylistic "centre of gravity" toward more open styles, albeit at different rates and to different extents. That such borough background factors do not unidirectionally tend towards openness is seen by the Bromley experience. The gradual politicization of Bromley council, the end of traditions of "independent men" representing "independent villages" on the council, mirrored the evolution of the borough's physical development from a series of exurban villages into a significant part of the suburban London commuter belt. Such variations in the openness and closedness of borough council styles need to be seen in the context of national political norms. While those norms certainly do not discourage inter-party competition, they do serve to put restraints on intra-party conflict.

I suggested in the opening chapter of this work that there is no necessary reason why traditions of Parliamentary party discipline, where survival of the government of the day is dependent on maintaining a continuing of Parliamentary majority, necessarily carried over into local government, where councils are elected to fixed terms of office. Nevertheless, those national traditions do work their way through lower levels of politics as well, and the politicization or more properly, the "partisanization", of the Bromley council Conservatives could be expected to reduce the tolerability of open conflict, and thus move the council toward more closed styles than had prevailed in earlier periods.

Although I will be emphasizing the explanatory power of leadership and rank-and-file councillor attitudes in accounting for variations in council styles, I have sought to show that such style-preference among current participants are not imposed on a *tabula rasa*, but that the political backgrounds of the boroughs studied produce tendencies toward openness or closedness in political style. These tendencies are not uniform, of course, just as the traditions, and patterns of economic evolution of the boroughs studied are not uniform.

In the case of Tower Hamlets, we find a borough with strong traditions of "working-class solidarity", a tradition I have associated with closed council styles. Although there has been some weakening of this tendency, it has by no means disappeared. In Islington, a relatively small change in borough population's class composition, and a much more comprehensive change in the make-up of the borough council, has produced far more comprehensive changes in borough politics. We would now expect to find a tendency towards openness as the Islington norm.

In Bromley, the fuller integration of the borough into metropolitan political life has brought with it a movement towards regional and national political norms, and these norms encourage more intra-party cohesiveness than had been the more traditional Bromley pattern. As shall be shown below, the tradition of "independent men" on the Bromley council has by no means disappeared, and so Bromley cannot be said to have moved towards an entirely "closed" council style. Nevertheless, for the reasons indicated above, we would expect to find evolution in this direction.

The Impact of Leadership Preferences on Council Political Styles

I have emphasized that patterns of council leadership in the three boroughs examined in this research changed over time in ways that mirrored the economic and political evolution of the boroughs. Nevertheless, the leaders are independent actors, whose personal views regarding preferred council styles form one significant element in determining what styles are actually followed by the councils they lead. And the leaders studied did vary in their style preferences.

As I have suggested above, attitudes towards preferred style can be considered as forming an openness/closedness continuum. Although we ought not expect to find the term "closedness" openly praised, the leaders studied did vary in the extent to which they discussed "openness" as a crucial characteristic which they saw as fundamental to council activities, and the extent, if any, to which they qualified their endorsement of the concept. Two crucial determinants of leadership attitude toward openness were their views on how rank-and-file councillors, on the one hand, and general publics, on the other, would use open council procedures.

For Cllr Southgate, the Islington leader, it was a point of pride that Islington was a "distinctively open council". Contrasting the situation in Islington with that of a neighbouring borough, he told of how a member of Islington council had gone to a meeting of the other council, and come back reporting that the contrast was very great: "He never appreciated quite how far the policy [of Islington openness] had gone, how far we had developed." Southgate shared this assessment, "I think we may lead in this field." And he believed that the general public was aware of the possibilities of access:

> People at some point feel an anxiety, and I think that when they feel an anxiety they go to a councillor or they come into town hall to find out precisely what the effect will be on them. I think we have managed to get this idea across that they can find out.

In contrast:

> I get the impression that our neighbours [in another borough] have got pretty closed doors.

Thus, for Southgate, a policy of openness was not only positively evaluated, it was a part of his sense of the distinctiveness of Islington.

But what does being a "distinctively open council" consist of? For Southgate, there seemed to be several elements. One major element involved relations with the press. As I suggested in the introduction to this chapter, the traditions of British politics, particularly in local government, suggest a rather wary and distant relationship between local governments and the local press, particularly for Labour-controlled councils. Southgate saw things differently, and recognized that his views were not necessarily held by all:

> They [the press] are pretty good as a whole. Some councillors possibly take a very secretive attitude and think we should tell the press nothing, whereas we tend to use it a great deal now.

Islington had changed its internal council rules so that much which had previously been discussed in closed party group meetings was now to be discussed in open council sessions. Southgate looked forward to the consequences of this change:

> After the recess, committees will begin to bring forward reports on major issues of policy [to the entire council, rather than to the party group]. And then there will be much more extended council meetings with a lot of debates upon controversial issues. . . . When they start coming up the council will . . . become a very much livelier, more vigorous body.

Southgate anticipated that there would still be some efforts to have disputes within Labour ranks settled privately in party group meetings:

> I would imagine it would happen where the group was split right down the middle and it was felt we should take a private decision rather than a public decision, presumably for reasons of saving face.

But Southgate did not agree:

> My argument would be that it would have to be a pretty strong case for doing this because if there is a split then there must be genuine differences of policy, and let's debate those in the open.

And Southgate felt that this increased openness would be constructively used. He perceived that there had been a significant change in the composition of the Islington council, and he felt that the new councillors, in particular, would be better able to act on increased information because they "understood the new budgetary jargon". In addition, their history of voluntary-group activism meant that they were sympathetic to extensive formal council consultation with community groups. Thus, such councillors would be regularly informed about meetings between council staff and community groups, and councillors would attend. Officers had been told to send out lists of proposed council activities and projects and indicate to ward councillors which projects might affect their ward. Although such types of information might seem unremarkable, as will be seen below it is by no means the universal practice of the boroughs studied.

Thus, for Southgate, openness included positive relationships with the press, encouragement of public debate on controversial issues, even if these divided the Labour Party, encouragement of citizen access to information about the council, and councillor involvement in council-sponsored community liaison. This package of attitudes and actions, Southgate felt, made Islington an atypical council, but he strongly approved of its atypicality.

The Bromley leader, Cllr Barkway, presents a different picture. Any evaluation of leadership attitudes towards openness of council procedures must take into account the leaders' evaluation of the utility and consequences of openness. Where Southgate saw openness as a vehicle for community groups and individual residents to express needs he regarded as legitimate, Barkway interpreted matters differently. In response to a question on whether citizens had sufficient information to be useful in helping councillors to decide borough questions, Barkway thought: "They're not well enough informed. . . . Usually when, in my view, they express a point of view, it is for a personal or pecuniary interest." And these were not the grounds on which the council ought to be deciding policy, in Barkway's view.

Given such an interpretation, we would not expect to find Cllr Barkway as enthusiastically supportive of open styles of council work as was Cllr Southgate. Although he felt that the press will, "on balance, give you a fair crack", he also felt that councillors should be more restrained in raising matters in local newspapers:

> I think that people [members of the council] often shout off to the press far too often. . . . You ought to give the system the opportunity to come up with the answers before criticizing the system. But one knows that there are many people to whom a secret is a burning issue and they can't actually relax until they've told someone.

Thus, for Barkway, use of the press by councillors ought to be more limited than it acutally is. And he felt that many councillors violated what he felt to be a proper norm of council conduct by overusing it.

Barkway's attitudes were paralleled by the expressions of appointed council officers and in council actions. Thus we find the Bromley town clerk, the top council officer, warning councillors against leaking confidential information to the press (in this case a report arguing that the borough needed more social workers). We also find the Bromley council, in an economy move, discontinuing its practice of directly informing residents of planning requests from their immediate area. Cllr Barkway, in announcing this change, reported that since lists of all planning requests continued to be available for inspection at the town hall, further direct information to residents was unnecessary. These two actions, consistent with Barkway's views as reported above, would seem inconceivable in the Islington setting, given the view of council leadership in that borough.

Cllr Beasley, the new leader of the Tower Hamlets council, presents an intriguing middle position between Cllrs Southgate and Barkway on appropriate norms of council openness. In his view, the Tower Hamlets council was moving in the direction of greater openness than had been true in the past, and this trend was consistent with local public opinion as he saw it: "People want a little more open-mindedness. The impression goes out that you are a sterile council. In areas of voluntary organizations, people wanted to feel we were a bit more receptive to them."

As was seen in Chapter 3, Cllr Beasley was far more receptive to voluntary organizations in addition to trade unions, than had been true for his predecessors. But, unlike Southgate in Islington, there were limits to his view of the proper role of voluntary organizations, and also unlike Southgate, openness was not at the top of his priorities for reforming the style of the Tower Hamlets council. Rather, Cllr Beasley saw the fundamental need in Tower Hamlets to be a reform of council structure to make the borough's functioning more efficient—what he called "the corporate idea". The council, in his view, had to project a "feeling for change. A feeling we've got to project a new image. Bring the whole thing up to date."

Councils could not continue to be run on what he described as "amateurish" basis. In order to make this shift, Beasley wanted to see more professionals on the Tower Hamlets council. But his goal in seeking some change in the composition of the council was to bring to it individuals who would do a better job of managing: "Long-time members can get stale."

Such a managerial view is not necessarily inimical to openness in council procedures, but is not strongly encouraging of openness either. And Beasley's views need to be seen in the context of the borough's political traditions described earlier, traditions which he wanted to modernize rather than break. Those traditions created and reinforced closedness, and as will be seen in the next section of this chapter, most rank-and-file Tower Hamlets councillors continue to adhere to these values. It would have required a major commitment on the part of council leadership in Tower Hamlets to produce major modifications in council style, and Beasley's efforts were not primarily directed toward this end.

We can see that the council leaders in the three boroughs examined do fall at different points along an openness/closedness dimension. Cllr Southgate, the Islington leader, saw an open council as one of Islington's marks of distinctiveness, and a fundamental break with past borough practice. Cllr Beasley, while perceiving a public desire for somewhat more council openness, placed this desire in the context of a desire for a more up-to-date and modern borough governmental structure. His prime means for achieving this was through managerial reform, rather than by any fundamental reform of the borough's political style. Cllr Barkway, the Bromley leader, did wish to change the borough's style, and make it more partisan. This involved changing a tradition of "independent men" on the borough council, who would independently represent the needs and views of their autonomous "villages". As the borough became a more integrated whole, Barkway sought to move its politics into a more "normal" British party system. Such a system, stressing inter-party competition and intra-party solidarity, led Barkway from some of the borough's tradition of open representation by independent village squirearchies.

The Impact of Rank-and-File Councillor Preferences on Council Political Styles

In Chapter 4, I suggested that councillors could be classified into distinctive types on the basis of their location on two dimensions—the scope of their ambition and the scope of their representation. In the introduction to this chapter, I suggested that those councillors who were broadly ambitious, who sought higher socio-political involvement, would be likely to favour more open council procedures.

The "broadly ambitious" councillors are of two types, the "traditional aspirants" and the "localists". Councillors with "narrow" ambition included "traditional rank-and-file" councillors and "parochials". As I will be showing in this section, distinctive types of councillors, as described above, do indeed hold distinctive views about the degree of openness of style they regard as appropriate for their councils.

We can view closedness as the traditional norm for British local government. It requires an active choice, therefore, for a councillor to advocate and assume a more open style of council work. In one sense, therefore, it might seem paradoxical to place the "traditional aspirant" councillors in the category of those expected to be supportive of open council procedures. What is important here, however, is that the aspirant who wishes to rise to higher political levels (and is not content merely with rising within his existing borough council political framework) must have some sort of access to wider attention. He must, therefore, begin to think of the necessity of having his name appear in the newspapers, and to be seen as an "active" councillor. To be sure, these advancement needs can put such a councillor in conflict with the norms of his council. As was noted in the last chapter, for example, the "traditional aspirants" among Bromley Conservative councillors had all failed, up to now, in their efforts at political advancement.

"Localists", however, are much more consciously anti-traditional in their views regarding council activity. As their background, reported on in the last chapter, shows, such councillors come largely out of a setting of voluntary organization, pressure-group activity. Many localists have to contest actively within their party organizations for their council nominations in the first place. We can expect that a history of participation in pressure groups, one of whose prime goals was often the opening of council procedures, would lead to on-council behaviour supportive of openness. Similarly, the nature of the intra-party conflicts that many localists went through prior to obtaining a council seat, where the new localist councillors quite consciously saw themselves as "opening up the system", would also lead us to expect them to take a similar view in their new official capacities as council members.

In addition to these distinctive features, localists also shared the ambition of the "traditional aspirants", and the same arguments operating for that category, need for publicity, and need to appear publicly competent, would work with equal force for the ambitious localist. With this combination of reinforcing factors, we would expect localist councillors to be strongly supportive of open council procedures, supportive to a much larger extent than the more cross-pressured traditional aspirants.

For the non-ambitious councillor categories, on the other hand, we have a different picture. Neither parochials nor traditional rank-and-file councillors sought higher levels of office. Publicity, therefore, of the type that might call such a councillor to the attention of Parliamentary selection committees, for example, was unnecessary. And, as I suggested above, in a political system where closedness has been the norm, it requires an active motivation for a councillor to behave differently, and councillors in neither of the two "non-ambitious" categories had such motivation.

It might be thought that parochials, motivated to seek borough council activity out of some very local or even personal grievance, might want open council procedures for the expression of this grievance. Such was not generally the case, however. Indeed, one of the major dividing lines between parochials and localists, both of which councillor groups saw themselves as expressing ward interests, was the extent to which a councillor put his ward grievance into a broader political context. For parochials, who did not do so, the relatively abstract issues of council procedures did not normally seem to be tied to the specifics of their grievance. The specifics of these councillors' style preferences, therefore, depended not on some general set of procedural values, but on the particulars of their local situation, and as shall be seen below, to a considerable degree on the norms of the councils on which they sat.

The procedural "status quo", in English local government, I indicated above, was a closed style. If parochials were "closedness-tolerant", because their interests did not really extend to general procedural matters, traditional rank-and-file councillors, the final councillor category to be considered here, were "closedness-supportive". Councillors I have characterized as "traditional rank-and-file" were heavily concentrated in Tower Hamlets, and formed a large majority of the councillors in that borough's sample.

Although the new council leader in Tower Hamlets had an at least partial willingness to see the borough council become more open, this view does not seem to have permeated the attitudes of the rank-and-file members of the borough council he led. Thus, although Beasley reported a personal willingness to see the council become more open, and perceived some public pressure in this direction, traditional rank-and-file councillors from Tower Hamlets retained their old attitudes. This can be seen most clearly when these councillors' attitudes towards use of the press is examined. One councillor answered flatly and simply: "We are not allowed to raise issues through the press." Another expected retaliation from the party if he pursued such forbidden activity, "Use the media? Do you want me to commit suicide?"

But this second councillor's attitude is instructive. Although he first responds in terms of personal political danger if the press were used by him, it later becomes clear that he opposes its use on his own: "The press is not a tool of the working-class movement", according to this Tower Hamlets traditional rank-and-file councillor.

For another traditional rank-and-file councillor, it was clear that the "press only wants sensational news". That his attitude was not limited to the local press of his own borough became clear when this Labour councillor cited Richard Nixon's treatment by American newspapers as an example of "the press setting itself above the government", clearly a bad thing in his view.

For a number of councillors the existence of the borough's own irregularly published newspaper, the *Tower Hamlets News*, distributed free to borough households, obviated the need to have any other press contact. Whatever information borough residents needed would get communicated to them in what these councillors felt sure was an unbiased way, by the council itself through its own paper: "We publish our own paper, where we give all the information that's necessary as far as the running of the borough is concerned."

The commercial press, by contrast, was only interested in publicity, and in bad publicity at that:

We're not too pleased with the local press, because they distort facts. . . . I don't think they like our methods.

You get the people complaining about their housing conditions, and they go to the press and they make front-page news of it. And when the official departments go dive into it, it's nothing like what they say at all. There are some bad places, agreed, but when you get something it's always front-page news.

And finally, raising intra-party controversies publicly was anti-democratic for one traditional rank-and-file councillor:

It's never right to raise [issues] with the press. . . . We're a one-party council. If a member of this council who follows the standing orders feels there is an aggrieved situation, then logically he ought to deal with it within the [party] group [on the council] rather than going to the press and outside bodies, because then it becomes an issue which is taken out of the council. . . . And after all is said and done, what democracy means is that after a decision is taken, whether for or against, then that decision ought to be binding on everybody else, that's democracy.

It becomes clear that for this group of traditional councillors, a closed council style is not simply something imposed from above on a group of reluctant followers, but a set of personally held views about what constitutes appropriate, and inappropriate, councillor behaviour.

Parochials, by contrast, lacked such systematic attitudes. As one parochial ambivalently put it: "We have the council's own paper . . . I suppose you could go to the press. I haven't."

Another parochial, reluctant to use the press, reported that "The press is biased against us. I don't know why." Such a view stands in contrast to those expressed by the traditional rank-and-file councillors cited above, who certainly felt they did know why the press was against them.

But not all parochials felt that way. A plurality of parochials came from the borough of Bromley. I described such councillors as hold-overs from the days when the now London borough was really a collection of independent villages. Although I have characterized the norms of English local political life as ones of closedness, such a description needs some qualification. In the case of Bromley, the "traditional" style once the borough was amalgamated was for parochial councillors to see themselves as representatives of their separate villages on the consolidated council, and to act to defend their "village" (now ward) interests. For such councillors, often acting out of only the most nominally partisan base, "independence" meant publicly stating the case for the concerns of their own local areas. The "traditional" stance in Bromley, therefore, was less closed than in the long urbanized boroughs of Islington and Tower Hamlets.

As such factors would indicate, it is not surprising to find Bromley parochials more willing to use the press, indeed to seek publicity, than their Inner London counterparts. It is also not surprising to see this use of the press being undertaken for explicitly ward-defensive reasons. Thus one ward-defensive suburbanite felt "the press is very good", "I have a good relationship with them." The basis for this feeling, it turned out, was that reporters for the local newspapers pointed out to him planning applications that might affect his ward, planning applications he would then oppose. In the formulation, the press became an information source for the particular councillor, rather than as a locale for publicity about the councillor.

But parochials were not averse to press publicity, at least when their ward-defensive role was challenged. One Bromley Conservative parochial used the press in a reactive way: "I use the press as a choppng block, rather than as a sounding board. If somebody has said something [in the papers] that I take exception to, I write to the press. . . . You might write in response to something." And his example of the sort of incident which would lead him to want to respond is instructive: "I objected to the view that the two Liberal councillors [from another part of the borough] represent Liberals throughout the borough. They don't represent Liberals in my ward."

For this parochial councillor, the concept of ward-defensiveness meant not only defending the ward against outside forces which might bring in unwanted forms of development, but also against claims that party ties might supplant territorial interest as the basis of council activity. On a question so fundamental, in his view, he would have to respond through the press.

It became clear, therefore, that when fundamental ward-based interests of the individual parochial councillor were challenged, going to the press became a permissible technique. Indeed, even in Tower Hamlets, with its apparent norms "forbidding" press contact, at least one parochial councillor was willing to use the local newspaper. Representing a ward which he saw as physically isolated from most of the borough, and therefore in danger of not having sufficient attention paid to it, he saw the press as a useful vehicle for bringing the ward and its problems to wider attention:

> We raised [the issue of vandalism] with the press. We were pushing for a community centre. And this is where the press can be useful, because it goes around and interviews people.

> We've managed to get them [the press] down here and get involved. They're always on the lookout for stories.

And this councillor was prepared to give them stories from his ward.

But unlike the "ambitious" councillors to be described below, those parochials who used the press did so in limited ways. As with the councillor above who would write to the press, but only in response to items which had been initiated by others and which had already appeared in the press, several parochial councillors drew a distinction between raising issues themselves or limiting their press-related activity to answering allegations made by others.

But basically, the press was not a first-choice for parochials and publicity not an end in itself. As one councillor put it in describing how he would try to promote the interests of his ward: "We would use the press for publicity as a last resort." And because parochial councillors' interests were essentially limited to matters affecting their own wards, they were unlikely to be very interested in challenging the overall direction of council styles.

For localist and traditional aspirant councillors, by contrast, use of the press seemed normal and routine, one of the first things a councillor might do, rather than a last resort. Especially among localist councillors, use of the press at the outset of a political effort seemed the most natural thing in the world.

For several Islington localists, the use of the press was explicitly seen as a means of bringing pressure to bear on the very council on which they served:

There's a local press we use when we want to bring pressure on the council. . . . [We] ring them up and tell them to come write a story. . . . You get a bigger reaction through . . . the national media.

[A local activist] has managed to get relevant contact in the national media. . . . We have one case where there's a single man aged about 50 whose mother died six months ago and his dog died and he was living in a house in appalling conditions, and his landlord tried to get him out and proceeded to pull down his back wall and to remove all facilities. Within 48 hours we got television involved, various papers involved and that helped a lot, actually, to bring pressure on the officers, *and on me* [emphasis added], to hurry up and get something done.

Thus this localist councillor, with extensive ties to neighbourhood voluntary organizations, saw use of the press as a means of mobilizing public attention on very specific local problems, and of using this attention not only to affect the behaviour of the council's employees, but also to aid her efforts to solve local problems by permitting her to point out to both council employees and fellow-councillors that she was under pressure from her ward to do so. The media were useful in making this argument more credible.

Another localist similarly saw the utility of putting specific incidents into the press spotlight: "Certainly, on some matters, if you really want to get action, get the media in and produce something dramatic. . . . Sometimes you let it happen. . . . People sitting down in the road [over a traffic complaint]. It worked." Here we have a councillor who was quite prepared to have demonstrations against current council policies staged by residents of his ward. His style would be to "get the media in", and "let it happen". Once again, this willingness to use the media to focus attention on specific local problems, and a willingness to act against existing policies of the council on which this localist sat, stands in sharp contrast to the much more collective sense of proper councillor–council relations held by traditional rank-and-file councillors presented earlier.

Localists recognized that using the press in these ways was not universally approved. As one localist put it: "It is thought wicked to use the press." Nevertheless, this councillor was perfectly prepared to do so and reported having done so over a planned local office development in the ward. (This linkage between preferred openness of council style and opposition to certain types of economic development will be discussed further in the next section of this chapter.)

Just as the councillor was willing to use the press to raise a local point of view despite the fact that he recognized that for some "it is thought wicked" to do so, so another localist was willing to use the press to avoid the constraints of the council's committee system. In this councillor's view, one of the most useful occasions for involving the press was when one wanted to raise questions where the committee structure was unclear, where responsibility for the problem involved might lie in the jurisdiction of more than one committee. Rather than seeking to clarify such situations within the council's internal procedures, this councillor believed that the best way to proceed would be to direct press attention to the problem, hoping thereby to generate sufficient publicity so that the entire council would be forced to deal with the matter.

Once again, we see that one of the essences of the "localist" political style is a much looser sense of the formalities and conventional proprieties of council life. But if localists were, in this sense "anti-establishment" in their use of the press and in their overall desires for open council procedures, no such characterization could be made of the attitudes and actions of the "traditional aspirant" councillors encountered in their study.

For most "traditional aspirants", use of the press was a way of becoming better known, rather than a device for challenging the council and its policies. And traditional aspirants generally felt they had friendly relations with the press. For one Bromley aspirant:

Our local press is very good. They always attend all our functions as well as our council meetings, and our ward committee always makes sure we get bags of publicity. . . . We feed them, my co-councillor and I, we're very press-conscious and know all the reporters.

Even one Tower Hamlets aspirant, while sharing most of his colleague's general distrust of the press, felt that "they're reasonably fair inasmuch as they will print the letters they get", and he had no trouble envisioning himself as a letter-writer.

And a newly elected aspirant in Islington was also conscious of the potential utility of the press for his own ambitions:

From my own point of view one of the things I hope to do is get a presence in the local paper. . . . I suppose through press releases saying what we're doing. We'll set up a surgery or when we take up a particular issue.

As this quote indicates, traditional aspirants can differ some-what from localists in their goals, even though they might not be all that different in their means. Localists councillors would be unlikely to be quite so consciously self-promoting. As another Bromley aspirant put it: "Sometimes you've got to play the gallery." And in order to do this effectively the press had to be sought out. For another aspirant, the press was useful "When you want to get a splurge of activity." When this councillor wished to oppose any housing construction in the Green Belt, a position he knew would be popular, he simultaneously wrote to the local residents' association and to the local press when he heard that there might be a request for planning permission to build on the Green Belt. This simultaneous raising of a popular question with both a local voluntary organization, and with the press, is a mark of an aspiring councillor:

I like to use the press. It gets the attention of residents . . . I keep on friendly terms with the reporter by tipping him off that certain things might be coming through . . . I have a good working relationship with [the press]. I'm useful to them and they're useful to me. It's as simple as that.

Of course, not all aspirants saw the press this way. For one such councillor, raising an issue in the press, would be "rather a confession of failure". But this ambitious councillor had alternative means of gaining publicity. An articulate and outspoken participant in council debates, frequently at odds with other councillors, he knew that his positions would receive extensive coverage by the local papers, and this sort of "use of the press" bothered him not at all.

But, of course, some aspirants were uncomfortable with much of any use of the press. For one aspirant, this was clearly a matter of personal style:

> I don't think one should go to the press at all. They might get in touch with me but I don't like to give off the cuff responses.

For another:

> I find the press a difficult subject locally, because they're really only interested in bad news. . . . They always seem to create the trouble, the press does, before they come and ask you for your views.

These two aspirants clearly felt that their ambitions could be satisfied without the type of press-cultivation most aspirants practised. Whether party structures provide sufficient routes for advancement without personal publicity, as these two councillors felt, is a question beyond the scope of this study. What is clear, however, is that most aspirants did not think so, and saw the press as a potential ally in the advancement of their political careers, and an ally whose support and interest was worth cultivation.

The reason why press cultivation was important for aspirants, of course, was precisely that they had higher ambitions. As I have suggested in this section then, ambition becomes a key element in predisposing rank-and-file councillors to support open council procedures. The two councillor categories made up of individuals with broad ambition, the traditional aspirants and the localists, seemed generally supportive of open procedures. Among the councillors with narrower ambition, the "traditional rank-and-file" councillors were most actively opposed to an opening of their councils, while parochials, by the narrowness of their concerns, tended to be indifferent or perhaps more precisely, tolerant of whatever norms characterized the councils on which they served. In practice, this usually meant a tolerance for closedness.

Borough Styles—Press Relations and Public Participation

One of the arenas in which whole-council style can be observed is in council relationships with the local press. Documenting variations in style among the boroughs in this regard must rely on a combination of impressionistic evidence and published sources. Unlike earlier sections of this chapter, which have been based largely on interview data, the material presented here draws much more heavily on reports of council activities presented in the local press of the three boroughs, and in the councils' minutes and agendas and other official documents. An examination of these sources shows some striking contrasts between the boroughs.

The three components of borough background, leadership attitudes, and rank-and-file councillor attitudes have varying impacts on the whole-council style of the three boroughs.

In none of the three boroughs were the three elements entirely consonant with each other. Islington is perhaps the closest to pure consonance, with a borough leader strongly committed to openness, a dominant council faction of similar persuasion, and a borough tradition of closedness understood to have been gravely weakened by the in-migration of new types of residents into the borough. In such a situation, we would anticipate that the actual styles of Islington council would tend strongly towards openness, and that those on the council who continue to oppose this pattern would be largely ineffectual in their opposition.

Tower Hamlets presents something of a paradox. In a borough with traditions of closedness, and continuing support for, or toleration of, closedness among majorities of rank-and-file councillors, we nevertheless find a leader with some interest in changing this pattern. But one element of the closed style would be deference to leadership. We would therefore expect to find Tower Hamlets making some moves in this direction, but always with the proviso that the council leader could limit this openness when he chose to do so.

In Bromley, we have the most "dissonant" pattern. Borough traditions would suggest open styles, but the underlying basis for these traditions has been eroding. A new leader had come to power committed to a party-unity "closed" style. Attitudes among rank-and-file councillors were sharply split, with no clearly dominant faction, as in Islington. Under such circumstances, we would anticipate that movements toward closure would be tentative, and directed particularly at those types of councillors with lesser influence. The most clear-cut example of such a shift would be a more sytematic exclusion of minority party participation in the essence of council decision-making. (And, as I shall suggest in the next section, it also leads to a policy I will be calling "focused development", where some sections of the borough are targeted for widespread change, while others, represented by still powerful "independent men" on the council, are largely left alone.)

Tower Hamlets clearly reports the least about its activities. Not only do council minutes indicate short council meetings, sometimes lasting less than an hour, but agendas report little information about the topics to be decided. The commercial borough weekly, the *East London Advertiser*, is only slightly a better source. Its main emphasis is on individual incidents, e.g., "Tenants Protest Conditions on Council Estate",[8] and it provides only limited coverage of council activities and almost nothing about council committees. At the last borough council election, the paper listed all candidates, but provided little other information about them.[9] The council's own paper, the *Tower Hamlets News*, is printed irregularly, and describes council policies, rather than council controversies about policy. Much of the council's own paper is taken up with feature stories about council programmes, e.g. "A Day at Eastbourne for the Elderly".[10] If one only read these sources, and Tower Hamlets residents have few other published sources, one would learn little about patterns of division among councillors. One would learn something about protest groups from the *East London Advertiser*, the so-called "action groups" which regularly attack the council, and write letters to the editor in virtually every issue, but little about either their strength or the extent to which any particular complaint has any significant support among the borough's elected representatives.

While these shortages of information are perhaps the best indication of the actual degree of openness practised by Tower Hamlets council, what published information is made available to residents is nevertheless instructive. National legislation in Britain now requires that all meetings of borough council committees must be open to the public. In accordance with this directive, the agenda of Tower Hamlets council duly notes that henceforth all committee meetings will be open.[11] In subsequent issues of the borough paper, committee meeting times are listed, along with an indication that the public may attend.[12]

All committees are listed except one, that deliberating on future use of the Docklands of the borough. The question of Docklands is in many ways the most controversial the borough will be facing in future years. For this single committee, no fixed meeting times are listed in the borough paper. Instead, residents are informed that the times of meetings will be posted on a bulletin board at the Town Hall, and those interested should consult this notice to discover meeting times.

This is not to say that the debate over Docklands takes place in secret. Indeed, the council has held several "public consultation meetings" regarding plans for Dockland development. Specifically, Cllr Beasley argued the need for greater public consultation, and cited Dockland discussions as an example of how Tower Hamlets was moving in this direction.[13] But old traditions die hard. Even two years after the first adoption of the formal requirement for open meetings, the borough paper was still publicizing the fact as if it were new, and with no indication that this was a nationally imposed requirement. And two years after the first adoption, each issue of the council paper also carried the notice that "If the public causes any disruption, the chairman of that committee is fully entitled to order [the persons involved] to leave the room."[14] And, in another issue, committee meeting announcements are prefaced with the notice that "The public cannot take part in these meetings as they are only admitted as spectators."[15]

Although more openness does come to characterize the Tower Hamlets council, it comes haltingly. And Cllr Beasley's praise of openness is not universally agreed with by his colleagues. Thus one councillor is reported by the [commercial] paper as feeling that residents of his ward "are suffering from too much advice" from government-sponsored advice centres.[16]

In a rare development, three councillors from one ward write a collective letter to the editor announcing that a community centre will be set up on one of the large housing estates of their

ward. Such a communication, announcing a public benefit by
the representatives of an area, seems peculiar only because of its
usual absence from the political life of Tower Hamlets. And the
context of the letter makes clear the reason for the deviation.
Rather than issuing a press release, these councillors are writing
specifically "in reply to a recent publicity".[17] This publicity
took the form of a series of articles in the commercial paper
complaining about the absence of such a centre.

Thus, although we see some response from councillors to
pressure from the press, it is an uncertain response. And it is
issued only in "reply to recent publicity", a technique which we
know from the interview material reported above, that the
rank-and-file councillors of Tower Hamlets generally viewed as
inappropriate in the first place. In such a context, it is not
surprising that information is sparsely provided, even though
the council leader feels that there ought to be more of it.

Residents of both Bromley and Islington are inundated by
available information, at least in contrast to Tower Hamlets.
Minutes and agendas of council meetings are voluminous, and
the local press carries far more information about council
controversies. But while Islington was moving towards more
open procedures during the period of this study, Bromley gave
signs of moving in a somewhat more closed direction. I have
already indicated that the Bromley leadership preferred a more
closed "party-unity" style of doing business. Perhaps the
clearest indication of the consequences of such a style came
when the Conservative council leadership decided to exclude all
opposition Labour representation on the council's policy and
resources committee.[18] This committee, made up of chairmen of
the council's substantive committees and the council leader,
functions as the borough's equivalent of a Cabinet in the British
national Parliamentary system.

Of course, in national government, the Cabinet would not
normally include members of the opposition party. It is a mark
of the less partisan history of Bromley borough that the leader of
the opposition party had been a regular member of the committee. However, beginning in the spring of 1975, Labour was
excluded. Cllr Barkway, speaking for the majority, argued that
this exclusion was necessary since Labour councillors had used
their access to information for partisan purposes. The Conservative council majority confirmed this decision.[19]

Movements in the direction of closedness were not limited to the opposition councillors, however. The council's chief appointed officer, the town clerk, warned councillors against leaking information to the press, and the council ended its policy of directly informing residents about planning requests that affected their immediate area. This type of policy shift affected councillors as well. Thus, when a councillor inquired (in reference to the closing of local tennis courts) why the ward councillors were not informed of the decision? the committee chairman responded: "It is not council policy to individually inform ward members of committee decisions affecting their particular ward."[20]

And when national legislation requiring open committee meetings came into effect, the borough press reported that Bromley had made no provision for publicity about this fact, and that the borough council used the proviso permitting secrecy for "confidential" committee discussions extensively.[21] In this vein it is not surprising to find the council defeating a motion to have the annual estimates (the borough budget) debated in public.[22]

I reported above on Tower Hamlets' lower levels of publicity on what may be its most divisive issue, Docklands development. Bromley's closest equivalent, at least in terms of divisiveness, is planning for the development, or non-development, of the borough-owned airfield at Biggin Hill. This issue received somewhat similar treatment. It is consistent with what has been reported above to find that although an "Airport Working Committee" of both residents and councillors was set up to examine the future of the airport, this committee was often asked by its Conservative councillor-members to meet in private.[23]

But these changes in Bromley were not comprehensively exclusionary. They clearly had the effect of limiting opposition party access to information, and they made it possible for the council leadership to restrict information from some Conservative councillors as well. But, as the interview data from Bromley Conservatives has shown, many of them continued to feel quite well-informed regarding council policy, certainly as it affected their own wards.

I suggested earlier that Bromley was in the process of creating a policy I called "focused development", in which unpopular schemes, but ones which were necessary from the council leadership's point of view, were concentrated in some areas of the borough. The specific developmental consequences of this policy will be discussed in the next section of this chapter. But at this point, it is relevant to point out that this policy of "focused development" has its analogues, or perhaps its antecedents, in council style. As I indicated in describing the Bromley leader, Cllr Barkway, and his views on access, all of his examples of "legitimate" access were drawn from situations which would characterize the borough's more affluent neighbourhoods.

While the council was taking steps to reduce the formal information flow somewhat, many councillors, particularly those from the more affluent sections, reported no difficulty in getting information. Focused development was tied to "focused access", a style in which the extent of the council's openness or closedness varied from councillor to councillor, depending on the type of area he represented.

In Islington, such qualifications would not be necessary to describe council procedures. To the degree that controversies continue in Islington over style questions, they centre on some more traditional councillors' view that the council wastes too much money on its public access programmes, and that council meetings have become far too lengthy. But it is clear that councillors who hold such views now form only a minority of the Islington council, and that there is a clearly dominant council faction with personal attitudes and experiences which are strongly supportive of open styles. Unlike Bromley, therefore, Islington not only produces voluminous information, but the tendency has been to increase its flow. Of the three boroughs studied, Islington clearly had the greatest degree of consonance between its leader's style preferences, and those of a majority of its rank-and-file councillors. That such a consonance does not necessarily suggest a "calm" council will be clear in the next section of this chapter, that dealing with council policies. But it is also clear that for the leader and for the council's majority, questions over the desirability of an open council style were considered as settled.

Islington politicians were often quite self-consciously distinctive. That is, they saw their borough as functioning differently from many others, and they liked the difference. This attitude is clear not only in the private interviews conducted for this research, but in the public communications of the council with the borough's residents. Thus, for example, although a number of boroughs, particularly in Inner London, publish their own borough newspapers (including Tower Hamlets, as indicated above) the Islington council was at pains to point out that its borough paper was to be unusual. An early issue indicated that "*Focus* [the borough-sponsored paper] has a marked difference from other borough papers. . . . One of its main aims is to get you, the reader, to take part in shaping the decisions and policies of the Council."[24] And the chairman of the council committee on "Public Consultation and Participation" (a committee not found in normal organization charts of English local governments), saw the publication of *Focus* as a: "step in the plans of the Council to provide people with the opportunity to contribute to the future of the borough."[25]

Thus, we can see the twin elements of the Islington council's self-definition, an emphasis on broad public participation (or at least publicity about broad public participation), and the sense that in making such an emphasis Islington was acting in a manner different from the operating procedures of many other London boroughs.

Although it would be hard to make any definite judgements about the effectiveness of such attempts to increase participation without much more data on individual resident attitudes and information, it is clear from the documentary evidence that the Islington council did take steps to encourage more public input. Thus, we find devices such as the introduction of "Question Time" at the opening of general council meetings. But unlike Parliamentary question times, the questioners were to come from the general public.[26]

And the council engaged in extensive use of public meetings and survey questionnaires prior to the formal adoption of new programmes. A council statement indicated the rationale for this, indicating that there were to be two purposes to neighbourhood participation: "Council should consult the people affected by its proposals before final decisions are taken", and: "People should say what their own needs are and make proposals to the Council and other bodies responsible for meeting them."[27]

It is clear that the general notion of council openness was to be closely tied to the representation of neighbourhood interests. In the Islington council formulations, these two aspects were inextricably intertwined. (The logical alternative, expression of "public input" by borough-wide or broader functional interest groups, does not appear to have been a significant element in the thinking of Islington councillors when they discussed or acted upon proposals to "open" the council.) The specific attention to neighbourhood as the source of public input, of course, can be tied to the predominance of "localists" in the Islington council: councillors who saw a ward scope of representation as the appropriate scope for a borough councillor.

But it is also clear that Islington council and its councillors recognized the likelihood of public scepticism about the consequences of formal "openness" innovations. We find an indication of concerns about this in one *Focus* headline and article. In a piece headed, "Action follows liaison forums" on play facilities, the borough-sponsored paper continues: "As you can see, Council has seriously considered proposals made at liaison forums, and acted on them."[28]

Indication that the council's intention to alter its procedures was not merely internal talk among councillors or formalistic public relations can be found in the reports of the borough's commercial weekly, the *Islington Gazette*. Thus, the *Gazette* would regularly have articles with headlines such as "More Public Consultation on Angel" (a redevelopment plan)[29] and reports that Islington council was holding more meetings per year than any other London borough.[30]

According to the *Gazette*, the Islington Labour Party had become accepting of the idea that internal conflicts within it were inevitable, and that the party had adopted a "more relaxed position" towards disagreement among Labour councillors.[31] Such "relaxation" is obviously a necessary concomitant of the more open procedures Islington had adopted. With an all-Labour borough council, the airing of divisions of opinion in public, which structural changes in the council had encouraged, would become intolerable unless such intra-party disagreement came to be a part of the accepted ways of doing business.

Both the opening of formal structures, and the reported changes in party attitude, stand in striking contrast to the continued sense of the importance of "working-class solidarity" among the rank-and-file councillors of Tower Hamlets. Despite the Tower Hamlets leader's interests in more visibility and openness for council functioning, that borough could never adopt formal changes such as Islington's innovation of ending most policy discussion in (closed) party group meetings and holding them instead in (open) council sessions. The attitudinal base for such a change simply did not exist among the rank-and-file of Tower Hamlets, while in Islington, the rank-and-file majority was coming to regard open disputes as normal.

This is not to say that conflict became more muted in Islington, quite to the contrary. Rather, conflict between "left-wing" and "right-wing" Labour councillors came to be regarded as a part of the usual style of borough politics, not something which could, or should be, hidden from view. Indeed, the varying factions within the Islington Labour party group were highly visible, and conflict between them acquired symbolic significance for its participants. Thus, two councillors, clearly identifiable as "left-wing" and "right-wing" on the council, had a brief fist-fight over the question of whether it was proper to display a bust of Lenin as part of a local art exhibit being staged at the town hall![32] While the next section of this chapter will deal more explicitly with the policy consequences of borough political styles, it is clear that one consequence of Islington openness was a much greater freedom for its councillors to engage in "symbolic politics", even within their own party.

But Islington "openness" was not limited to purely symbolic matters. Thus, in sharp contrast to the direction of the Bromley council described above, Islington council was taking steps to ensure that ward councillors were officially informed of prospective council actions that might affect their ward, and that "Where a report relates to matters affecting a ward interest, ward members will have sight of it before it is considered by the committee concerned."[33] While both Bromley and Islington were somewhat altering their councillor-information policies during the course of this study, the direction of change was completely opposite.

Distinctions between Islington and the other boroughs studied could also be found in how the various councils promoted citizen–councillor contacts. In Bromley, such contacts were not really promoted by formal council action at all. It could be argued that the extensiveness of voluntary-organization activity in Bromley and the ties of ward councillors to the areas they represented, provided sufficient citizen–councillor contact without additional council stimulus. But not all areas of Bromley were uniformly suburban, middle-class, voluntary-organization rich, and yet the idea of council-sponsored settings for citizen–councillor contact (ward surgeries) never really surfaced at all. Indeed, the Bromley council explicitly decided that "neighbourhood councils", proposed ward-based groups which might be organized by the council, were unneeded in Bromley precisely because of the number of voluntary organizations in the borough.[34]

In Tower Hamlets, surgeries were conducted in a highly formalized way by the borough Labour Party, with councillors serving on a rota system which required them to be present in party offices several times a year. But because of the rotating nature of these surgeries and because they were centralized, they really could not be considered as regular opportunities for residents to raise problems directly with the councillors who represented their own ward. Although the Tower Hamlets leader, Cllr Beasley, mentioned with approval one experiment where ward councillors were regularly conducting a week-end surgery under the auspices of a legal advice centre, this arrangement was unusual and not directly sponsored by the council.

Only in Islington were there organized efforts by the council as a collective and official body to organize settings for borough-sponsored surgeries. Although party-tied surgeries also existed in Islington, they were not as formalized as in Tower Hamlets, and much more likely to be located in the individual ward and to be run by the ward councillors. But Islington council nevertheless was willing to organize and pay for such surgeries as a governmental activity. This change carried with it a necessary break with party politics in the conduct of the surgeries, a break explicitly recognized by the council committee which reported favourably on the idea.[35] It is a mark of the relative weakness of the concept of "party activity" in Islington that this was taken by borough councillors as a matter of course and not as a reason to object to borough-sponsored surgeries. It seems much less likely that a change of this type would have been acceptable to the rank-and-file councillors of Tower Hamlets.

As I indicated at the outset of this section, evidence on council openness cannot be conclusive, but examination of the available public materials clearly suggest that Islington council was far more rhetorically committed to open procedures than were either Bromley or Islington, and insofar as could be ascertained with the procedures available to this study, this commitment was not simply a sham.

Saying this, however, does not suggest that Islington's distinctively "open" council styles necessarily provided for "better" or "more representative" citizen input into council decisions. Indeed, some councillors among the remaining minority of "old guard" working-class councillors in Islington explicitly argued to the contrary. Their articulate spokesman, Cllr Bayliss, suggested that the major reason why Islington had to engage in such formalized efforts was because its council majority was no longer representative of the borough's working-class population. In his view, the council's efforts at "organized participation" were a "joke", inadequate attempts to substitute formal structure for the normal daily contacts which, he argued, characterized traditional relationships between working-class councillors and their working-class constituents.

Bayliss argued that very few residents ever came to the myriad of meetings organized by the council for "citizen input". And, indeed, the *Islington Gazette* often reported sparse attendance at such meetings,[36] and also indicated that an attempt by the council to survey opinion by questionnaires had been a failure. Of 110,000 questionnaires on a proposed development plan distributed, the paper reported, only 1500 had been completed and returned to the council.[37] Thus, although the claims of Islington council to have attempted to be a "distinctively open" council appear to be correct, it remains an unresolved question as to just how much impact these efforts had on the borough's citizenry.

I suggested at the outset of this chapter that variations in borough characteristics, leadership preferences, and rank-and-file councillor attitudes, would form important determinants of variation in the openness or closedness of borough political styles. I suggested several ways in which these factors might have impact. Borough "traditions" might be strongly supportive of closedness, as in the case of Tower Hamlets, or of more open procedures, as in "pre-urbanization" Bromley. Leaders might vary from individuals such as Cllr Southgate in Islington, who saw himself and his council as making names for themselves by distinctive openness, to Cllr Barkway in Bromley, whose more partisan interests led him to seek to move the borough's Conservative Party councillors to close ranks.

For rank-and-file councillors, I suggested several dimensions of variations which could be expected to have impact on their support for open or closed procedures. Those councillors with a broad scope of ambition, I argued, were likely to "need" open council procedures for their own personal advancement, while councillors with narrower ambition were less likely to do so. Councillors who looked strongly to political party for behaviour cues were likely to support party-solidarity closedness, while councillors whose primary political reference groups were neighbourhood voluntary organizations were much less likely to do so.

Finally I suggested that those councils where these various elements were in "consonance" were more likely to have a clear-cut direction to their council styles, while those councils where borough characteristics, leadership preferences, and rank-and-file attitudes were in "dissonance", would have mixed policies with regard to council styles of doing business.

These hypotheses have been confirmed by the evidence presented in this and preceding sections of this chapter. We can clearly see a "consonance" in Islington, with leadership and rank-and-file majorities supportive of openness, and a recent borough history which suggests at least a toleration of openness — that is, a lack of strong resistance to the in-migration of non-working-class residents. Both Bromley and Tower Hamlets, by contrast, present more "dissonant" displays. In Tower Hamlets, borough tradition is strongly supportive of "working-class solidarity" and majorities of rank-and-file councillors continue to adhere to this norm. The new borough leader, however, is interested in at least a partial opening of council procedures. His main goals, however, lie in improving the technical competence of the council, and openness seems deisrable less as an end in itself but as another demonstration that Tower Hamlets is becoming a more "up-to-date" council. Under such circumstances, we would expect to find only halting steps towards more open council procedures, and we do.

Bromley is potentially the most "dissonant" of the three boroughs studied. Borough traditions, I have suggested, are from a "pre-urban", or perhaps more precisely, "pre-suburban" period. Many councillors continue to see themselves as "independent men" representing the values of the village life and on the council to defend these "villages" from intrusion. But suburbanization of the borough has reduced the viability of such a stance for many parts of the borough, and the council's leadership clearly is not this type. When I indicate that the Bromley leadership took some steps in the direction of council closure, it ought to be remembered that Bromley begins with the highest base of voluntary organization activity of the three boroughs, and that therefore its movements in the *direction* of closure do not alter its relatively high level of continuing access, at least for the representatives and residents of some parts of the borough. (It will be recalled from Cllr Barkway's comments that he was obviously more deferential to the "parochial" needs of the wealthier parts of the borough than those raised by other sections.)

In general, then, variations in council openness can be seen to be related to the three underpinnings of borough political life which have been discussed successively in preceding chapters, the borough's political traditions, leadership preferences, and rank-and-file councillor attitudes. Variations in openness–closedness "fit" with variations on these factors.

But having shown that style variations can be understood in this way does not definitively indicate what the consequences of these style variations might be. An examination of the potential links between style and policy is the subject of the concluding section of this chapter.

B   THE LINKAGE TO POLICY

Any conclusion about the impact of variations in council styles on mass publics are problematic. The entire question of whether we ought to expect to find linkages between variables in political styles and other political variables has been debated in the political science literature inconclusively.

What I would like to suggest in this section, however, is that the adoption of relatively open, or relatively closed styles of conducting council business does have some impact on the nature of policy decisions taken by the council. One fruitful arena in which to examine such a possible linkage is in the field of economic development policy. I am suggesting that those councillors with a borough scope of representation would be more likely to support economic development plans than councillors with ward scopes of representation.

This hypothesis is based on a recognition that most development plans are in some way disruptive of established patterns of local life, and therefore are likely to be opposed by neighbourhood-based interest groups. Councillors with a ward scope of representation, in this argument, are clearly more closely tied to such neighbourhood-based groups than are councillors with a broad scope of representation, and more importantly, ward-scope councillors will, by the very definition of their roles, see such protests as legitimate and entitled to council support.

I am arguing, therefore, that those boroughs with larger percentages of "broad-scope" councillors, and those boroughs with leaders of similar persuasion, will more readily adopt economic development plans than boroughs with fewer such councillors and different leadership orientations. But I further wish to suggest that the likelihood of significant movement towards adoption and implementation of such plans is mediated by council openness. Those councils with more "open" styles will be less likely to implement development, precisely because the openness of procedure gives opposing groups more opportunities for raising complaints and attempting to veto plans.

But despite the likelihood of objection, each of the three boroughs is under some pressure to adopt economic development plans. Although systems of "revenue-sharing" are far more extensive in English local government than in the United States, each borough nevertheless has a stake in increasing its local tax base and thereby relieving pressure on local property taxes. (Although there has been some debate in England about the possible utility of local income taxes, property tax revenues —"the rates"—remain the only form of local government taxation in the country.) Under such circumstances, it is predictable that boroughs would like to entice more business and industry to locate within their borders, thereby increasing rateable properties.

But in addition to concerns about revenue, boroughs have other motivations for pursuing economic development as well. The Tower Hamlets leadership particularly was concerned about the need for development in order to stabilize its population base. Tower Hamlets, like most "inner city" areas in developed countries, has been gradually losing population for many decades. Borough leaders feared that if this trend was not reversed, or at least if population stability was not achieved, there was some danger to the continued existence of Tower Hamlets as an independent borough. Already the smallest in population of the London boroughs, its leaders feared forced amalgamation with neighbouring units if its population continued to drop. While neither Bromley nor Islington leaders expressed such concerns explicitly, it is clear that leaders in all three boroughs saw attempts at economic expansion as necessary for the economic health of their areas, and indirectly for the political health of those now in power in each of the boroughs.

But all aspects of sub-national government and politics need to be seen as operating within a pattern of constraint imposed by national economic and political decisions. This is particularly true with regard to plans for economic development. In a unitary state, on a crowded island, and one with long traditions of more centralized land-use planning, it is especially relevant to ask whether borough decision-makers hold any power at all over such questions. As I have indicated earlier, it is the contention of this study that they do. And I am further arguing that variations in the openness–closedness of council procedures are one element useful in understanding variation in borough government attitudes towards local economic development.

What must still be investigated, and not assumed, is whether this potential for policy variation gets translated into actual policy differences or not.

The Impact of Borough Background

For each of the boroughs examined in this research, I have identified one or two major economic development proposals which have been the subject of controversy during the course of this research. These projects would all involve some change in the economic base of the boroughs, and have potential consequences for borough population mixes as well.

In Tower Hamlets, I will be examining council action with regard to Dockland development. Changes in shipping patterns have moved most commercial shipping into and out of the Port of London farther downstream to the east, leaving dockland areas in Tower Hamlets largely underutilized and/or abandoned, and ripe for redevelopment. While debate over the future of the Dockland affects a number of East London boroughs on both banks of the Thames, I will be focusing on alternative development plans for Dockland within Tower Hamlets, and particularly the borough council's stance toward what types of development it favours.

In Islington, I will be examining the council's reaction to proposals for office development in parts of the borough near the City of London. Once again, changes in land use have left warehouse areas disused and/or underutilized, and under pressure for land use shifts toward office development from the expanding City of London financial district. In Bromley, I will be directing my attention towards plans for the commercial and office development in Bromley town centre, and plans for expanded use of the borough-owned airfield at Biggin Hill, issues I will argue are closely related, and a second controversy over redevelopment of single-family housing areas into apartment use in Copers Cope Ward.

As I have suggested throughout this research, patterns of economic life in London as a whole are undergoing change, and it will be noted that all these development plans, in one way or another, involve potential for increasing London's specialization in "central office headquarters" functions. The bases for such changes can be found in technological change and in the nature of the national (and international) economy. But the specifics of development have aroused lively local controversy in each of the three boroughs.

These controversies take two forms, one overt, one less visible. At the overt level, each proposal for development has aroused considerable local reaction from neighbourhoods immediately affected, and this reaction has almost always been adverse. But, rather less visibly, another type of "controversy" takes place about the extent to which development itself ought to be a priority matter for the borough concerned, or whether attention gets absorbed in other matters on the local political agenda.

The first of these can be examined directly, by determining positions of the participants and the political resources they can bring to bear on policy decisions. The second is less easy to investigate, and is most usefully looked at by examining the relative importance debate on development policy plays in local political life of the borough concerned.

In Bromley, I will suggest, discussion of development strategies (or of anti-development strategies) lies at the core of borough political life and regularly at the centre stage of borough political controversies. In Islington, by contrast, debate over development often gets submerged by other issues, particularly having to do with the council's "social policy", especially towards the problem of "homelessness" and "squatters". These latter issues, which have no precise American analogue, have to do with how the council responds to immigration, but not necessarily to ethnic or class change. Traditional English law permits the occupation of unused property for residential use by "squatters", and eviction is legally quite complicated. Boroughs vary considerably in their response to squatting, and how they respond affects other aspects of social policy as well. Opponents of squatting, for example, argue that since squatters typically live in the poorest of housing conditions, they end up at the top of priority lists for public housing. Often bitter debate about what Islington ought to do about this tends to push development controversies into the background.

While Tower Hamlets also has a considerable amount of squatting, and the consequent debate over what the appropriate council response should be, the issue of development remains more central and more publicly visible than in Islington. One major reason for this difference is the greater potential for development in Tower Hamlets, where Dockland areas occupy a significant fraction of the borough's land area, and decisions about its future use have more obviously direct consequences for the future of the borough than do development alternatives in Islington.

The Impact of Leadership on Council Policy

But in addition to the "objective" reasons for variations in the intensity and centrality of development controversies, I am suggesting that the attitudes of the borough political leadership, the mix of councillor types, and the consequent openness or closedness of borough political styles, have impact as well.

Since development policies are almost always opposed by

local groups from affected areas, I am arguing that openness of council styles predisposes a council to veto or de-emphasize development, while a closed council style is associated with the adoption of development policies favoured by the borough's political leadership, even where these are controversial.

In a related, but distinct point, I am suggesting that councillors with a ward scope of representation will be most likely to oppose economic development plans, while those with a broader scope of representation will either be supportive of development, or at least be tolerant of it.

But any detailed consideration of economic development plans must first take into account the borough leadership's policy preferences, and the place of economic development issues on the leadership's agenda of borough concerns. Substantial variation was found among the leaders of the three boroughs in their attention to this question.

For Cllr Southgate, the Islington leader, economic development issues seemed of low salience. When he discussed development, for example, his focus was largely upon housing needs. He hoped to reorganize borough planning processes so that all social services needs in given neighbourhoods could be co-ordinated on an area basis, instead of being separately administered by each individual department of the borough government. While such concerns do not exclude economic development, by assigning higher priority to other matters economic development questions inevitably get pushed into the background.

And in his emphasis on housing policy, an opposition to certain forms of development was clear. Thus Cllr Southgate supported residents of one Islington neighbourhood, Kings Cross, in their plans to "fight rogue developers".[38] What "rogue developers" might do would be to replace working-class housing with housing designed for more affluent residents. Although controversy over economic development was certainly not absent in Islington, as shall be seen below, for Cllr Southgate it was controversies about the borough's residential base rather than its economic base that were at the heart of his concerns.

Both Cllr Beasley, the Tower Hamlets leader, and Cllr Barkway, the Bromley leader, gave economic development concerns high priority. In their interviews, and in their published comments in local papers, both mentioned such questions with far greater frequency than did Cllr Southgate. Although questions of business development could not be divorced from questions of the borough's residential base in either Tower Hamlets or in Bromley, economic development questions per se were obviously more important.

One major explanation for this variation in emphasis is that the class base of both Bromley, as a largely middle-class area, and Tower Hamlets, as a working-class borough, were seen as secure by their borough leaders. In each case, the class base of borough life might need some defending, but political majorities in each borough were sufficiently secure so that there was no question about borough policy in this regard. In Islington, however, with its more class-mixed population, and with possibilities for further class and ethnic change in the future, such questions inevitably occupied more of the agenda of political controversies than in either Tower Hamlets or in Bromley, where the basic population compositions were taken very much more as givens, even though they might need some defending from time to time.

For Cllr Beasley in Tower Hamlets, the need for attention to economic development was a consequence of the borough's success in housing policy, as he saw it. Having built extensively, attention could be turned to other issues, both social service delivery and economic development. But it was in the areas of economic development that he hoped new councillors would make a difference. Questions would be raised by these new councillors:

> mainly over development, particularly Dockland development. . . . How it's going to be financed, what the planning elements are. How much industry you're going to have, how much housing, what proportions of open space.

New councillors the "young, more professional people", would be:

> more interested in promoting quicker Dockland development; they are more concerned with the financial side of things.

And Beasley shared this view:

In the past the borough has been concerned only with the provision of services and not with the financial side of running the borough. It is necessary to have mixed development of Dockland.

For Cllr Beasley, therefore, economic development of the borough was rooted in the borough's financial needs. He worried about the fact that 60 per cent of the borough's revenue was coming through the rate support grant (revenue sharing) and felt a need for the borough to develop industrially and commercially, so that its own independent tax base would be secure.

In Bromley, Cllr Barkway also regarded development as necessary, but he anticipated more opposition. He recognized that especially in the more affluent parts of the borough, development plans would not be greeted favourably: "People want to protect the value of their expensive homes." But although he recognized opposition, Barkway was still committed to development: "You are either a doer or you're not", and it was "extremists" who "fanned up opposition" to development plans for Bromley town centre. Although he recognized concerns about Biggin Hill airfield as more legitimate, "people understand what has happened at Heathrow and Gatwick [the two major airports of London] and they don't want it to happen to Bromley", he nevertheless supported improvements to the airfield to make it more viable commercially and more useful to the overall economic development of the borough.

As I have suggested earlier, Cllr Barkway's response (and the Bromley council's collective response) to opposition to economic development plans was not to abandon them, but to adopt a strategy I have referred to as "focused development". Under this approach, economic development plans were centred on particular sections of the borough, and not on the areas where people had "one and two-acre gardens" and were both hardliners against development and mainstays of traditional Conservative strength.

In summary, then, economic development was clearly more significant for Cllr Beasley in Tower Hamlets and Cllr Barkway in Bromley than for Cllr Southgate in Islington. And in comparing the environments in which Cllrs Beasley and Barkway had to act, Cllr Barkway in Bromley had at least to take account of more opposition than did Cllr Beasley. As I have suggested, the traditions of closedness in Tower Hamlets made Cllr Beasley's task the easier one, despite his own interests in increasing openness. And remaining traditions of openness in Bromley served as a constraint on Cllr Barkway, despite his own interests in a more unified (and therefore closed) partisan style. But Barkway could solve his problem by deflecting development away from those sections of the borough where opposition within Conservative Party ranks was strongest by adopting a strategy of focused development in a limited range of areas.

The Impact of Rank-and-File Attitudes on Council Development Policies

As I suggested earlier, the different types of councillor identified in this study held differing views on the desirability and appropriateness of economic development programmes in their boroughs. Since the mix of councillor types varied from borough to borough, the impact of rank-and-file attitudes on actual development programmes similarly varied.

It is clear that the two types of councillors with broad scopes of representation were generally supportive of development plans, or at least tolerant of them when they were supported by higher authority. Traditional rank-and-file councillors tended, by their role definition, to be deferential to council leadership and council officers. Such councillors, it will be remembered, are heavily concentrated in Tower Hamlets. Given the leadership's support for development, traditional rank-and-file tolerance for it is to be expected.

Even when a traditional rank-and-file councillor clearly has his doubts about the wisdom of development, he nevertheless expects it to happen. Thus, one long-serving Tower Hamlets councillor indicates that "If you look at the plans for Dockland, you can see they're going to close the docks. They've got plans for yachting centres, and golf courses, and equestrian centres, in areas where men are still working." But despite this extreme view of the class consequences of redevelopment of Dockland, this councillor nevertheless expected such plans to be adopted and indicated no plans to attempt to prevent it.

For another councillor, such passivity was reasonable since

"In the main you are the agent of the national government" and national policy, he believed, supported Docklands redevelopment.

For other traditional rank-and-file councillors, economic development was acceptable as long as the council had a significant role in shaping the development. For those councillors, economic development was the natural successor to council housing policy: "This borough is becoming well-developed [in housing]", and additional non-housing development could be undertaken. Similarly, one councillor drew sharp distinction between development undertaken by purely private parties, which he would oppose, and development undertaken in conjunction with the borough council, which he would be willing to support even if local residents' groups opposed it.

Some traditional rank-and-file councillors were supportive of economic development plans as beneficial in their own right, not simply because representatives of what they regarded as higher authority levels supported it: "We think Dockland development should be mixed development [i.e., not simply public housing], but the people who live there are very parochial." And two Bromley traditional rank-and-filers supported these views. One supported Biggin Hill as "very useful for business purposes", even though local residents were "terrified by the idea of small jets": "They can't understand this. I know something about flying, so I understand it better than they do."

What we note here is that both a Bromley Conservative traditional rank-and-file councillor and a Tower Hamlets Labour councillor both are willing to support borough development, although the general economic stances of their respective parties are still present in their views. For the Tower Hamlets Labour councillor, development was made acceptable by the inclusion of the local government in the development plan, for the Bromley Conservative, the notion of aiding business made airport development reasonable. Both retained their separate ideological positions, but both supported development plans advocated by their boroughs' leaderships.

Traditional aspirant councillors may not have been quite so deferential to leadership, but they even were more supportive of development programmes. It will be noted that such councillors were heavily concentrated in Bromley. Even though these aspirants had not necessarily been successful in achieving their own personal political ambitions, their development-supportive attitudes obviously were of assistance to that borough's leadership in implementing its own development strategies.

One such councillor reported his reaction to local opposition to a (now-defeated) highway plan:

> Action groups formed as they did all over London. Although I could sympathize with them as individuals, because of the wider interests I couldn't go along with the idea that the concept was wrong. I believe that a Ringway is necessary.

Even when redevelopment was proposed in his own ward, where old large houses were being "subjected to improvement", and "from the local point of view it's dynamite", nevertheless, "from the interests of the borough, you know that a thing should be proceeded with".

Most importantly, traditional aspirants were interested in the overall reputation of their borough (perhaps expecting that a borough reputation for modernity would enhance their own career aspirations). Thus one aspirant indicated that development of Bromley town centre was necessary by comparing his borough with a neighbouring suburban borough:

> I always maintain Croydon is very much more go-ahead with regard to redeveloping and replanning their area. We're a conservative borough, I don't mean [just] politically. We could do a lot more.

But desired development, for this councillor, still had its limits. He strongly opposed any plans for additional low-income housing, for example, believing that it ought not be located in the suburbs at all:

> The Greater London Council [Labour-controlled] says we have a lot of open space, which is fair comment. But they don't realize that the people who've moved out here, paid good money, taken large mortgages, have moved here because of the environment, and we, the Conservatives on the council, we're defending this to the end. If a person wants to have an expensive house in a nice area like this, then he has every right. What annoys me is that in the Inner London boroughs

there is more than sufficient derelict land to house everyone on the whole of London's housing list. The Dockland areas, for example. They prefer to come out here and take our pleasant fields and woods.

While such sentiments might be equally shared by many of Bromley's Conservative parochials, the distinctive "aspirant" aspect of this councillor's attitudes lay in his coupling of suburban neighbourhood defensiveness with strong support for economic development of the borough's commercial centre, a matter which would not seem important to the borough's parochials.

Although "aspirants" were concentrated in Bromley, they were not limited to the borough. One Tower Hamlets aspirant was similarly interested in promoting economic development in his borough, although once again the general ideological distinction between Conservative and Labour could be seen:

What sort of industry do we want in the borough? . . . We don't want office complexes, but to a certain extent we've got to have some . . . [but] I refuse to allow any development in the dockland until it can be development that we [the council] want. To give way an inch means we'll have about a million square feet of office development down there, and I won't allow it.

Once again, several "aspirant" attitudes can be noticed, beyond the Labour commitment to government involvement in planning. One is the sense that development of Dockland did have to go forward, and another is the sense of personal efficacy—"I won't allow it."

Under such circumstances, the attitudes of aspirants towards the *type* of development they saw as desirable is obviously an important influence on actual borough development policies. Aspirants, unlike traditional rank-and-file councillors, are not likely to be passive supporters of whatever development strategies the borough leadership supports.

Despite this reservation, both traditional rank-and-file councillors and traditional aspirants were likely to be supportive of development proposals. The two remaining councillor types, localists and parochials, were not. Opposition among parochials was clearly the weaker, and more easily handled by development-minded leaders. As the concept "parochial" itself suggests, such councillors' concern with development was really limited to matters which might affect their own wards directly: "some [developers] are just for pulling down all old buildings. . . . There's a move at the moment to keep the High Street [of my village] a shopping precinct" and similarly: "I've been fighting on development. It's on blocks of flats [in my ward] and that sort of thing. I got them turned down." But despite this staunch anti-development ward-defensiveness of his own area, this same councillor rather neutrally described how "In Copers Cope Ward in some of the roads the old Victorian houses, they have been pulled down and flats are being put in." By contrast: "[my own ward] was fairly well-developed in the 1930s. There hasn't been a great deal of what is happening in Copers Cope." For such a councillor, a policy of "focused development" in Copers Cope would be sufficient to deflect his criticism of flat-building.

Another Bromley parochial, who saw his main function as a councillor as "protecting the environment in my ward" from applications for building permits, nevertheless was also an obvious candidate for deflection by focused development. In his view, parochialism was something engaged in by members of the opposition Labour Party: "I have found there is not one socialist member of the authority that is not a parochial."

Conservative development plans in Bromley almost always met with party-political opposition from the borough Labour Party. But the problem for the council leadership was not in dealing with the opposition, but in making sure of its strength among the Conservative majority on the council. For councillors such as the Conservative parochial quoted above, the opposition of the Labour Party to the leadership's specific development plans made it easier for the leadership to garner his support. Always excepting, of course, any development that might specifically affect the ward he represented.

If the ward was challenged, the parochial could be very resistant. Thus one councillor from Copers Cope ward, one of the Bromley areas I have suggested was subject to "focused development", complained that "When I talk about one-bedroom flats and overdevelopment in Copers Cope Ward, they say, some old story. You get out of sympathy. If you keep on the same old story then no one's listening." Although this councillor was clearly an opponent of development, he recognized that his opposition was not especially effective. As I have suggested, such opposition was tolerable for the Bromley leadership since it was likely to come from only the relatively few wards directly affected by development. Even though the opposition was within the Conservative Party, and therefore had to be taken more seriously than if it had come from a Labour-controlled ward, unaffected councillors, combined with development-supportive councillors, would be sufficient to overcome opposition from parochials directly affected by the Bromley council's development plans.

The opposition of localist councillors to development plans was more wide-ranging. Thus we find one Islington localist opposing economic development that might increase the borough's gentrification. Office development is a particular danger, in this view, since it would make renewable housing in the borough even more attractive as a residential location close to work for middle-class professionals and businessmen. If one was interested in "introducing council policies which will stop gentrification" it became important to also oppose office development. Since, in this interpretation, office development anywhere in the borough would pose this same threat, a policy of "focused development" would not allay localist opposition as it might among parochials.

Similarly, the localist willingness to use the press made their opposition more significant. Speaking specifically of an office development scheme at The Angel, one councillor reported: "stirring things up in the press over the issue . . . shows you mean business". Once again, this type of opposition poses a more serious threat to development plans than less publicity-conscious opposition characteristic of parochials.

Finally, localists, particularly in Islington, had other items on their agendas. Thus one councillor described his view of the borough's proper priorities as being "community development" rather than economic development. "Community development", which meant both the construction of community centres and spending on social service staffing of such centres, came higher on the agenda for such councillors. Not only did such projects cost money, they also cost the time and attention of the borough's decision-makers. And left less for concern with the internal economic development of the borough. The strategic position of localists on the Islington council, therefore, meant that economic development questions were unlikely to receive the same priority as they would get in either Bromley or in Tower Hamlets.

Borough Decisions on Economic Development Policy

Any discussion of the actual content of borough economic development decisions must begin by identifying the influences on those decisions from higher levels of authority. Although it is clear that general economic trends in Britain (and internationally) affect the general climate in which development decisions are taken, I shall be concerned in this section with more specific local economic-development decisions. Under British planning procedures, however, the national government plays a role at this level as well. Its development aims for London have been codified in the *Greater London Development Plan*. This plan, required by the Town and Country Planning Act of 1971, had been published in preliminary fashion and was the subject of detailed discussion throughout the course of this study. A "final" version was published as this study was concluding.[39]

The plan is quite detailed, listing specific locales for housing, industry and commerce, and transportation plans of similar specificity. But despite its detail, the plan's authors recognize that one of the fundamental elements which will determine the degree of actual implimentation is:

> Action by the London Borough councils which ensures that local planning and development, whether by public authorities or private enterprise, supports the intention of the Plan.[40]

It is therefore clear that nationally encouraged planning is not wholly determinative of what the individual boroughs will do.

There are numerous references in the plan which are relevant to the economic development goals of the three London boroughs being studied here. Bromley town centre is identified as a "strategic centre", where preferred office development ought to take place.[41] Bromley had not been included as a major employment growth area in the original draft of this plan, but its subsequent revisions changed this. As shall be seen below, this change was not displeasing to the Bromley council leadership.

In addition to identifying the Bromley town centre as a

"strategic centre", the Greater London Development Plan affected Bromley in two other ways which are relevant here. One major point is the plan's conclusion that "The advantages which [the Green Belt] confer on London living would be irreplaceable"[42] and that therefore extensive housing construction on such land would be undesirable. (Suggestions have been made from time to time for the use of the Green Belt land for housing. Such a shift in land use, almost always in the context of additional public housing, is anathema to the Bromley political leadership and its council majority. The Greater London Development Plan, by reducing the danger, permits the Bromley council to pursue the policy I have called "focused development" with less external threat than might be the case if the plan had taken a different approach to this question.)

The plan also affects Bromley by listing the St Mary Cray area as one of its "preferred industrial locations".[43] This area, on the eastern outskirts of the borough, is the site of a large public housing "overspill" estate which predates the formation of the current Bromley borough. It is a mark of the current council's choice of economic emphasis that this aspect of the plan received almost no public attention in Bromley, while plans for the Bromley town centre were often at the centre of council attention and controversy. Finally, in an interesting omission, the plan makes no specific reference at all to one form of economic development which was highly significant to Bromley politics, the redevelopment of old housing into new middle-class apartment use in the Copers Cope area.

In Islington, the Angel area is also referred to as a possible area for additional office location,[44] and two areas on opposite ends of the borough, north and south, Holloway, and South Shoreditch, as possible locales for additional industrial development.[45] As with Bromley, controversy has centred on the areas targeted for office development rather than on those listed for industrial development. But the level of controversy, as I have indicated, was lower. In Islington, economic development conflicts were submerged by conflicts over social policy. Although the plan makes passing mention of a need to be concerned about the "effects of population composition",[46] it really does not deal with the two elements of this concern which most exercised Islington during the course of this study—gentrification by the middle (and upper) classes, and squatting by the poor.

The most important issues in Tower Hamlets are clearly those which revolve around the future use of Docklands. Although the plan identifies much of Docklands as "obsolete for riverside commercial and industrial purposes",[47] it also declines to spell out specific redevelopment strategies pending the reporting of the separate "Docklands Joint Committee".[48] (This is a committee of all Docklands boroughs and the Greater London Council.) Thus, the Greater London Development Plan itself, which is clearly promoting some sort of Dockland redevelopment, gives little guidance as to what type of development this might be.

For all three boroughs, therefore, it seems clear that whatever encouragements or discouragements specific development schemes might receive from the national government, the boroughs were left sufficient "operating space" to press their own development strategies. What must now be examined is whether the boroughs used this "operating space" actually to pursue differing policies, or whether the impact of larger economic forces was sufficient to overwhelm variations in borough styles, and in the policy preferences of the borough's political participants.

The Bromley strategy of "focused development" can be seen from an examination of council documents and local news reports. We can observe regular rejections of development proposals that come from areas outside the ones I have identified as targets for development. In upper-middle-class sections of the borough, 3,000 signatories from Petts Wood supported the Bromley council's refusal to grant planning permission for residential development.[49] And in the Shortlands ward, the council's development committee rejected applications for shop-to-office conversion permission despite the fact that the council's officers had recommended approval.[50] In the Beckenham section, plans for a "town centre" were rejected by the council. Cllr Barkway specifically enunciated the policy: "Any involvement with the scheme for Beckenham may detract from the plans for Bromley High Street [the town centre]."[51]

But protests from areas slated for development received lukewarm council reaction. Biggin Hill Ratepayers' Association demanded that all council meetings on the airport be open meetings,[52] and the Bromley North Residents' Association, directly affected by traffic plans for Bromley town centre development, called the council "two-faced" for claiming that the Greater London Council was imposing a traffic plan when, the Residents' Association argued, it was really a borough decision.[53] Despite protests from Copers Cope residents' groups, the council regularly approved additional development proposals. Its ward councillors protested that planning decisions were being taken by too few council members, and they were being excluded, and its residents association complained that in one year (1973) 87 of 92 single-family homes demolished in the entire borough were in Copers Cope Ward.[54]

But the policy of the council seemed clear-cut. Even when the council refused to increase the weight limit of planes allowed to use Biggin Hill airport, the relevant committee chairman indicated that of the competing interests at stake, the "interests of the ratepayers as a whole" came before the "interests of the local residents".[55] And at the conclusion of this study plans were announced for the construction of a hotel at the airport,[56] and the airport management committee approved the layout of the industrial site at the airport.[57]

In Bromley town centre, the council's policy committee (in effect the borough Cabinet) welcomed the designation of Bromley town centre as a "strategic centre" in the Greater London Development Plan, the council's large central library/ theatre project went forward, and a major department store chain announced plans for "one of our larger units" next door to the library/theatre project.[58]

As this brief review of development policy indicates, the Bromley council had the political means to achieve its development goals, so long as these did not spread all over the borough's landscape. And opposition to its "focused development", while vigorous and at times with the ability to delay, did not seem able to defeat any of the council's central development goals.[59]

I have argued above that development policy was far less central to the Islington council. While Bromley council documents and borough papers were filled with residents' groups protesting development and council action on economic development, in Islington these matters received less attention. It must be noted that this lesser attention, therefore, was not a product of closed policy-making, but of attention to other matters. Thus, time and energy occupied with economic development in

Bromley got directed towards population-composition and social-policy questions in Islington.

But economic development issues were not entirely absent. A private developer, for example, proposed modernizing a block of flats it owned without rent increases, in return for council permission to build offices. This proposal was rejected by the borough council, on the grounds that economic development should take the form of industrial use rather than office space.[60]

Although the *Greater London Development Plan* proposed using land at the Angel for office development, the local residents' association was in opposition: "We do not wish to see Angel become an . . . extension of the City."[61] And another residents' association in a different part of the borough also argued that whatever development took place at the Angel should be in the form of factory jobs.[62] And, as I indicated earlier, the council was committed to public consultation about Angel development.[63] But the outcome of that consultation was only spotty public participation.

And despite the opposition, some office development at the Angel was finally approved. In its approval, council statements indicated the hesitant nature of its action:

> There are very few offices at the present at The Angel. But like many parts of London there is pressure for new office development. . . . Council policy is that offices should not change the character of The Angel. They must fit existing scale, and other housing and shopping.[64]

And the council reduced the number of square feet the office development would be permitted to have.[65] But perhaps the clearest reason for the final permission to proceed with development could be found in the council's indication that:

> Office development can provide large capital profits. If the owner is the council, then these profits can be used for the benefit of the whole community. It is already very difficult for the Council to find money for many worthwhile schemes, and building offices is one way of increasing money for the Council.[66]

What we have here is a reconciliation of permission for office development and ideological position of Islington councillors, many of whom described themselves as "left-wing socialists". What the council would be doing, of course, would be constructing socialized office buildings for use by private firms. During the course of this study, therefore, council policy went from opposition to grudging permission for development to proceed. Two reasons can be found for this change. One is that the localist councillors in Islington were increasingly occupied with other issues, questions of squatting and gentrification. Although the proposals for development were not on their own "priority list", they were priorities for others. But the other is more national in impact. The general British economic crisis was leading the national government to impose more and more stringent reductions in aid to local governments and greater restrictions on local government spending. Although Islington councillors at first might have hoped this policy would be only temporary, as time went on, revenue-raising alternatives like council-sponsored office development obviously became more acceptable.

Despite its very different political environment, the course of economic development in Tower Hamlets follows somewhat similar lines. Once again we find a pattern of local residential opposition to office development, and arguments for industrial rather than office jobs in both Dockland and other parts of the borough where office development might occur. In the end, however, at least through the time of this study, office development comes to be an important part of development plans.[67]

We see a shift of council policy from one favouring housing and industry,[68] to agreement with private developers for mixed usage, to include office development as well.[69] In an especially significant development for Tower Hamlets, the council also approves the construction of private housing in Dockland, in a project to be mixed council house, private housing in nature.[70] And the council also approves new forms of council-housing ownership, in which residents will become "partial owners".[71] Cllr Beasley described the council's involvement in Dockland development as a "historic decision . . . we set out to get a good slice of the developers' cake and we got it."[72] But this "historic development" would be changing the nature of Dockland. Thus, in related developments, the offices at the controversial "World

Trade Centre" in Dockland will be permitted to expand,[73] and in a development simultaneously symbolic and substantive, an old brewery in Docklands is to be converted into an inn[74]—an inn whose clientele will be middle and upper class, and not characteristic of most pubs in Tower Hamlets.

These new forms of "balanced development" are not without their critics. Thus the "Dockland Action Group" argued that the concept of "a balanced community . . . is a justification for bringing the higher income groups from elsewhere into the area which will lead to the neglect of the interests of the people now in the docklands."[75] But, as the Council's own newspaper described it, when announcing plans for a borough plan which will include office development, "times change, trends change, population changes".[76]

Thus, both Islington and Tower Hamlets move in the direction of permitting economic development, including office development. But the plans for Tower Hamlets seem to be considerably more far-reaching. But what really distinguishes the Tower Hamlets case, however, is that it never goes through the stage of intense on-council opposition which characterized Islington decision-making. The nature of the membership of the Tower Hamlets council, and its style of doing business, precludes such possibility.

It is of course beyond the scope of this study to describe definitely what the evolution of policy would have been had the national economic environment been different, but the available evidence suggests that Islington political forces were far better mobilized than those of Tower Hamlets to resist office-centred economic development. But even with Islington's councillors' far greater degree of organization, access to public attention, and influence in the inner workings of the council, in the end they could not completely prevent such development from taking place.

C CONCLUSION

The theme of this chapter has been the interplay of borough characteristics, leadership preferences, and rank-and-file councillor attitudes on whole-council styles and policies. Previous chapters suggested clear variations among the boroughs studied in these three elements. The first major section of this chapter, dealing with council styles, found that these elements combined to produce distinctive styles among the three boroughs studied. With regard to style, therefore, the councils could surely be said to be making independent choices.

When the examination turned to actual council policies, however, the situation became more problematic. For one thing, there is a larger body of formal constraints operating on local government policy in England than on local council styles. I have argued, nevertheless, that despite the strictures of the Greater London Development Plan, that councils had consider-able freedom to manoeuvre and to adopt different emphases on their own. But the need for revenue, particularly in times of budgetary stringency, imposed limits on the councils' freedom of choice. This was particularly true for the two Inner London boroughs studied. These boroughs are far more dependent on external aid than the relatively prosperous suburban borough of Bromley. As such, the economic attractions of office develop-ment given these inner boroughs' proximity to the City of London, made such development irresistible.

Compromises with "socialist" ideology became necessary in two ways. First, in periods of unemployment, even the less-desirable office jobs became better than none at all. If industrial development could not be stimulated to the degree desired, then office construction was an acceptable alternative under the circumstances. Second, borough ownership, or at least major local government participation in the development of office projects, meant they could be presented as compatible with "socialism". Although it is clear that approval for development in the Angel and in parts of Dockland was granted reluctantly, it was granted nevertheless in both Tower Hamlets and in Islington.

It is clear, therefore, that autonomy is greater in matters of style than in matters of policy. Two questions remain, however. One is how much relative influence each of the three elements— borough background, leadership preferences, and rank-and-file councillor attitudes—have on council style. I have suggested earlier in this chapter that the various elements I have listed can be thought of as being in consonance or dissonance with each other. Islington, with the most "consonant" set, had the most clearly open style. Both Tower Hamlets and Bromley had more "dissonant" circumstances. Bromley had traditions of openness but a leader interested in greater closedness. The evidence presented in this chapter suggests that his policy of "focused development" and closure of council procedure successfully achieved his goal. Tower Hamlets, on the other hand, had traditions of closedness, and a set of rank-and-file councillor attitudes still supportive of this tradition, but a leader interested in some changes toward openness. The evidence regarding Tower Hamlets council's styles of operating suggest that this was a less successful leadership effort. It would seem that leaders have a harder time "imposing" openness than they do attempting to "close" council decision-making. Style preferences of rank-and-file councillors, therefore, may be just as important as leader preferences in determining whole-council operating styles.

The second remaining question is whether the evidence on council policy choices should be taken to mean that council styles are irrelevant in determining policy outcomes. Although there is no way to be definitive on this question, I am arguing that this is not the case. Rather, I am suggesting that style variations predispose councils with regard to policy, but are not determinative. In the case of Bromley, a more closed style, and a policy of focused development were tied together. In the case of Tower Hamlets and Islington, their very different council styles did not produce greatly varied policy outcomes. But the explanation for this does not lie in any irrelevance of style, but in the ability of significant external economic factors to overwhelm the policy preferences of local-level units of government.

These findings raise significant questions both for theories of representation and for theories of local government. It is these implications which will be the subject of the concluding chapter of this research.

6 Implications

Earlier chapters of this work have shown that the boroughs studied here demonstrated very different patterns of representation, and that variations in individual councillor style translated into variations in whole-council styles as well. Any assessment of the implications of such findings must take into account the need to distinguish between several competing goals of systems of representation.

More "open" council styles, I suggested, can enhance the opportunities for area residents to know about council activities and to express their opinions. But in a borough like Islington, this "openness" was achieved by a change in the composition of the Council's membership, a change which probably reduced the opportunities for individual participation in the formal political process by the borough's working-class residents. Paradoxically, opportunities for influencing the council may be enhanced at precisely the same time as opportunities for participating as a councillor are being reduced.

In this chapter I will be considering the implications of these earlier findings for more general questions about urban political life. I have divided these implications into two broad categories: an "urban" component and an Anglo-American comparative component. In this first section I am returning to a question raised at the outset of this work, where I suggested that problems of representation are different at the urban level than at the national, and I now want to argue that the evidence of this study confirms such a view.

My second category of implications also returns to questions raised at the outset. I indicated there that this study had its origins in political questions which had risen to prominence in American political debate. Controversies about urban decentralization and representation showed how matters often thought of as being of interest only to political theorists could become matters on the active political agenda. In the second section of this chapter I am again asking these questions, and showing what evidence can be brought to bear upon them from a detailed look at three London boroughs.

A THE "URBAN" COMPONENT

The nature of population distribution in large Western cities has been characterized by class geographic compactness. This class compactness ensures that there will be predominantly working-class neighbourhoods in some sections of the metropolis, and predominantly middle-class neighbourhoods elsewhere. Given the relationships between social class and political party affiliations, these geographic patterns are likely to translate into domains of one-party dominance. Many theories of democratic functioning take inter-party competitiveness for granted. This study has investigated the impact of variations in representational functioning in arenas where one-party systems are the norm, but these are one-party systems which result from voter choice rather than authoritarian external controls.

In a political system such as London's, these factors produce a situation in which political control of the "home base" of the borough can be regarded as more or less certain, while political control of the metropolitan area as a whole, and of the entire nation, will be closely contested. Under such circumstances, we should expect to find varying patterns of response from those with local political authority. Some can be expected to centre their political attention on the "safe" borough, while others will direct their energies and attention to politically more precarious regional and national politics. As I have suggested in earlier chapters, the councillors studied in this research do indeed vary on this dimension, which I have referred to as the scope of ambition.

A second distinctively urban component identified in this study is tied to the geographically specific nature of urban decisions. Specific sites are set for development programmes, for example, and the benefits (and costs) of such programmes are likely to be divisible and differential. We would therefore expect to find those in local authority continually being forced to choose between competing small-area demands. What this research has discovered is that councillors vary in the degree to which they see this dilemma. I have referred in earlier chapters to councillors' scope of representation, the range of territory which they understand to be their prime responsibility. We would expect variations in this "scope of representation" to be an especially meaningful matter for political jurisdictions, such as London boroughs, which must make many geographically specific policy decisions. It is, I have argued, distinctively "urban" to have to make such choices *within* class-homogeneous neighbourhoods.

A final "urban" component of the findings reported on earlier in this study focuses not so much on the urbanness of the locale, as on the fact of "sub-nationality". The existence of higher levels of formal (and informal) authority in the nation-state suggest that decision-making at the local level is necessarily constrained compared to the authority which can be exercised by national-level representative systems. Under such circumstances, I argued, the policy freedom of local governments is likely to be limited, and variation in representational modes get channelled into style questions, where higher authority is less likely to be controlling.

In the next section of this chapter I will be examining the distinctively "British" features of the political systems I have studied, but many of the patterns of politics reported on here show commonalities with patterns of local-level politics in metropolitan areas of other large Western industrial countries. Specifically, the presence of Islington "gentrifiers" provides a social base for political activity not dissimilar from that provided by middle-class central city residents for Reform Democrats in the United States. "Suburban defensiveness", coupled with "focused development" programmes, the characteristic stance of Bromley policy-makers, also has strong analogues in American suburban politics. What I am arguing, then, is that comparable patterns of urban development, and of urban population distributions, can produce analogous patterns of political development as well.

B   LESSONS FOR URBAN AMERICA

An American, observing the evolution of local government elsewhere, is inevitably drawn to the question of parallels with and differences between the system he is studying and comparable systems in the United States. As I indicated in the Preface in this research, it was the existence of a stable, ongoing, form of "neighbourhood government" in London which first drew this researcher's attention to its being a useful arena for gaining insight into problems of decentralization which have been raised in the American urban setting.

If one observes the overall functioning of the three borough governments, Bromley's seems the closest to American patterns. I characterized its overall position as one of "suburban defensiveness", and this pattern of suburban politics is familiar to observers of almost any American metropolitan area. (Certain differences are obvious. Bromley's resistance seemed more a question of class, without the racial overlay so characteristic of American suburban defensiveness. The formal rules of government and the political history of the country mean that Bromley is not nearly so free an actor as American suburban governments are.[1] Nevertheless, the basic outlines of policy look quite similar.)

By contrast, the political pattern of Tower Hamlets seems the most different from the American experience. While it would be tempting to see parallels between the positions, styles, and values of "traditional" politicians in Tower Hamlets and the "traditional" American local style—the political machine—such comparisons would be largely misleading.

While modes of recruitment and attitudes of Conservative suburban councillors from Bromley would not seem unusual in any comparable American setting, few American communities would have a politics which looks (or looked) like that of Tower Hamlets. The key difference, of course, is the difference between the British Labour Party and any American parties.

What is important about the distinction, for the purpose of this analysis, is not the seemingly age-old question of why the United States has never had a strong socialist party, but rather the existence in Britain, and not in the United States, of a political mechanism formally tying local trade unions to the political party system. As I suggested in Chapter 4, the "traditional" members of the Tower Hamlets Council could never have entered politics in any major way if it were not for this link. The largely working-class nature of the Tower Hamlets Council is rooted in this relationship, and there is little like it in the United States.[2]

Islington presents a middle case. If the politics of Bromley seems familiar to an American, and that of Tower Hamlets largely different, Islington presents a mixed, and therefore especially intriguing pattern. While its traditional politics are not very different from Tower Hamlets, and therefore at some remove from American experiences, its political evolution in recent years is much more comparable. As I indicated above, the "localists" on the Islington council come out of a population base of "gentrification", and patterns of this sort are not at all unknown in large American cities. In New York, for example, both politicians and general publics speak of some neighbourhoods as undergoing a "brownstone revival", and inner-city rehabilitation projects can be observed in many other American cities as well. In neighbourhoods of this type, and in other, more demographically stable middle-class inner-city neighbourhoods, Reform Democratic political organizations have now become the dominant forces on the local political landscape.

In describing New York City Reform Democrats, James Q. Wilson argued that demographic shifts were at the base of the growth of the political group.[3] Thus, the Reform Democrats of Greenwich Village were individuals "for whom Manhattan has an irresistible fascination", and who regard the "atmosphere of Village life as culturally and intellectually stimulating".[4]

These middle-class-professional migrants are similar in personal characteristics to the Islington gentrifiers described in Chapter 2, and their politics have a similar cast to them as well. Among the distinctive features of the "localist" style was a much greater turning to interest groups as legitimate sources of information about the ward and policy cues as to desirable council policies. This does suggest some rather considerable departures from British political norms, and, to this extent at least, makes Islington politics look more "American".

In the standard literature on British politics, it is now a commonplace to suggest that interests are more likely to be represented by the diversity of legislators themselves, rather than indirectly through pressure group activity.[5] In quite another portion of the "standard" literature, Almond and Verba describe differences in American and British publics in their preferred personal methods for influencing local government.

More than twice as large a percentage of British residents, they report, would attempt to influence local government by personal contact with an elected official than is true in the United States. Forty-five per cent of British respondents might use such a tactic, compared with only 20 per cent in the United States. By contrast, the American sample was considerably higher in its willingness to use organized group activity to influence local government decisions. Fifty-six per cent of the American sample could imagine using this tactic, compared with only 34 per cent in Britain.[6]

The Almond–Verba findings fit with what this study has shown to be the modes of interaction with the citizenry preferred by traditional councillors. While it would be inaccurate to say that the traditional rank-and-file councillors of Islington and Tower Hamlets had no group contacts, they were clearly suspicious of groups which did not have explicit ties to the Labour Party.

Such councillors can be seen as engaging in a form of "typical" representation, where they see their own personal interests as identical to those of their working-class neighbours. But this pattern of representation by immersion in the community also suggests that contact with constituents will largely be of the informal, street-conversation sort. While I would not wish to suggest that the localist councillors avoided personal contact with their constituents (indeed, most of them emphasized their efforts in this direction), they stand in contrast to their traditionalist colleagues in their class-distinctiveness from the wards they represented, and in their much greater reliance on ward-based group articulation of interests. While this particular study has no survey evidence to confirm the proposition, we can nevertheless expect that if the perspective of the new Islington councillors has permeated the communities they represent, then the patterns shown in the Almond–Verba study regarding methods of influencing local government would today look considerably closer to the American data, at least for Islington.

But despite some such similarities, patterns of urban politics in Britain are likely to remain distinct from those in the United States, especially at the most local level. In an examination of urban government in the United States, Yates has characterized its mode of functioning as "street-fighting pluralism".[7] Despite the role of a diverse set of voluntary organizations in Bromley, and the rise of power of "localists" in Islington, such a characterization could not be made of the London Boroughs.

Although, as I have suggested, economic and demographic changes in the boroughs have brought with them changes in the boroughs' political structure, political authority remains concentrated in the hands of the council. As I indicated in Chapter 1 of this study, small-area governments, such as London boroughs, are a standard feature of British political life, and have none of the experimental quality that characterizes American experience with "neighbourhood government". As such, the London units are far less susceptible to having their formal decision-making power challenged by appeals to other levels. Despite the legal possibility for the reversal of London borough decisions by the national government, it is clear that the boroughs have unquestioned "legitimacy". The same could not be said for any of the American neighbourhood government experiments.

Because of this authority, the London boroughs are likely to remain more attractive units for participation by the politically ambitious than is the case in the United States. Joseph Schlesinger has argued that the rise of politicians to power in America needs to be understood as a combination of personal ambition and available opportunity structures.[8] London boroughs provide such an opportunity structure at the neighbourhood level, and the United States does not have it.

I alluded earlier to the similarities in style between Islington localists and New York Reform Democrats. But the opportunity structures of London and New York politics differ significantly, and such actors have a far easier time acceding to power in London than they do in New York, precisely because of the existence of "neighbourhood" government in the form of the London boroughs.

When James Q. Wilson studied American "amateur Democrats", he reported that the reformers were "cosmopolitan" in their political outlook, while the local elected politicians were "locals".[9] I have suggested throughout this study that Islington localists transcend this distinction by articulating very local problems, but placing them in broad social perspectives. I now wish to argue that their possibility for doing this, and the relative weakness of comparable American efforts, lies in the fact that proponents of an "ideology of localism" in London have an available arena for these efforts which is not part of the normal political structure of American cities. Thus "inner-city" politics of London and of New York look very different indeed.

But, as I suggested above, suburban patterns are not quite so distinctive when compared with the United States. Thus the boroughs studied in this research vary not only among themselves, but also in the extent to which comparable forms of local political activity can be found in other societies. One problem with many analyses of British local government, particularly those undertaken by Americans with an eye on comparisons with the United States, is that they tend to describe all British local government as if its dominant characteristics were unvarying from unit to unit. We have descriptions of British local government as showing little interest-group activity,[10] as being not particularly responsive to business interests,[11] or as "unlikely to develop a taste for grass-roots democracy".[12] None of these characterizations would describe all of the boroughs studied in this research. But some American observers have called attention to variations among local units of government in Britain, and to the potential variations in policy consequences which might result from these patterns of distinctiveness.[13]

A borough like Bromley, for example, violates a number of the standard American understandings of the functioning of British local government. Comparisons are more usefully sought in the literature on American suburbs. Thus, when Prewitt describes Bay Area City Council memberships as an extension of a community voluntary organization role,[14] he describes a pattern of political activity very similar to that practised by Bromley's parochials.

But even with this similarity, once again the variations in opportunity structures produce variations in political patterns even between otherwise similar units, such as the American suburbs that Prewitt describes, and Bromley. Prewitt suggests that the prominence of voluntary organization activity in the communities he studies, what he calls the "ethic of volunteerism", weakens those communities' non-partisan electoral systems.[15] In Bromley, by contrast, the increasing integration of the borough's political system into national politics weakens the role of ward-based voluntary organizations, rather than the other way around.

In his revisionist account of much of the American–British comparative local government literature, L. J. Sharpe suggests that the existence of a "social-democratic" party is an important variant in the British experience, which "redresses the balance for the working-class elector" and is not present in American urban politics.[16] This point is clearly exemplified by the traditional political structure of Tower Hamlets, a borough whose traditional activists, I suggested above, would have few American counterparts.

Sharpe catalogues a variety of distinctions between American and British urban political forms which he finds in the literature. Although he rejects most of the reported distinctions, he does accept the argument that American urban politics is more "open" than is the urban politics of Britain.[17] He nevertheless suggests additional criteria of "functional effectiveness", "public trust", and "public interest", dimensions on which he regards British performance as superior.[18]

The evidence of this study suggests that although "closedness" may have been the norm for British local government, it is by no means a universally followed norm today. The Islington evidence specifically suggests that changes in council composition can produce significant changes in council style, and Tower Hamlets indicates that declines in "social closedness" make possible at least some movement toward a more open political style.

What is less clear, however, is what consequences such changes have for the dimensions Sharpe suggests are more important—functional effectiveness, public trust, and public interest. While any definite judgements about "public trust" and "public interest" would require public opinion data not now available, this study did report on the relatively low levels of public participation in Islington's attempts at more open formal public participation in council decision-making. While Islington is obviously now a more "interesting" borough for its "attentive publics", it is uncertain whether council openness has been translated into increased interest (or trust) for the bulk of its population.

Any judgement about "functional effectiveness" necessarily requires certain value judgements about the desired policy outcomes sought from local government. In the one arena of policy decision-making reported on in this study, plans for economic development, the openness of council style in Islington produced certain modifications of the borough's plans for economic change, but no basic alteration in overarching economic imperatives. Whether such a result could be characterized as "functional effectiveness" would depend on the perspective of the observer.

By what standards, then, should the London borough political systems studied in this research be evaluated? In the opening chapter of this work I suggested that the various reorganizations of English local government, and the official reports which stimulated those reorganizations, contained a set of goals which could serve as benchmarks for evaluating the impact of the systems of local government they helped to create.

The variety of official commissions which have examined the structure of English local government have operated on very different theoretical assumptions about the desired forms of council and councillor activity. To briefly recapitulate, one view, expressed by the Royal Commission on Local Government in Greater London (the Herbert Commission), placed emphasis on recruitment of "better" councillors.[19] In another interpretation, found in the reports of the Committee on the Management of Local Government (the Maud Committee), greater attention is given to the need to have councillors who are socio-economically representative of the communities they represent.[20] A third view, expressed by the report of the Royal Commission on Local Government in England (the Redcliffe-Maud Commission) placed greater emphasis on the need to have councillors who accurately articulated the interests of the communities from which they were elected.[21]

Of course, these three emphases are not necessarily incompatible, but the authors of all of the reorganization studies seemed to feel that the first of these emphases was in some conflict with the latter two. But all commissions, no matter what their position on desirable councillor characteristics, suggested a need for additional links between councils and local voluntary organizations. We can now ask how well the councils and councillors reported on in this research meet these criteria.

Conclusions about the final point mentioned above, the need for greater ties between councils and voluntary organizations, is the easiest to discuss. It is clear that both Islington and Tower Hamlets councils were moving in the direction of greater links of this type. For Islington in particular, the building of links between ward-based voluntary organizations and the council, was an especially high council priority, shared by both the council leader and its most influential rank-and-file members. While moves towards links with voluntary organizations were somewhat weaker in Tower Hamlets, there too it is clear that the council was moving in the direction of closer liaison, and that the range of local voluntary organizations regarded as "legit-imate" by council leadership and rank-and-file members was expanding. While Bromley council could be seen as moving somewhat in the opposite direction, it began from a very high base of voluntary organization activity, and, as I have suggested throughout this study, the influence of such organizations in Bromley remains high.

While this study has no time-series data on councillor types, it is clear that the overall mix of councillors must steadily have been moving in the direction of greater ties with voluntary organizations. The growth of localist councillors in Islington, in particular, suggests that expression of the interests of organized community groups was growing during the period of this study. In Tower Hamlets, with less dramatic changes in the com-position of its borough population, and with more "traditional" councillors, the ties between councillors and voluntary organiz-ations, besides trades unions, also became relatively more important, as the single comprehensive role of union organiz-ations as expressers of community interests declined.

In so far as one of the criteria of "functional effectiveness" for borough councils ought to be the vigorous expression of the sentiments of local voluntary organizations, we can confidently say that the councils studied here were moving towards better performance.[22] But having found a greater articulation of "community group" interests cannot be regarded as necessarily identical with the expression of "community" interests. Since this study does not include any data on underlying popular attitudes in the boroughs studied, it is beyond the scope of this research to assess the effectiveness of the councils in representing opinions of individual constituents.

It is possible, however, to comment on the "effectiveness" of the councils in meeting the two other criteria described above:

the recruitment of technically knowledgeable councillors, and the recruitment of councillors who are socio-economically representative of their communities. Once again, the most intriguing councillor category for analysis are the localists. It is clear that councillors of this type were more technically sophisticated, with a better grasp of the jargon of government administration. It is also clear that they were less likely to reflect the demographic characteristics of the wards they represented. These two findings are as the various government commissions predicted.

But two "unpredictable" findings emerge from an examination of the localist councillors. First, the emergence of councillors of this type is dependent on the presence in the local population of individuals potentially recruitable to serve on the borough council. Islington could not have seen an influx of "localists" on to its borough council had it not previously seen an influx of "gentrifiers" into the borough's residential population. (Note, by contrast, that the Tower Hamlets leader, although interested in recruiting more "managerial types" on to the borough council, had a much smaller population pool from which to draw, and that few such individuals emerged in the rank-and-file Tower Hamlets sample.) Thus, although localist councillors may not have been "representative" of their neighbourhoods' total population, the growth of middle-class professionals as a significant sector of neighbourhood population was a pre-condition for their presence on the council.

In a second "unpredictable" finding, it is clear that the localists also felt that they bridged a gap which the various government commissions had identified. Particularly in the Maud and Redcliffe-Maud reports, distinctions are made between "two types of councillors; one at home dealing with individual cases, and the other with broad policy and general management",[23] and a view that "it is very unlikely that the same person will want or be able to play both [roles]."[24]

But it is nevertheless the case that the localists in Islington did not reflect the overall population composition of the wards they represented. What consequences flow from this? In their study of the 1972 Democratic presidential convention in the United States, Sullivan *et al.* argued that there were two basic arguments for what they called "group" representation (and what Pitkin has referred to as "typical" representation).[25] Sullivan *et al.* suggest that "members of the category may feel decisions are more legitimate if a sizeable number of the category have participated in the decision-making"[26] and "a greater number of group members would permit more articulation and clearer definition of group interests."[27]

While the evidence from this study cannot be brought to bear on the first of these hypotheses, it is possible to comment on the second. The emergences of localists in Islington, and the consequent diminution of traditional working-class councillor styles in that borough, did not bring with it any diminution in the articulation of group interests. Quite to the contrary, the expression of such interests in council debate increased. As I suggested earlier, the paradox of the localist style is precisely that it articulates the group interests of precisely those working-class individuals whose personal participation in borough government is reduced. The Islington experience suggests that the second proposition by Sullivan *et al.* need not necessarily be correct. What remains undecided, however, is what long-term consequences the reduction in working-class participation on organs of government such as the Islington borough council will have.

One final comparison with the American experience needs to be made. It is frequently asserted that American political realities require that little attention be given to long-range planning.[28] In Britain, on the other hand, it is often suggested that the evolution of local government forms has produced a structure more amenable to longer term thinking.[29]

The available evidence in this research suggests some cautionary notes regarding the British experience. Even in the relatively secure electoral environments of the boroughs studied, the pressure of the moment did not seem conducive to long-range thinking and planning. There are two important "dogs that did not bark" in this research; the impact of the British economic crisis and the state of big-city British race relations. Although both of these matters have come to widespread attention and discussion in the period since these interviews were conducted, they were both almost entirely absent from the comments of the elected representatives of London boroughs in the summer of 1974.

C   A FINAL WORD

A major theme of this work has been the complexity of political change. One concomitant of this complexity is that the changes observed and reported on in this research have been multi-directional. Even political change which I have identified as springing from a common source: the predispositional impact of greater economic integration of the boroughs studied into the economy of Greater London, had varying impact on the boroughs studied. In Bromley, it produced a political style relatively less responsive to voluntary organizations; in Islington it had the opposite impact.

Population change in Islington led to the emergence of a new group of political activists, practitioners of what I have referred to as an "ideology of localism". This set of views, in practice, led to a council more open to the residents of this still largely working-class borough in terms of public visibility of decision-making, but less open in terms of working-class access to actual council membership.

In each of the boroughs, a significant proportion of councillors were concerned with "community defence", but the concepts of "community" varied, and so did the "defence" tactics. For both Tower Hamlets and Bromley, boroughs at opposite ends of the socio-economic scale, "community" meant class homogeneity, and "defence" required the maintenance and establishment of economic bases to support the boroughs' class bases. In both boroughs, however, challenges to this homogeneous sense of community were developing. As I have indicated earlier, I am arguing that metropolitan-area-wide economic changes under-lay these "threats" to the boroughs' status quo.

In Islington, the "community" in the mind of the politically dominant localists was a far more heterogeneous one. But this concept of community needed defending as well. The risk to Islington, as the localists saw it, was the gradual disappearance of much of its working-class population in parts of the borough underlie these "threats" to the boroughs' status quo.

With such mixed patterns of change, it would be misleading to infer any common patterns of future development. What is clear, however, is that the structure of local government in London permits local actors to adopt distinctive political styles and to attempt to direct policy outcomes in directions consistent with their stylistic preferences.

In discussing the evolution of American political parties, Samuel Hays has argued that American parties are paradoxical in expressing national ideologies, but doing so by mobilizing activists whose own political values are formed "within the parochial context of community".[30] As this study has shown, the concept of community need not be parochial in nature, but can be linked to a more general understanding of societal functioning.

In discussing the evolution of European political systems, Samuel Huntington has argued that "expansion of participation was linked to the centralization of power" in national governments.[31] The United States, by contrast, was seen by Huntington to be a unique arena in which expansion of participation took more varied forms, including access to autonomous local power.[32] He regarded the United States as, in this sense, maintaining "Tudor" interpretations of the desirable polity. As this study has shown, "post-Tudor" England shows a re-emergence of autonomous local power in its London Boroughs, not unlimited, but real nonetheless.

I have argued that this re-emergence is predicated on two elements: the development of an "ideology of localism", in which neighbourhood concerns are seen as an arena for the resolution of questions of wider relevance; and the greater economic integration of the neighbourhoods studied into the regional and national economy, making borough decision-making "important" beyond its own borders. But as a result of these basically integrative trends, we see something of a return to older styles of more autonomous local politics. While the full policy consequences of this development have yet to be determined, the viability of local political settings as arenas for political activity is unquestionably enhanced.

Appendix 1
Councillor Interview
Schedule*

Let me begin by asking you a little bit about   (borough)   and
about   (ward)   in particular:

1   When local residents think of the neighbourhood, do they
    think in terms of the ward, or what?
        What would most people around here call this area?

2   What's this area like?
        What kinds of housing do most people live in?
        What sorts of jobs do most people around here have?
        What sorts of incomes do they earn?
        What's the political composition of the area?
        Have any of these things changed much in the last few
            years?

3   Are most people around here pretty much alike? Are they of
    the same social class?

Now let me ask you a few general questions about the job of a
councillor and your relationship with your constituents:

4a   In general, how would you describe the job of a councillor,
     what are its main points as you see it?

4b   From your own experience, how do you best get to know
     about the needs and attitudes of people in your ward?

* Interviews were sought with one councillor per ward in each of the three
boroughs, a total of 64 wards. Interviews were actually conducted with rank-
and-file councillors in 63 of the 64 wards.

Do you get letters from constituents? About how many a
week? What are they about?

Do people approach you on the street or in shops? Do
they call or telephone?

Is there a local press which is at all useful in learning
about the ward? About the borough?

What about election canvassing? Is that a useful way to
learn about the ward? Would you do that only in
borough elections, or at other elections as well?

5 On the whole, how important would you say the views of
constituents are in helping you to make up your mind on
issues before the council?

6 Some people say that there are two theories of political
representation. The first says the representative should be
the voice of the people and should act as they want him to.
The second says that the representative should exercise his
own judgement and act according to his own conscience and
his own assessment of the situation. Which do you agree with
most?

Now, speaking of constituents and their problems:

7 How often do constituents come to you with problems?

8 What types of problems do they bring to you?

(IF NOT MENTIONED, ASK SCHOOLS, HOUSING,
AMENITIES, ROADS, CULTURE, RATES)

9 How do they come? (PROBE: SINGLY, OR IN GROUPS)
Would that be different for different issues, and are there
some problems groups would be more likely to raise,
and others that individuals would be more likely to
raise? What would they be?

10 IF GROUPS MENTIONED: How do you feel about
efforts of groups to make their views known to you and seek
your support?

11 Are there any groups in your ward that are particularly
active?

12 Any that are particularly influential?

13 When people (or groups) bring problems to you, where do they usually do it? (PROBE: HOME? SURGERIES? ARE THEY PARTY SURGERIES?)

14 Why do you think they brought the problem to you in particular? (PROBE: FOR DISTINCTION FROM OTHER WARD COUNCILLORS AND/OR OFFICERS)

15 Are there any sorts of problems that wouldn't be brought to you, that people would think best to take someplace else? (PROBE: WHY AND WHERE?)

16 Thinking of the problems that people bring to you, how often, if ever, are they in conflict? Do different individuals or groups in your ward ask you to do opposite sorts of things? How often does this happen?

17 In the time you've been on the council, have there been any changes in the types of problems people bring to you?

18 Now, with regard to the sorts of problems people do bring to you; if you decided to try to help with a   (issue mentioned by councillor)   problem, where would you go, what would you do?

FOR ANY OF FOLLOWING NOT MENTIONED SPONTANEOUSLY:

Have you ever raised this   (see below)   ?
IF YES, what happened?
    How responsive were they?
    How was problem dealt with?
IF NO, what do you think would happen if you did?

a   directly with officers involved
b   through the media
c   within the party organization
d   within the party group on the council
e   with relevant committee chairman
f   with the council leadership
g   to a higher level of government
h   directly, in council committee
i   directly, in general council debate

19 What does the leadership of the council think a councillor should do if someone comes in with a problem?

20 Can a member push "too hard" for the interests of his own ward? PROBE: What would that be like? Has that happened at all?

21 How would the local party leadership feel about this? Just how is the   (party name)   organized here in   (borough)   ? IS THAT THE BOROUGH PARTY, THE CONSTITUENCY PARTY, THE WARD PARTY, OR WHAT? (FOR ANY PARTS OF PARTY NOT SPECIFICALLY MENTIONED)

22 What advice, if any, were you given about the representation of ward interests when you were first elected to the council?

23 What advice would you give a new councillor about this?

24 Do you think there is any difference between the parties in   (borough)   on this? (For Tower Hamlets and Islington, "I realize the council is completely made up of Labour Party councillors, but what about the other parties which contest council seats?")

25 IF YES: Why is this?
(PROBE FOR NATIONAL PARTY DIFFERENCES AND/OR ROLE OF OTHER PARTIES IN MAJORITY OR OPPOSITION ON BOROUGH COUNCIL)

26 Is there much competition between the parties in this ward? Would you regard this as a marginal ward?

27 How do you think this affects the way you carry out your job as a councillor?

28 Do you think the specific policies you support are important in determining the election outcome? or in changing many votes in the ward?

29 Does the vigorous promotion of ward interests make a difference in this?

30 We were talking before about the   (name)   party structure here in   (borough)   . On the ward level, could you tell me a little bit about how candidates for the council get designated in this ward?
How were you designated?

Now I wonder if I could ask you a few questions about yourself?

31 Could you tell me how you first got involved in political activity?

32 How did you come to stand for the council?

33 You mentioned you've been on the council since   (date)
      Have you always represented this ward?
      Did you ever stand in another ward?

34 Thinking to the future, how long do you expect to stay on the council? (IF ANSWERED IN TERMS OF POSSIBLE ELECTORAL DEFEAT):
      If you're able to get re-elected, how long would you like to stay on the council?

35 Are there any other levels of politics you think you might like to be involved in? (IF NOT INCLUDED IN ANSWER, PROBE FOR STANDING FOR GLC OR PARLIAMENT)

36 Could you tell me a little bit about your own position on the council. What committees you're on?

37 IF NOT NOW A CHAIRMAN: Do you think you'd like to be a committee chairman at some point? IF YES: Do you think you'll be able to do that?

38 How long have you lived in   (borough)   ? Do you live in   (ward represented)   ? IF NO: How did you come to stand in   (ward represented)   ?

39 May I ask what your occupation is?

40 Is that in   (borough)   ?

41 And your educational background? What was the last type of full-time school you attended? Any further education?

Well, that completes my list of questions. What else ought I have asked about the job of a councillor in   (borough)   ?

Do you think   (borough)   is a typical borough in how a councillor functions?
IF NO: How is it different?

Appendix 2
London Maps and
Map Codes

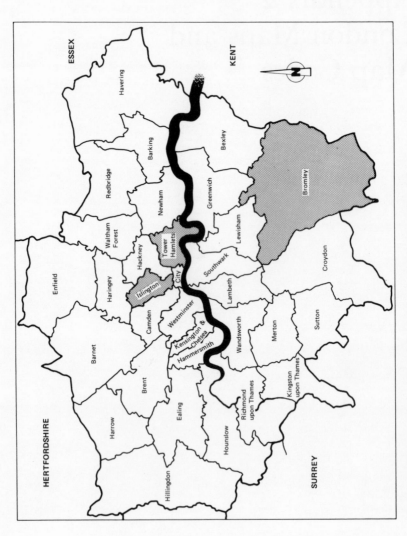

MAP 1   Greater London boroughs (and City of London)

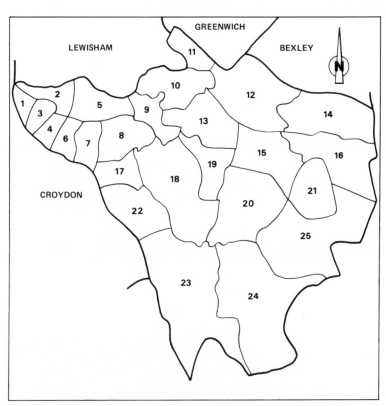

MAP CODE

1	Anerley
2	Lawrie Park and Kent House
3	Penge
4	Clock House
5	Copers Cope
6	Manor House
7	Eden Park
8	Shortlands
9	Martins Hill and Town
10	Plaistow and Sundridge
11	Mottingham
12	Chislehurst
13	Bickley
14	St Paul's Cray
15	Petts Wood
16	St Mary Cray
17	West Wickham North
18	Keston and Hayes
19	Bromley Common
20	Farnborough
21	Goddington
22	West Wickham South
23	Biggin Hill
24	Darwin
25	Chelsfield

MAP 2   Bromley ward map

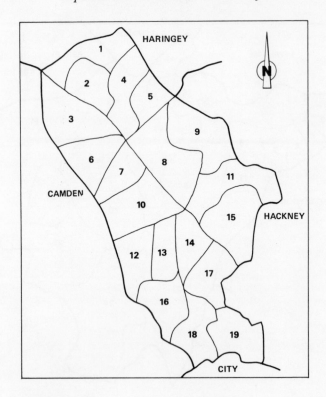

MAP CODE

1	Highview	11	Mildmay
2	Hillrise	12	Thornhill
3	Junction	13	Barnsbury
4	Parkway	14	St Mary
5	Station	15	Canonbury
6	St George's	16	Pentonville
7	Hillmarton	17	St Peter
8	Highbury	18	Clerkenwell
9	Quadrant	19	Bunhill
10	Holloway		

MAP 3   Islington ward map

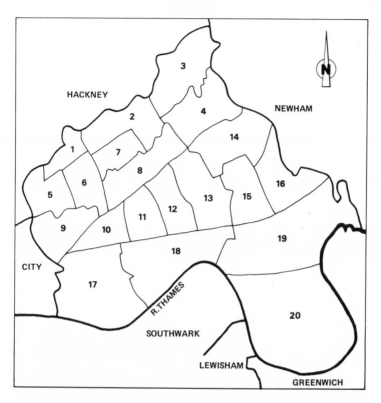

MAP CODE

1	Bethnal Green North	11	Redcoat
2	Bethnal Green East	12	St Dunstan's
3	Bow North	13	Limehouse
4	Bow South	14	Bromley
5	Bethnal Green West	15	Poplar West
6	Bethnal Green South	16	Poplar East
7	Bethnal Green Central	17	St Katherine
8	Holy Trinity	18	Shadwell
9	Spitalfields	19	Poplar South
10	St Mary's	20	Poplar Millwall

MAP 4 Tower Hamlets ward map

Notes

INTRODUCTION

1. A literature has grown up comparing the American and British urban experience, and a subset of this literature explicitly compares London and New York. See, for example, L. J. Sharpe, "American Democracy Reconsidered, Parts I and II", *British Journal of Political Science*, vol. 3 (January and April, 1973) pp. 1–28 and 129–67), and Kenneth Newton, "Community Decision-Making in Britain and the U.S.A.", in Terry Clark (ed.) *Comparative Community Politics* (New York: John Wiley, 1974) pp. 55–86, for some general American-British comparisons. Specific New York–London comparative literature includes H. V. Savitch, "Leadership in New York City and London", *Policy and Politics* vol. 2, no. 2 (December 1973) and Andrew Glassberg, "The Linkage Between Urban Policy Outputs and Voting Behavior: New York and London", *British Journal of Political Science* vol. 3, part 3 (July 1973) pp. 341–61. For an example of the argument that the two cities cannot be compared, see Wallace Sayre, "The Relevance of the Greater London Governmental Experience to New York City Government", in State Study Commission for New York City, *The Neighborhoods, the City, and the Region* (New York: State Study Commission, 1971).

2. Douglas Yates, *Neighborhood Democracy* (Lexington, Mass.: Lexington Books, 1973) p. 159.

3. The issue of changes in the nature of Labour Party representation, particularly at the local council level, has been extensively debated in both the academic literature of political science and in the more popular literature of British politics. A seminal, but very controversial, statement can be found in Barry Hindess, *The Decline of Working-Class Politics* (London: Paladin, 1967), a study of Liverpool political participation.

Hindess argues that there has been a systematic reduction in working-class participation in Labour Party ranks, and a replacement by middle-class activists. His findings have been challenged by a number of other analyses. See, for example, R. Baxter, "The Working Class and Labour Politics", *Political Studies*, vol. 20 (1972) pp. 97–107, which argues that Hindess's finding is incorrectly limited to participation in ward meetings, and that working-class membership on the council in Liverpool, and elsewhere in England, was actually on the increase. This coincides with L. J. Sharpe's earlier conclusion that working-class participation on local councils increased considerably from the 1930s to the 1950s in England. L. J. Sharpe, "Elected Representatives in Local Government", *British Journal of Sociology*, vol. XIII (1962) pp. 189–209.

Several other authors make congruent points. Tom Forester argues that Labour councillors have always been predominantly middle class, but that there has been no increase in this pattern recently. Tom Forester, *The British Labour Party and the Working Class* (New York: Holmes & Meier, 1976) pp. 89–90. Ian Gordon argues that middle-class Labour councillors demonstrate high rates of social mobility, with almost half such "middle-class" councillors coming from working-class backgrounds. Ian Gordon, "The Recruitment of Local Politicians", *Policy and Politics*, vol. 7 (1979) p. 16. Thus, an examination of the current socio-economic status of Labour councillors may understate the extent to which such councillors are of working-class origin. Another recent report suggests that, "many of the ostensibly middle-class councillors think of themselves as working class and share attitudes very similar to those of actual working-class councillors", Ian Gordon and Paul Whiteley, "Social Class and Political Attitudes: The Case of Labour Councillors", *Political Studies*, vol. 27, no. 1 (1979) pp. 112–13.

For the purposes of this study, such controversies were of lesser importance. The intention here is to examine the political styles of different types of councils and councillors. The councils chosen for study were not chosen because they represented a cross-section of local government, but rather because they represented clear examples of differing political styles. As I shall be demonstrating, the two entirely Labour councils studied here show very different patterns of class composition, and very different political styles as well.

4. See John Dearlove, *The Politics of Policy in Local Government* (Cambridge: Cambridge University Press, 1973) on Kensington and Chelsea; Ruth Butterworth, "Islington Borough Council: Some Characteristics of Single-Party Rule", *Politics*, vol. I, 1 (May 1966) pp. 21–31; Paul Cousins, "Voluntary Organizations as Local Pressure Groups, The Situation in Bromley", *London Review of Public Administration*, no. 4 (October 1973) pp. 17–26; Kenneth Young and John Kramer, *Strategy and Conflict in Metropolitan Housing* (London: Heinemann, 1978) on Bromley.

5. H. V. Savitch, "Leadership in New York City and London", *Policy and Politics*, vol. II, no. 2 (December 1973) pp. 113–33; Paul Kantor, "The Governable City: Islands of Power and Political Parties in London", *Polity*, vol. VII, no. 1 (fall 1974) pp. 4–31.

6. Greater London Council Intelligence Unit, *Research Report No. 9, Classification of the London Boroughs* (London: Greater London Council, February 1971): Greater London Council Intelligence Unit, *London Borough Council Elections* (2 May 1974).

7. See Savitch, op. cit. regarding Tower Hamlets; Cousins, op. cit. and Young and Kramer op. cit. regarding Bromley; and Butterworth, op. cit. and Savitch, op. cit. regarding Islington.

CHAPTER I

1. Douglas Yates, *Neighborhood Democracy* (Lexington, Mass.: Lexington Books, 1973) p. 91.

Notes

207

2. John Wahlke, *et al.*, *The Legislative System*, ch. 12 (New York: John Wiley, 1962) pp. 267–86.

3. A bibliography of applications of this typology may be found in Vincent Hauge, "City Councillors as Representatives", 1974 American Political Science Association Annual Meeting Paper.

4. Wahlke, *et al.*, op. cit., chs 12 and 13, pp. 267–310.

5. Op. cit., pp. 289–91.

6. Hanna Pitkin, *The Concept of Representation* (Berkeley: University of California Press, 1967) p. 211.

7. A. H. Birch, *Representation* (New York: Praeger, 1971) p. 48.

8. J. R. Pennock, "Political Representation: An Overview", in J. R. Pennock and J. W. Chapman (eds), *Representation: Nomos X* (New York: Atherton Press, 1968) p. 23.

9. For evidence on this point in London politics, see John Dearlove, *The Politics of Policy in Local Government* (Cambridge: Cambridge University Press, 1973) p. 44.

10. Samuel Huntington, *Political Order in Changing Societies* (New Haven: Yale University Press, 1968) pp. 106 ff.

11. Loc. cit.

12. Committee on Political Parties, American Political Science Association, "Toward a More Responsible Two-Party System", *American Political Science Review*, vol. XLIV, no. 3, part 2 (September 1950) pp. 18, 22.

13. Robert Dahl, *Who Governs?* (New Haven: Yale University Press, 1961) p. 305.

14. James D. Barber, *The Lawmakers* (New Haven: Yale University Press, 1965) pp. 209 ff.

15. Thomas R. Dye, *Politics, economic and the public: Policy outcomes in the American States* (Chicago: Rand McNally, 1967).

16. Noel Boaden, *Urban Policy-Making* (Cambridge: Cambridge University Press, 1971).

17. Hanna Pitkin, "The Concept of Representation", in Hanna Pitkin (ed.), *Representation* (New York: Atherton Press, 1969) p. 18.

18. Committee on Public Participation in Planning, *People and Planning* (London: HMSO, 1969) p. 9.

19. Op. cit., p. 1.

20. The three major reports are those of the "Herbert Commission", Royal Commission on Local Government in Greater London, *Report* (London: HMSO, 1960); the "Maud Committee", Ministry of Housing and Local Government, *Report and Research Studies* (London: HMSO, 1967); and the "Redcliffe-Maud Commission", Royal Commission on Local Government in England, *Report* (London: HMSO, 1969).

21. Royal Commission on Local Government in England, *Report*, vol. I, p. 2.

22. Op. cit., p. 11.

23. Royal Commission on Local Government in Greater London, *Report*, p. 179.

24. Op. cit., p. 180.

25. Loc. cit.

26. Op. cit., p. 62.

27. Op. cit., pp. 62–3.

28. Loc. cit.
29. Loc. cit.
30. Op. cit., p. 64.
31. Loc. cit.
32. Loc. cit.
33. Op. cit., p. 63.
34. Loc. cit.
35. Ministry of Housing and Local Government, Committee on the Management of Local Government, op. cit., vol. II, p. 7.
36. Op. cit., vol. II, p. 2.
37. Op. cit., vol. II, p. 3.
38. Royal Commission on Local Government in England, op. cit., vol. I, p. 164.
39. Op. cit., vol. I, p. 128.
40. Ministry of Housing and Local Government, Committee on the Management of Local Government, op. cit., vol. I, p. 143; Royal Commission on Local Government in England, op. cit., vol. III, p. 129.

CHAPTER 2

1. Greater London Council, *Intelligence Unit Research Report*, no. 9 (February 1971) p. 21.
2. Thomas Anton and Oliver Williams, "On Comparing Urban Political Systems: Residential Allocations in London and Stockholm" (1971 American Political Science Association Annual Meeting Paper) p. 38.
3. Councillor Ann Page, quoted in *Labour Councillor* (February 1976) p. 20.
4. Unpublished 1971 Census data on housing stock and socio-economic group data, by wards. Made available by Intelligence Unit, Greater London Council.
5. Darwin Ward itself is larger than either Islington or Tower Hamlets Boroughs. Greater London Council, *1971 Census Data for London* (London: Greater London Council, 1974) pp. 44–61.
6. Michael Young and Peter Willmott, *The Symmetrical Family* (New York: Pantheon, 1973) pp. 21–3.
7. London Borough of Islington, *Official Guide* (2nd edition) (Cheltenham: E. J. Burrow & Co., n.d.) p. 25.
8. Unpublished 1971 Census ward housing stock data.
9. Alan W. Evans, *Economics of Residential Location* (New York: St Martins, 1973) p. 142.
10. Evans, loc. cit.
11. Anne Chisholm, "The Blighted Angel", *New Statesman*, vol. 85, no. 2187 (16 February 1973) p. 231.
12. Maurice Ash, "Green Belt or the Green City", *Town and Country Planning*, vol. 42, no. 1 (January 1974) p. 8.
13. Jon Rowland, *Community Decay* (Harmondsworth: Penguin, 1973) p. 41.
14. K. G. Blythe, *Islington Borough Development Plan, Report of Studies, Topic Paper 3, Recreational Open Space, Summary* (April 1973), p. 1.
15. Peter Willmott and Michael Young, *Family and Class in a London Suburb*

(London: New English Library, 1967) p. 10.
16.   John Rex and Robert Moore, *Race, Community and Conflict: A Study of Sparkbrook* (London: Oxford University Press, 1967) p. 9.
17.   *Labour Councillor* (February 1976) p. 8.
18.   Rex and Moore, p. 24.
19.   Op. cit., p. 25.
20.   Unpublished 1971 Census ward immigration data.
21.   Richard Minns, "Who Builds More?", *New Society*, vol. 28, no. 603 (25 April 1974) p. 186.
22.   Donald Hoodless (chairman of the Islington Council Housing Committee), letter to the editor, *New Society*, vol. 28, no. 605 (9 May 1974) p. 334.
23.   Lindsay Knight, "A Tenants Cooperative", *New Society*, vol. 28, no. 679 (16 August 1974) p. 420.
24.   Unpublished 1971 Census ward housing stock data.
25.   Anton and Williams, p. 25.
26.   Bleddyn Davies, *Social Needs and Resources in Local Services* (London: Michael Joseph, 1968) p. 236.
27.   Rex and Moore, p. 9.
28.   It should be pointed out that this distinction between the two types of council housing in Tower Hamlets is far from perfect, because Tower Hamlets is itself an amalgamation of three separate historic political entities, Stepney, Bethnal Green, and Poplar. Tower Hamlets borough housing, while heavily populated by residents from the borough, may still be seen by local residents as populated by "outsiders" if the particular development has a large fraction of its population from outside the immediate neighbourhood. But although these new developments may seem to be populated by "outsiders" from the perspective of local residents, to the borough political leadership, at least, they are very much "locals".
29.   In some boroughs a different policy has been followed. Anton and Williams report that Barking borough took over GLC housing specifically to gain control of the entry rules, so that the borough could use vacancies for local residents (Anton and Williams, p. 52).
30.   Unpublished 1971 Census ward housing stock data.
31.   Willmott and Young, *Family and Class in a London Suburb*, p. 105.
32.   Andrew Blowers, "London's Out-County Estates: A Reappraisal", *Town and Country Planning* vol. XLI, no. 9 (September 1973) p. 412.
33.   Loc. cit.
34.   Op. cit., p. 414. However, suburban resistance to council housing in England is sometimes more overt. In the classic case, a wall was erected to separate middle-class neighbourhoods from a housing estate in Oxford. Peter Collison, *The Cutteslowe Walls* (London, Faber & Faber, 1963). Bromley itself had walls of this type on the boundary of the borough, separating a middle-class neighbourhood from a housing estate in the adjoining, largely working class borough of Lewisham. Kenneth Young and John Kramer, "Local Exclusionary Policies in Britain", in Kevin Cox (ed.) *Urbanization and Conflict in Market Societies* (Chicago: Maaroufa, 1978) p. 231 and Young and Kramer, *Strategy and Conflict in Metropolitan Housing*, op. cit., p. 25.
        It is significant to observe the difference in reaction when the housing estate is surrounded by middle-class and affluent neighbourhoods and thus can exist

in ignored isolation, and the much greater extent of resistance when the estate is perceived as an indication of an expansion of a largely working-class area into a middle-class neighbourhood.

35.   Anton and Williams, p. 33. For a comprehensive account of Bromley's successful resistance to additional council housing within its borders, see Young and Kramer, *Strategy and Conflict in Metropolitan Housing.*
36.   Minutes of the Bromley Borough Housing Committee, 28 November 1973.
37.   Ash, p. 8.
38.   Minutes of the Bromley Borough Council, 7 January 1974.
39.   Minutes of the Bromley Borough Council, 21 March 1974.
40.   Bromley Local Government Committee of the Labour Party, *People and Priorities: Labour's Plan for Bromley* (n.d.) p. 24.
41.   *Bromley Times* (28 March 1974) p. 1.
42.   Simon Jenkins, "The Politics of London Motorways", *Political Quarterly* vol. 44 (1973) pp. 257, 265.
43.   Kenneth Leech, "The Role of Immigration in Recent East London History", *East London Papers* vol. X, no. 1 (1967) p. 16.
44.   Op. cit., p. 10.
45.   Op. cit., p. 16.
46.   Op. cit., p. 13.
47.   Michael Young and Peter Willmott, *Family and Kinship in East London* (Glencoe: Free Press, 1957) p. 78.
48.   Op. cit., p. 26.
49.   Loc. cit.
50.   Op. cit., p. 81 (footnote).
51.   John Goldthorpe *et al., The Affluent Worker: Political Attitudes and Behaviour* (Cambridge: Cambridge University Press, 1968) p. 74.
52.   Op. cit., p. 75.
53.   Young and Willmott, *Family and Kinship in East London*, pp. 142–3.
54.   *Tower Hamlets News* (December 1973) p. 1.
55.   *East London Advertiser* (3 May 1974) p. 1.
56.   Young and Willmott, *Family and Kinship in East London*, p. 102.
57.   R. E. Pahl, *Patterns of Urban Life* (London: Longman, 1970) p. 84; Richard Hoggart, *Uses of Literacy* (Fair Lawn, N.J.: Essential Books, 1957) p. 34; Suzanne Keller, *The Urban Neighborhood* (New York: Random House, 1968) pp. 28 ff.
58.   Great Britain, General Register Office, *Census 1961, England and Wales, Workplace Tables*; Great Britain, General Register Office, *Census 1966, England and Wales, Workplace and Transport Tables*; Great Britain, General Register Office, *Census 1971, England and Wales, Workplace and Transport Tables.*
59.   Rowland, p. 41.
60.   Ruth Butterworth, "Islington Borough Council: Some Characteristics of One-Party Rule", *Politics*, vol. I, no. 1 (May 1966) p. 21.
61.   Young and Willmott, *The Symmetrical Family*, p. 3.
62.   Loc. cit.
63.   Willmott and Young, *Family and Class in a London Suburb*, p. 114.
64.   Loc. cit.
65.   Unpublished 1971 Census ward immigration data.

66. Great Britain, General Register Office, *Census 1966, England and Wales, Economic Activity, County Leaflet, Greater London.*
67. Evans, pp. 11–12.
68. Op. cit., p. 141.
69. Paul Abramson and J. W. Books, "Social Mobility and Political Attitudes in Britain", *Comparative Politics* vol. 3, no. 3 (April 1971) p. 424.
70. Young and Willmott, *Family and Kinship in East London*, p. 142.
71. Willmott and Young, *Family and Class in a London Suburb*, p. 22.
72. Howard Biel, "Suburbia and Voting Behavior in the London Metropolitan Area", *Tijdschrift voor Economische en Sociale Geografie* vol. LXII, no. 1 (1972) p. 43.
73. P. Davies and K. Newton, "An Aggregate Data Analysis of Turnout and Party Voting in Local Elections", *Sociology*, vol. 8, no. 2 (May 1974) p. 222.
74. Willmott and Young, *Family and Class in a London Suburb*, p. 79; David Thorns, *Suburbia* (London: MacGibbon & Kee, 1972) pp. 149–50.
75. Paul Cousins, "Voluntary Organisations as Local Pressure Groups: The Situation in Bromley", *London Review of Public Administration*, no. 4 (October 1973) p. 19.
76. Loc. cit.
77. See, for example, Bromley Council minutes, 15 January 1974, where the Rotary Club paid for local park benches.
78. Kenneth Young, "Orpington and the Liberal Revival", in C. Cook and J. Ramsden (eds), *By-Elections in British Politics* (New York: St. Martins Press, 1973) pp. 212–13.
79. Colin Bell and Howard Newby, *Community Studies* (New York: Praeger, 1971) p. 206.
80. Loc. cit.
81. Young, p. 212.

CHAPTER 3

1. Ralph Stodgill, *Handbook of Leadership* (New York: Free Press, 1974) p. 23.
2. Lord Redcliffe-Maud and Bruce Wood, *English Local Government Reformed* (London: Oxford University Press, 1974) p. 101.
3. Ruth Butterworth, "Islington Borough Council: Some Characteristics of Single Party Rule", *Politics*, vol. 1, no. 1 (May 1966) p. 31.
4. Loc. cit.
5. Op. cit., p. 27.
6. Op. cit., p. 26.
7. H. V. Savitch, "Leadership in New York City and London", *Policy and Politics*, vol. 2, no. 2 (December 1973) p. 127.
8. In no ward in Islington did the percentage of the population in professional or managerial occupations go above 18 per cent, according to the 1971 Census, and for the borough as a whole the percentage was 11.5 per cent. *1971 Census Data for London* (London: GLC, 1974) pp. 53–4.
9. Frank Parkin, *Middle-Class Radicalism* (New York: Praeger, 1968).
10. *1971 Census Data for London*, p. 60.
11. Op. cit., p. 29.

12.   For a description of this lifestyle, see Michael Young and Peter Willmott, *Family and Kinship in East London* (Glencoe: Free Press, 1957).

13.   John Goldthorpe, David Lockwood, Frank Bechhofer, and Jennifer Platt, *The Affluent Worker in the Class Structure* (Cambridge: Cambridge University Press, 1969) pp. 45–6.

14.   See Kenneth Young, "Orpington and the 'Liberal Revival'", in C. Cook and J. Ramsden (eds), *By-Elections in British Politics* (New York: St. Martin's Press, 1973) pp. 198–222.

15.   See R. E. Pahl, *Whose City?* (London: Longman, 1970).

16.   This pattern of increasing politicization is not unique to Bromley. Other studies in the same part of England have shown shifts among Conservatives from stands as essentially independent councillors to a more party-political position. T. Brown, M. J. C. Vile, and M. Whitemore, "Community Studies and Decision Taking", *British Journal of Political Science*, vol. 2 (1972) p. 145.

17.   Emile Durkheim, *Division of Labor in Society* (Glencoe: Free Press, 1933) pp. 129–32.

18.   See G. W. Jones, *Borough Politics* (London: Macmillan, 1969).

19.   This and all succeeding quotations are from tape-recorded interviews conducted in 1974.

20.   See Geoffrey Green, "National City and Ward Components of Local Voting", *Policy and Politics*, vol. I, no. 1 (1972) pp. 45–54.

21.   Stein Rokkan, *Citizens, Elections, Parties* (Oslo: Universitetsforlaget, 1970) pp. 191–2.

22.   S. H. Lipset, *Political Man* (Garden City: Doubleday, 1959) pp. 74–6.

23.   As I indicated earlier, the term "council" is ambiguous in its meaning. In this context, the speaker would be referring to the borough's bureaucratic structure.

24.   V. H. Vroom and P. W. Yetten, *Leadership and Decision-Making* (Pittsburgh: University of Pittsburg Press, 1973) pp. 200–1.

25.   This is a national phenomenon in England. For example, the proportion of residents who work within the local government area where they live has been steadily dropping. See Bruce Wood, "Urbanization and Local Government", in A. H. Haley (ed.), *Trends in British Society Since 1900* (London: Macmillan, 1972) pp. 260–1.

CHAPTER 4

1.   Each of the three boroughs studied had council membership of 70 at the time of this study. At the time of interviewing, each council still had 10 appointed aldermen serving on the council, although these positions were scheduled for elimination after the next set of borough elections. Bromley's 60 elected councillors represented 25 different wards, with ward memberships ranging from one to three per ward. (only one ward was a single-member district, and this was the only such ward in any of the three boroughs. Islington's 60 elected councillors represented 19 different wards, while Tower Hamlets' 60 councillors represented 20 wards.)

Since this study was particularly interested in areal representation, aldermen were eliminated from the sample. Interviews were then sought with a sample of one councillor per ward from each of the total of 64 wards in the three boroughs. In each borough initial contact was made with the leader of the council, and the leader's cooperation was obtained. Letters were then written to councillors in the sample requesting interviews, followed by telephone contacts. Unlike council leaders discussed in the previous chapter, rank-and-file councillors were promised anonymity and their responses will not be individually identified. Use of this procedure produced agreement from 63 of the 64 sampled councillors, and these 63 form the councillor sample used in the study. All but one of the interviewed councillors agreed to have his interview tape-recorded, and the interview excerpts reported on here are drawn from those tapes.

The high rate of response obtained in this survey can be attributed to several factors. First, the research was presented to the councillors in a complimentary fashion. Councillors were told that this research project grew out of American interest in learning more about the structure of borough councils in London, and that there had been specific discussion in New York about emulating the London model. Many councillors saw the interview as an opportunity for information-gathering of their own, and asked questions about the structure and politics of American local government.

The fact that this research was conducted by an outsider also helped to gain access to some otherwise wary councillors. Although respondents were aware that they were participating in a research project, and had agreed to have their responses tape-recorded, many interjected comments indicating that they did not expect their remarks to have the same type of repercussions that comparable remarks to a British academic researcher might have had. "I can say this to you, I wouldn't say it to people around here" was a typical comment.

The interview schedule used with councillors can be found in Appendix I.

2.   These classifications are drawn largely from answers to two questions in the councillor interview schedule. "Scope of representation" was classified primarily on responses to Question 20, which asks, "Can a member push 'too hard' for the interests of his own ward?" This formulation produced a rich and varied pattern of answers, illustrations of which appear throughout this chapter. This question, and the way councillors answered it, seemed more discriminating than more traditional questions about role orientations, which produced largely ritualized responses. The formulation used here permitted councillors to discuss their feelings about proper councillor representational style, and then move into a discussion about their own personal methods. In this fashion, it avoids some of the difficulties of appearing to have a "correct" answer. This is a particular problem in the study of British politics, with its Burkean traditions.

"Scope of ambition" was classified on responses to Question 35, "Are there other levels of politics you think you might like to be involved in?" As will be seen in the body of this chapter, I have suggested that councillors might be "ambitious" in ways outside formal political participation. Some councillors showed aspirations to leadership of national interest groups, for example. Where such indications were shown in an interview, a councillor was classified as "ambitious", even though he might have shown no particular interest in higher elective office.

3.   Ambition beyond the local council is not typical for most local councils in England. In a study of two Essex councils, Blondel and Hall report that a large Majority of councillors consider the local council to be the ultimate level of their political careers. J. Blondel and R. Hall, "Conflict, Decision-Making and the Perceptions of Local Councillors", *Political Studies*, vol. XV (1967) p. 327.

4.   These two dimensions are often presented as if they were in conflict. In one classic example of such an interpretation, the Maud Report, which was fundamental to the restructuring of London local government, indicated that there are "two opposite views of councillors' role; 'director and controller of policy', and 'watchdog' for the interests of electors." Quoted in Martin Minogue (ed.) *Documents on Contemporary British Government. Volume II, Local Government in Britain.* (Cambridge: Cambridge University Press, 1977) p. 145.

I am suggesting that an important group of councillors studied in this research would not have agreed that these were necessarily "opposite views".

5.   Other studies of British local politics have shown this to be a common view among Labour councillors. In his study of Birmingham, Newton reports that:

> Labour group members are more sensitive to the workings of social and economic processes which set the parameters of individual lives. Hence Labour members are less likely to assume the parochial, individual problems, ward representative style of the Conservatives, and to see their role as city governers and public policy-making agents."

Kenneth Newton, *Second City Politics* (Oxford; Clarendon Press, 1976) p. 444.

This study has identified an important group of Labour councillors with a different perspective.

6.   John Wahlke *et al.*, *The Legislative System* (New York: John Wiley, 1962).

7.   Greater London Council Intelligence Unit. *Greater London Research: Research Report No. 13. Characteristics of 12 Clusters of Wards in Greater London* (July 1971).

8.   *1971 Census Data for London* (London: GLC, 1974).

9.   Department of the Environment, *People and Planning: Report of the Committee on Public Participation in Planning* (London: HMSO, 1969). In their study of Glasgow politics, Budge, Brand *et al.* report more councillors with a city-wide orientation: Ian Budge, J. Brand, M. Margolis, and A. L. M. Smith, *Political Stratification and Democracy* (London: Macmillan, 1972) p. 85. Newton reports a similar finding for the Birmingham Council: Kenneth Newton, *Second City Politics*, p. 125.

10.   G. W. Jones, *Borough Politics* (London: Macmillan, 1969).

11.   This councillor would certainly have agreed with Norman Dennis's argument that, "the more the dissident councillor imagines he has to complain about, the more quickly the councillors of the rank and file will tire of him and control him." Norman Dennis, "Councillors, Officers, and Public Participation in Urban Renewal", in Richard Rose (ed.) *The Management of Urban Change in Britain and Germany* (London: Sage Publications, 1974) p. 168.

12.   The sporadic nature of such activity mirrors Forester's finding that membership in local organs of the Labour Party is usually low, "but can rise or fall quite dramatically in exceptional periods". While Forester's argument related to national politics, a comparable point can be made to explain the

sudden development (and politicization of parochial concerns at the local level as well). Tom Forester, *The British Labour Party and the Working Class*, p. 85.

13. But reluctance to have councillors too heavily involved in voluntary-organization activity is not limited to the Labour Party. In his study of Kensington and Chelsea, John Dearlove reports that the local Conservative leadership discouraged its rank-and-file councillors from too much contact with outside pressure groups. John Dearlove, *The Politics of Policy in Local Government* (Cambridge: Cambridge University Press, 1973) p. 126. But Dearlove also reports that many new councillors challenged this view (p. 145). Newton, in his examination of Birmingham council, suggests that few councillors in his sample consulted voluntary organizations on policy questions, even though most were at least members of many such organizations. Kenneth Newton, "Links Between Leaders and Citizens in a Local Political System", *Policy and Politics*, vol. I (1973) p. 298.

14. For a history of this growth and decline of Liberal fortunes in Bromley, see Kenneth Young, "Orpington and the Liberal Revival", in C. Cook and J. Ramsden (eds), *By-Elections in British Politics* (New York: St. Martins, 1973) and Kenneth Young and John Kramer, *Strategy and Conflict in Metropolitan Housing*, pp. 187–9.

15. A critical account of this trend can be found in Cynthia Cockburn, *The Local State* (London: Pluto Press, 1977), ch. 6. From a quite different perspective, McKay and Cox describe the development of the British "Inner Cities Programme", and the growing belief that inner-city neighbourhoods had distinctive problems, and that these could not simply be addressed by nationally uniform policies. David McKay and Andrew Cox, *The Politics of Urban Change* (London: Croom, Helm, 1979) pp. 234 ff. One natural consequence of such a change in view would be a movement of social activists into areally based local political disputes.

16. Alan Evans, *Economics of Residential Location* (New York: St. Martin's Press, 1973).

17. That such a pattern is unusual can be seen not only within this study, but by comparison with another recent study of five English local authorities. Ian Gordon reports that over three-quarters of the councillors in his sample were asked to stand for office by some individual or organization, usually trade unions or local political party organizations. Ian Gordon, "The Recruitment of Local Politicians", p. 22.

18. Ruth Butterworth, "Islington Borough Council: Some Characteristics of One-Party Rule", *Politics*, vol. I, no. 1 (May 1966) pp. 21–31.

19. Austin Ranney, *Pathways to Parliament* (Madison: University of Wisconsin Press, 1965) p. 197.

20. Op. cit., p. 238.

21. Op. cit., p. 239.

CHAPTER 5

1. Harvey Cox and David Morgan, *City Politics and the Press* (Cambridge: Cambridge University Press, 1973) p. 13.

2. Wallace Sayre, "The Relevance of the Greater London Governmental

Experience to New York City Government", in State Study Commission for New York City, *The Neighborhoods, the City, and the Region* (New York, 1971) p. 20.

3. Edward Banfield, "The Management of Metropolitan Conflict", in Edward Banfield (ed.), *Urban Government* (New York: Free Press, 1969) p. 42.

4. Paul Peterson and Paul Kantor, "Political Parties and Citizen Participation in English City Politics", *Comparative Politics*, vol. 9, no. 2 (January 1977) p. 207.

5. Loc. cit.

6. L. J. Sharpe, "American Democracy Reconsidered, Part I", *British Journal of Political Science*, vol. 3 (January 1973) p. 8.

7. O. Tapper, "Poplar on Trial", *East London Papers*, vol. 3, no. 2 (1960) p. 59.

8. *East London Advertiser*, 19 March 1974.

9. Op. cit., 19 April 1974.

10. *Tower Hamlets News*, April 1974.

11. Tower Hamlets Council Agenda, 23 January 1974.

12. *Tower Hamlets News*, June 1974.

13. *East London Advertiser*, 25 April 1975.

14. *Tower Hamlets News*, June 1976.

15. Op. cit., April 1975.

16. *East London Advertiser*, 27 September 1974.

17. Op. cit., 28 March 1975.

18. *Bromley Advertiser*, 24 April 1975.

19. Op. cit., 1 May 1975.

20. Bromley Council Minutes, 8 October 1973.

21. *Bromley Times*, 30 May 1974.

22. *Bromley Advertiser*, 11 December 1975.

23. Op. cit., 5 September 1974.

24. *Focus on Islington*, spring 1973.

25. Islington Council press release, 30 January 1973.

26. *Focus on Islington*, autumn 1974.

27. Op. cit., summer 1973.

28. Op. cit.

29. *Islington Gazette*, 23 May 1975.

30. Op. cit., 5 December 1975.

31. Op. cit., 17 January 1975.

32. Op. cit., 13 February 1976.

33. Islington Council Minutes, 2 October 1973.

34. *Bromley Advertiser*, 19 September 1974.

35. Islington Council Agenda, 6 May 1975.

36. *Islington Gazette*, 2 May 1975.

37. Op. cit., 18 July 1975.

38. Op. cit., 11 October 1974.

39. *Greater London Development Plan* (London: Greater London Council, 1976).

40. Op. cit., p. 9.

41. Op. cit., p. 29.

42. Op. cit., p. 12.

43. Op. cit., p. 31.

44. Op. cit., p. 29.
45. Op. cit., p. 31.
46. Op. cit., p. 19.
47. Op. cit., p. 91.
48. Op. cit., p. 122.
49. *Bromley Times*, 2 May 1974.
50. *Bromley Advertiser*, 2 January 1975.
51. Op. cit., 12 February 1976.
52. *Bromley Times*, 15 August 1974.
53. Op. cit., 27 June 1974.
54. *Bromley Advertiser*, 25 March 1976.
55. Op. cit., 27 June 1976.
56. Bromley Council Agenda, Airport Management Committee Report, 5 July 1976.
57. Op. cit., 1 December 1975.
58. Bromley Council Agenda, Policy and Resources Committee Report, 10 February 1976.
59. *Bromley Advertiser*, 21 August 1975.
60. *Islington Gazette*, 27 September 1974.
61. Op. cit., 18 April 1975.
62. Op. cit., 25 July 1975.
63. *Focus on Islington*, winter 1973.
64. Op. cit., June 1975.
65. Op. cit., autumn 1975.
66. Op. cit., June 1975.
67. *East London Advertiser*, 4 July 1975.
68. Op. cit., 13 September 1974.
69. Op. cit., 4 April 1975.
70. Op. cit., 6 June 1975.
71. Op. cit., 30 May 1975.
72. Op. cit., 27 June 1975.
73. Op. cit., 8 August 1975.
74. Op. cit., 13 February 1976.
75. Op. cit., 28 November 1975.
76. *Tower Hamlets News*, June 1975.

CHAPTER 6

1. For a description of the persistence of political autonomy in American suburbia, see Robert Wood, *Suburbia* (Boston: Houghton-Mifflin, 1958) pp. 83 ff.
2. Even in American communities with labor unions committed to high political activity, their influence on local government has been far weaker than the British norm. David Greenstone has argued that nonpartisan local politics are one major reason why this is so. See David Greenstone, *Labor in American Politics* (New York: Vintage Books, 1969) pp. 120 ff.
3. James Q. Wilson, *The Amateur Democrat* (Chicago: University of Chicago Press, 1966) p. 42.
4. Loc. cit.

5. See Samuel Beer's discussion of "functional representation" in Samuel Beer, *The British Political System* (New York: Random House, 1974) pp. 180 ff.

6. Gabriel Almond and Sidney Verba, *The Civic Culture* (Princeton: Princeton University Press, 1963) p. 191.

7. Douglas Yates, "Service Delivery and the Urban Political Order", in Willis Hawley and David Rogers (eds), *Improving the Quality of Urban Management*, vol. 8, *Urban Affairs Annual Reviews* (Beverly Hills, California: Sage Publications, 1974) p. 215.

8. Joseph Schlesinger, *Ambition and Politics* (Chicago: Rand McNally, 1955) ch. 1.

9. J. Q. Wilson, op. cit., p. 10.

10. Wallace Sayre, "The Relevance of the Greater London Governmental Experience to New York City Government", in State Study Commission for New York City, *The Neighborhoods, The City, and the Region* (New York, 1971) p. 19; Stephen Elkin, *Politics and Land Use Planning* (Cambridge: Cambridge University Press, 1974) pp. 94 ff.

11. Delbert Miller, "Decision-Making Cliques in Community Power Structures: A Comparative Study of an American and an English City", *American Journal of Sociology*, vol. 64 (1958) p. 307.

12. Edward Banfield, "The Management of Metropolitan Conflict", in Edward Banfield (ed.), *Urban Government* (New York: Free Press, 1969) p. 41.

13. James Fesler, "Understanding Decentralization", *Journal of Politics*, vol. XXVII (1965) p. 552; Douglas Ashford, "Territory vs. Function", 1976 American Political Science Association Annual Meeting Paper, p. 24.

14. Kenneth Prewitt, *The Recruitment of Political Leaders* (Indianapolis: Bobbs-Merrill, 1970) p. 212.

15. Loc. cit.

16. L. J. Sharpe, "American Democracy Reconsidered, Part II", *British Journal of Political Science*, vol. 3 (April 1973) p. 166.

17. L. J. Sharpe, "American Democracy Reconsidered, Part I", *British Journal of Political Science*, vol. 3 (January 1973) p. 7.

18. L. J. Sharpe, "American Democracy Reconsidered, Part II", p. 129.

19. *Royal Commission on Local Government in Greater London* (London: HMSO, 1960) pp. 179–80.

20. Great Britain Ministry of Housing and Local Government. Committee on the Management of Local Government, *The Management of Local Government*, vol. 2: *The Local Government Councillor* (London: HMSO, 1967) p. 2.

21. *Royal Commission on Local Government in England* (London: HMSO, 1969), vol. I, p. 164.

22. This finding stands in some contrast with the American data reported on by Verba and Nie. They argue that as communities "begin to lose the clear boundaries that separate them from other communities", that "communal participation" declines. While I have described the London boroughs studied in this research as undergoing such a loss of "clear boundaries", communal participation in their formal council activities at least, has increased, not declined in Inner London. See Sidney Verba and Norman Nie, *Participation in America* (New York: Harper & Row, 1972) p. 242.

23. Op. cit., *Research Studies*, vol. 1: *Local Government in Southeast England*, p. 20. See also, *The Management of Local Government*, vol. 1, p. 143.

24. Loc. cit.

25. Hanna Pitkin, *The Concept of Representation* (Berkeley: University of California Press, 1967) pp. 75 ff.

26. Dennis Sullivan *et al.*, *The Politics of Representation* (New York: St. Martin's Press, 1974) p. 34.

27. Op. cit., p. 35.

28. Edward Banfield and James Q. Wilson, *City Politics* (New York: Vintage, 1966) pp. 202 ff.

29. Lord Redcliffe-Maud and Bruce Wood, *English Local Government Reformed* (London: Oxford University Press, 1974) pp. 149 ff.

30. Samuel Hays, "Political Parties and the Community–Society Continuum," in W. Chambers and W. D. Burnham (eds), *The American Party Systems* (2nd edn, New York: Oxford University Press, 1975) p. 157.

31. Samuel Huntington, *Political Order in Changing Societies* (New Haven: Yale University Press, 1968) p. 129.

32. Op. cit., pp. 128–9.

Bibliography

Abramson, Paul, and Books, J. W., "Social Mobility and Political Attitudes in Britain", *Comparative Politics*, vol. 3, no. 3 (April 1971).

Almond, Gabriel, and Verba, Sidney, *The Civic Culture* (Princeton: Princeton University Press, 1963).

American Political Science Association, Committee on Political Parties, "Toward a More Responsible Two-Party System", *American Political Science Review*, vol. XLIV, no. 3, part 2 (September 1950).

Anton, Thomas, and Williams, Oliver, "On Comparing Urban Political Systems: Residential Allocations in London and Stockholm", 1971 American Political Science Association Annual Meeting Paper.

Ash, Maurice, "Green Belt or the Green City", *Town and Country Planning*, vol. 42, no. 1 (January 1974).

Ashford, Douglas, "Territory vs. Function", 1976 American Political Science Association Annual Meeting Paper.

Banfield, Edward, "The Management of Metropolitan Conflict", in Edward Banfield (ed.), *Urban Government* (New York: Free Press, 1969).

Banfield, Edward, and Wilson, James Q., *City Politics* (New York: Vintage, 1965).

Barber, James D., *The Lawmakers* (New Haven: Yale University Press, 1965).

Baxter, R., "The Working Class and Labour Politics", *Political Studies*, vol. 20 (1972) pp. 97–107.

Beer, Samuel, *The British Political System* (New York: Random House, 1974).

Bell, Colin, and Newby, Howard, *Community Studies* (New York: Praeger, 1971).

222   *Representation and Urban Community*

Biel, Howard, "Suburbia and Voting Behavior in the London Metropolitan Area", *Tijdschrift voor Economische en Sociale Geografie*, vol. LXII, no. 1 (1972).

Birch, A. H., *Representation* (New York: Praeger, 1971).

Blondel, J. and Hall, R., "Conflict, Decision-Making and the Perceptions of Local Councillors", *Political Studies*, vol. 15 (1967) pp. 322–50.

Blowers, Andrew. "London's Out-County Estates: A Reappraisal." *Town and Country Planning*, vol. 41, no. 9 (September 1973).

Blythe, K. G., *Islington Borough Development Plan, Report of Studies, Topic Paper 3, Recreational Open Space* (Spring 1973).

Boaden, Noel, *Urban Policy-Making* (Cambridge: Cambridge University Press, 1971).

Bromley Advertiser (newspaper).

Bromley Labour Party, Local Government Committee, *People and Priorities: Labour's Plan for Bromley* (n.d.).

Bromley Times (newspaper).

Brown, T., Vile, M. J. C., and Whitemore, M., "Community Studies and Decision-Taking", *British Journal of Political Science*, vol. 2 (1972) pp. 133–53.

Budge, Ian, Brand, J., Margolis, M., and Smith, A. L. M., *Political Stratification and Democracy* (London: Macmillan, 1972).

Butterworth, Ruth, 'Islington Borough Council: Some Characteristics of Single-Party Rule", *Politics*, vol. 1, no. 1 (May 1966).

Cockburn, Cynthia, *The Local State* (London: Pluto Press, 1977).

Collison, Peter, *The Cutteslowe Walls* (London: Faber and Faber, 1963).

Cousins, Paul, "Voluntary Organizations as Local Pressure Groups: The Situation in Bromley", *London Review of Public Administration*, no. 4 (October 1973).

Cox, Harvey, and Morgan, David, *City Politics and the Press* (Cambridge: Cambridge University Press, 1973).

Chisholm, Anne, "The Blighted Angel", *New Statesman*, vol. 85, no. 2187 (16 February 1973).

Dahl, Robert, *Who Governs?* (New Haven: Yale University Press, 1961).

Davies, Bleddyn, *Social Needs and Resources in Local Services* (London: Michael Joseph, 1968).

Davies, P., and Newton, K., "An Aggregate Data Analysis of

Turnout and Party Voting in Local Elections", *Sociology*, vol. 8, no. 2 (May 1974).

Dearlove, John, *The Politics of Policy in Local Government* (Cambridge: Cambridge University Press, 1974).

Dennis, Norman, "Councillors, Officers, and Public Participation in Urban Renewal", in Richard Rose (ed.) *The Management of Urban Change in Britain and Germany* (London: Sage Publications, 1974).

Durkheim, Emile, *Division of Labor in Society* (Glencoe: Free Press, 1933).

Dye, Thomas, *Politics, Economics, and the Public: Policy Outcomes in the American States* (Chicago: Rand McNally, 1967).

East London Advertiser (newspaper).

Elkin, Stephen, *Politics and Land Use Planning* (Cambridge: Cambridge University Press, 1974).

Evans, Alan, *The Economics of Residential Location* (London: Macmillan, New York: St Martin's Press, 1973).

Fesler, James, "Understanding Decentralization", *Journal of Politics*, vol. 27 (1965).

Focus on Islington (newspaper).

Forester, Tom, *The British Labour Party and the Working Class* (New York: Holmes & Meier, 1976).

Glassberg, Andrew, "The Linkage Between Urban Policy Outputs and Voting Behaviour: New York and London", *British Journal of Political Science*, vol. 3 (1973) pp. 341–61.

Goldthorpe, John *et al.*, *The Affluent Worker: Political Attitudes and Behaviour* (Cambridge: Cambridge University Press, 1968).

Goldthorpe, John *et al.*, *The Affluent Worker in the Class Structure* (Cambridge: Cambridge University Press, 1969).

Gordon, Ian, "The Recruitment of Local Politicians", *Policy and Politics*, vol. 7 (1979) pp. 1–37.

Gordon, Ian and Whiteley, Paul, "Social Class and Political Attitudes: The Case of Labour Councillors", *Political Studies*, vol. 27 (1979) pp. 99–113.

Great Britain, Department of the Environment, Committee on Public Participation in Planning, *People and Planning* (London: HMSO, 1969).

Great Britain, General Register Office, *Census 1961*.

Great Britain, General Register Office, *Census 1966*.

Great Britain, General Register Office, *Census 1971*.

Great Britain, Ministry of Housing and Local Government,

Committee on the Management of Local Government, *Report*, (London: HMSO, 1967).

Great Britain, Royal Commission on Local Government in England, *Report* (London: HMSO, 1969).

Great Britain, Royal Commission on Local Government in Greater London, *Report* (London: HMSO, 1960).

Greater London Council, *Greater London Development Plan* (London: GLC, 1976).

Greater London Council, *London Borough Council Elections, 2 May 1974* (London: GLC, 1974).

Greater London Council, *1971 Census Data for London* (London: GLC, 1974).

Greater London Council, Intelligence Unit, *Research Report No. 9, Classifications of the London Boroughs* (London: GLC, February 1971).

Greater London Council, Intelligence Unit, *Research Report No. 13, Characteristics of 12 Clusters of Wards in Greater London* (London: GLC, July 1971).

Green, Geoffrey, "National, City, and Ward Components of Local Voting", *Policy and Politics*, vol. 1, no. 1 (1972).

Greenstone, David, *Labour in American Politics* (New York: Vintage Books, 1969).

Hauge, Vincent, "City Councillors as Representatives", 1974 American Political Science Association Annual Meeting Paper.

Hays, Samuel, "Political Parties and the Community–Society Continuum", in W. Chambers and W. D. Burnham (eds), *The American Party System*, 2nd edn (New York: Oxford University Press, 1975).

Hindess, Barry, *The Decline of Working-Class Politics* (London: Paladin, 1971).

Hoggart, Richard, *The Uses of Literacy* (Fair Lawn, N.J.: Essential Books, 1957).

Hoodless, Donald, "Letter to the Editor", *New Society*, vol. 29, no. 679 (16 August 1974).

Huntington, Samuel, *Political Order in Changing Societies* (New Haven: Yale University Press, 1968).

Islington Gazette (newspaper).

Jenkins, Simon, "The Politics of London Motorways", *Political Quarterly*, vol. 44 (1973).

Jones, George W., *Borough Politics* (London: Macmillan, 1969).

Kantor, Paul, "The Governable City: Islands of Power and Political Parties in London", *Polity* vol. VII, no. 1 (fall 1974).

Keller, Suzanne, *The Urban Neighborhood* (New York: Random House, 1968).

Knight, Lindsay, "A Tenants' Cooperative", *New Society*, vol. 29, no. 679 (16 August 1974).

Labour Councillor (newspaper).

Leech, Kenneth, "The Role of Immigration in Recent East London History", *East London Papers*, vol. 10, no. 1 (1967).

Lipset, S. M., *Political Man* (Garden City: Doubleday, 1959).

London Borough of Bromley, Borough Council Minutes and Agendas.

London Borough of Islington, Borough Council Minutes and Agendas.

London Borough of Islington, *Official Guide*.

London Borough of Tower Hamlets, Borough Council Minutes and Agendas.

McKay, David and Cox, Andrew, *The Politics of Urban Change* (London: Croom Helm, 1979).

Miller, Delbert, "Decision-Making Cliques in Community Power Structures: A Comparative Study of an American and an English City", *American Journal of Sociology*, vol. 64 (1958).

Minogue, Martin (ed.), *Documents on Contemporary British Government, vol. II, Local Government in Britain* (Cambridge: Cambridge University Press, 1977).

Minns, Richard, "Who Builds More?" *New Society*, vol. 28, no. 603 (25 April 1974).

Newton, Kenneth, "Links between Leaders and Citizens in a Local Political System", *Policy and Politics*, vol. 1 (1973) pp. 287–305.

Newton, Kenneth, "Community Decision-Making in Britain and the U.S.A.", in Terry Clark (ed.) *Comparative Community Politics* (New York: John Wiley, 1974) pp. 55–86.

Newton, Kenneth, *Second City Politics* (Oxford: Clarendon Press, 1976).

Pahl, R. E., *Patterns of Urban Life* (London: Longman, 1970).

Pahl, R. E., *Whose City?* (London: Longman, 1970).

Parkin, Frank, *Middle-Class Radicalism* (New York: Praeger, 1968).

Pennock, J. R., "Political Representation: An Overview", in

J. R. Pennock and J. W. Chapman (eds), *Representation: Nomos X* (New York: Atherton Press, 1968).

Peterson, Paul, and Kantor, Paul, "Political Parties and Citizen Participation in English City Politics", *Comparative Politics*, vol. 9, no. 2 (January 1977).

Pitkin, Hanna, *The Concept of Representation* (Berkeley: University of California Press, 1967).

Pitkin, Hanna, "The Concept of Representation", in Hanna Pitkin (ed.), *Representation* (New York: Atherton Press, 1969).

Prewitt, Kenneth, *The Recruitment of Political Leaders* (Indianapolis: Bobbs-Merrill, 1970).

Ranney, Austin, *Pathways to Parliament* (Madison: University of Wisconsin Press, 1965).

Redcliffe-Maud, Lord, and Wood, Bruce, *English Local Government Reformed* (London: Oxford University Press, 1974).

Rex, John, and Moore, Robert, *Race, Community and Conflict: A Study of Sparkbrook* (London: Oxford University Press, 1967).

Rokkan, Stein, *Citizens, Elections, Parties* (Oslo: Universitetsforlaget, 1970).

Rowland, Jon, *Community Decay* (Harmondsworth, Middx: Penguin, 1973).

Savitch, H. V., "Leadership in New York City and London", *Policy and Politics*, vol. 2, no. 2 (December 1973).

Sayre, Wallace, "The Relevance of the Greater London Governmental Experience to New York City Government", in State Study Commission for New York City, *The Neighborhoods, the City, and the Region* (New York: 1971).

Schlesinger, Joseph, *Ambition and Politics* (Chicago: Rand McNally, 1966).

Sharpe, L. J., "Elected Representatives in Local Government", *British Journal of Sociology*, vol. 13 (1962) pp. 189–209.

Sharpe, L. J., "American Democracy Reconsidered, Parts I and II", *British Journal of Political Science*, vol. 3 (January and April 1973).

Stodgill, Ralph, *Handbook of Leadership* (New York: Free Press, 1974).

Sullivan, Dennis *et al.*, *The Politics of Representation* (New York: St Martin's, Press, 1974).

Tapper, O., "Poplar on Trial", *East London Papers*, vol. 3, no. 2 (1960).

Thorns, David, *Suburbia* (London: MacGibbon & Kee, 1972).

Tower Hamlets News (newspaper).

Verba, Sidney, and Nie, Norman, *Participation in America* (New York: Harper & Row, 1972).

Vroom, V. H., and Yetton, P. W., *Leadership and Decision-Making* (Pittsburgh: University of Pittsburgh Press, 1973).

Wahlke, John *et al.*, *The Legislative System* (New York: John Wiley, 1962).

Willmott, Peter, and Young, Michael, *Family and Class in a London Suburb* (London: New English Library, 1967).

Wilson, James Q., *The Amateur Democrat* (Chicago: University of Chicago Press, 1966).

Wood, Bruce, "Urbanisation and Local Government", in A. H. Halsey (ed.), *Trends in British Society since 1900* (London: Macmillan, 1972).

Wood, Robert, *Suburbia* (Boston: Houghton-Mifflin, 1958).

Yates, Douglas, *Neighborhood Democracy* (Lexington, Mass.: Lexington Books, 1973).

Yates, Douglas, "Service Delivery and the Urban Political Order", in Willis Hawley and David Rogers (eds), *Improving the Quality of Urban Management*, vol. 8, Urban Affairs Annual Reviews (Beverly Hills: Sage Publications, 1974).

Young, Kenneth, "Orpington and the Liberal Revival", in C. Cook and J. Ramsden (eds), *By-Elections in British Politics* (London: Macmillan; New York: St Martin's Press, 1973).

Young, Kenneth and Kramer, John, "Local Exclusionary Policies in Britain", in Kevin Cox (ed.) *Urbanization and Conflict in Market Societies* (Chicago: Maaroufa Publications, 1978).

Young, Kenneth, and Kramer, John, *Strategy and Conflict in Metropolitan Housing* (London: Heinemann, 1978).

Young, Michael, and Willmott, Peter, *Family and Kinship in East London* (Glencoe: Free Press, 1957).

Young, Michael, and Willmott, Peter, *The Symmetrical Family* (New York: Pantheon, 1973).

Index